OUTLAWS ON HORSEBACK

The History of the Organized Bands of Bank and
Train Robbers Who Terrorized the Prairie Towns of
Missouri, Kansas, Indian Territory, and Oklahoma
for Half a Century

HARRY SINCLAIR DRAGO

Introduction to the Bison Books Edition
by Richard Patterson

UNIVERSITY OF NEBRASKA PRESS
LINCOLN AND LONDON

◎ The paper in this book meets the minimum requirements of American
National Standard for Information Sciences—Permanence of Paper for
Printed Library Materials, ANSI Z39.48-1984.

First Bison Books printing: 1998
Most recent printing indicated by the last digit below:
10   9   8   7   6   5   4   3   2   1

Library of Congress Cataloging-in-Publication Data
Drago, Harry Sinclair, 1888–1979.
Outlaws on horseback: the history of the organized bands of bank and train
robbers who terrorized the prairie towns of Missouri, Kansas, Indian Terri-
tory, and Oklahoma for half a century / Harry Sinclair Drago; introduction
to the Bison books edition by Richard Patterson.
    p.   cm.
Originally published: New York: Dodd, Mead, 1964.
Includes bibliographical references and index.
ISBN 0-8032-6612-X (pbk.: alk. paper)
1. Outlaws—West (U.S.)—History.   2. Frontier and pioneer life—West
(U.S.)   3. Bank robberies—West (U.S.)—History.   4. Train robberies—West
(U.S.)—History.   5. West (U.S.)—History—1860–1890.   6. West (U.S.)—
History—1890–1945.   I. Title.
F594.D7   1998
978'.02—dc21
97-32634   CIP

Reprinted from the original 1964 edition by Dodd, Mead & Company, New
York.

To my fellow Westerner

HOMER CROY

companion of some memorable days and
many pleasant evenings. May I always
find my way to his campfire.

Contents

Illustrations

INTRODUCTION TO THE BISON BOOKS EDITION

Richard Patterson

Although Harry Sinclair Drago (1888–1979) did most of his writing within a cab ride of New York's Hudson River, he probably knew parts of the American West better than some who spent their lives there. A committed researcher, Drago once memorized the names of over a thousand counties in the western states and territories. To avoid mistakes, he kept pages of an 1890 atlas pinned to the wall of his office.

In *Outlaws on Horseback*, Drago concentrates on Missouri, Kansas, Oklahoma, and Indian Territory to create an in-depth look at sixty years of banditry that began with the depredations of William Clarke Quantrill in the early 1860s and ended in 1921 with the death of Henry Starr, the last of what Drago calls the "authentic horseback outlaws."

Drago covers the major badmen of the period—Frank and Jesse James, the Younger brothers, the Dalton brothers, and Bill Doolin—and adds to the mix with the exploits of Belle Starr, the career of the righteous hanging judge Isaac Parker, and the misdeeds of a host of lesser lawbreakers, plus the adventures of many of the law officers of the day.

As a former novelist, Drago could tell a good tale, but he knew the boundaries and never stretched the truth to give a story more zip. In fact, in most of his nonfiction works, he devoted considerable space to unmasking legends and correcting other writers' mistakes.

Among the myths he debunked in *Outlaws on Horseback* was the story that the James brothers were related to the Younger brothers and the Youngers were related to the Daltons, and therefore the same outlaw blood ran through their veins, creating some sort of inherited criminal propensity. Sheer literary nonsense, says Drago. The Youngers and the Daltons were second cousins, but that was it.

According to Drago, another misconception was that the Jameses and Youngers were not killers. On the contrary, he says; over the years the combined body count of the two clans was at least ten (eleven if you included the locomotive engineer killed in the wreck at the Adair, Iowa, express-car robbery in 1873). And Drago reminds us not to forget the long list of trainmen, bank employees, and just plain citizens injured during the James-Younger escapades.

Another error Drago felt compelled to correct in *Outlaws on Horse-back* was the belief that the James-Younger episode at Adair was the first peacetime train robbery in the United States. Credit for *that*, Drago correctly points out, goes to the Reno gang, which held up a Mississippi & Ohio express car near Seymour, Indiana, in 1866.

Drago savored such debunking and would spend days running down a fact to catch a colleague's mistake. For years writers had repeated an early Dalton biographer's misstatement that Bill Dalton was once elected to the California state legislature. Drago had misgivings about this story, so he obtained an official list of past members of both the California Senate and General Assemblies. The name Bill Dalton was nowhere to be found. He discovered that the error likely originated in a letter Bill had written in which he indicated that he was dabbling in local California politics and was *aspiring* to a seat in the legislature.

Although Drago was contemptuous of the errors of most of his fellow writers and did not hesitate to correct them, he seemed strangely tolerant of fiction boldly panned off as fact. Maybe it was because he knew many of the writers personally, but he seemed overly sympathetic, and not just toward those who carelessly repeated the mistakes of others, but even toward those who intentionally misled their readers. Foremost among these was former outlaw Al Jennings, who dreamed up outrageous accounts of derring-do in his *Through the Shadows with O. Henry* (1921). Another was Oklahoma pioneer Fred Sutton, author of *Hands Up! Stories of the Six-Gun Fighters of the Old Wild West* (1927). Drago seemed especially tolerant of Sutton, who claimed (falsely, according to Drago) to have been personally acquainted with Wyatt Earp, Bat Masterson, Wild Bill Hickok, and other frontier notables, and who put himself at the scene of some of their most exciting adventures.

Drago was a fairly careful writer himself. He had his critics, but he would have received fewer complaints had he cited his sources more often and perhaps allowed a little room for the opinions of others. For example, Drago was among a handful of writers who believed that Cole Younger was the father of Bell Starr's daughter, Pearl. While some writers had reservations about this, Drago was positive of the fact and said so. He probably had good proof, but in his text he simply states that, at age sixteen, the girl resembled Cole. If he had other evidence, he kept it to himself.

While reviewers usually praised Drago's work, because of his anecdotal approach, narrative style, and hesitancy to cite sources, he was reproached occasionally for disappointing serious researchers. Most of his critics, however, were mindful that he wrote for the mainstream reader and not academia.

As to citing sources, to be fair to Drago, it may not have been his fault that most of his books were short on footnotes. Drago wrote almost exclusively for New York trade publishers, many of whom believed that footnotes and endnotes discourage sales. Perhaps it was partly to compensate for this lack that Drago occasionally referred to sources in his text, but in doing so he usually mentioned only the author and title of a work, thus leaving devoted students of outlaw history to find the page numbers themselves. Subsequent authors who consulted Drago for their own works sometimes found his style disconcerting, knowing that he probably had in his files just the clipping or quote they needed. Just how generous Drago was in sharing these with colleagues, we don't know.

While Drago may have done most of his writing in New York, he was not desk-bound. He periodically headed west to rummage through old courthouse records and dusty newspaper archives. Moreover, he began these jaunts early in his writing career, collecting background material for his novels when there were still old-timers around who had been on the scene.

Although it is not obvious to the casual reader, Drago relied heavily on local and regional newspapers of the day for his source material; maybe too heavily, a reviewer once commented, suggesting that occasionally Drago came to the conclusion that something hadn't happened simply because it wasn't mentioned in the newspapers.

Such comments aside, *Outlaws on Horseback* has held up well under the scrutiny of later writers who have been as demanding as Drago himself. Oklahoma outlaw historian Glenn Shirley, who offers no quarter to careless researchers, treats *Outlaws on Horseback* kindly in his *West of Hell's Fringe* (1978) and *Belle Starr and Her Times* (1982). Likewise, the late Professor William A. Settle, whose *Jesse James Was His Name* (1966) remains the most faithful work on Jesse, had little to complain about in Drago's treatment of his favorite outlaw. Both of these authors, however, like Drago, relied heavily on contemporary newspaper accounts. Therefore, their sources were largely the same as Drago's.

Drago's reliance on newspapers may have stemmed from his early career as a reporter in Ohio. It was around 1906 when he left the University of Toledo to take a job at the *Toledo Bee*. However, as a cub reporter, Drago wasn't all that proficient, at least in the opinion of his editor, who was about to let him go when Drago persuaded him to let him try his hand at feature stories. With features Drago did better, and the editor kept him on.

For several years Drago wrote for the *Bee* and also for a companion newspaper, the *Toledo Times*. He specialized in stories about the theatrical companies that came through Toledo, and this led to an interest in the theater and in acting. In 1910 Drago chucked his newspaper job and headed for New York City to give the stage a try. Broadway didn't open its arms for him, but he did find an acting job with a touring stock company. The company, however, folded in mid-season, leaving the cast stranded in Pennsylvania.

Rather than return to Toledo and face a chorus of "I told you so" from his friends at the *Bee*, Drago headed for Detroit and a job in a bookstore. The store, Macauley Brothers, did a brisk wholesale business, and Drago was put on the road. He did well and soon acquired a fairly sound knowledge of the book business. This led to big ideas, and Drago got the urge to go into publishing himself. He found an acquaintance, H. K. Fly, then a salesman for the Bobbs-Merrill publishing company, who had similar aspirations, and they formed the H. K. Fly Company, specializing in theatrical books. For the next several years, Drago was involved, on a small scale, in nearly every aspect of publishing.

The fledgling company had its ups and downs, and in 1918 or 1919 Drago left Fly and went to work for the A. L. Burt Company, a small New York City publishing house. While working for Burt, Drago became acquainted with ex-outlaw Al Jennings, who was popping in and out of the Burt offices trying to write his fanciful account of his bandit days and his chance friendship with William S. Porter, also known as O. Henry. Two things apparently resulted from Drago's relationship with Jennings: he developed an interest in the American West, and he decided that he could probably write a book as good if not better than many of those being turned out by the New York houses.

Drago began with novels. His first effort, *Suzanna* (1922), a romance set in early California, was an immediate success. He quickly followed with *Out of the Silent North* (1923), for which he sold magazine and motion picture rights.

Seeing a future in frontier fiction, Drago moved to Nevada, where he fell in love with the West and also with a young Nevada woman who soon became Mrs. Drago. For the next several years, the couple toured the West while Drago gathered frontier lore and background material for his novels.

In 1927, Hollywood beckoned, and the Dragos moved to Los Angeles, where Harry wrote for Twentieth Century Fox, MGM, and several of the independents. Over the next few years he turned out scripts for Tom Mix, Buck Jones, and other cowboy stars. With the coming of the talkies, however, the studios cut back on westerns, and writers who specialized in the oaters were no longer in demand. In 1931, the Dragos moved to New York, and Harry returned to novels.

Over the next twenty years, Drago produced an average of three novels a year under a half-dozen pen names, mostly westerns, but also a few romances and gangster stories.

In 1952 Drago and a handful of fellow writers founded the Western Writers of America, an enthusiastic group dedicated to improving the lot of western authors. Drago served as the organization's first vice president.

In the late fifties, probably to acquire additional material for his westerns, Drago joined the New York City Posse of the Westerners, the nationwide organization of frontier history buffs. There he became friends with publisher Clarkson Potter, who suggested that he take a break from his novels and try nonfiction. Drago considered it an interesting challenge, but more than that, he had become increasingly discouraged over the state of the western fiction field. The sales of hardcover western novels had peaked in 1953 and then began a downward trend. As a result, most publishers were making only token efforts to promote the hardcovers, relying instead on 50 percent of the income from paperback reprints, which were still doing well. The authors got the other 50 percent on reprints, but only the highly prolific writers were making good money. Drago and other western novelists were pushing for a smaller cut for the publishers on reprints, or in the alternative, the publication of original paperbacks, but they were making slow progress. Drago decided that it would be a good time to try nonfiction.

Drago was well suited for the field. His first work, *Wild, Wooly and Wicked* (1960), won the Buffalo Award for best western book of the year. In 1962, he published *Red River Valley*. The present volume, *Outlaws on Horseback*, appeared in 1964, followed by *Great American Cattle Trails* (1966), *Lost Bonanzas* (1966), and *Notorious Ladies of the Frontier* (1969). And in 1971, when Drago was eighty-three years of age, his *Great Range War* won the Western Heritage Award for the most outstanding western nonfiction book of 1970.

Using the same battered Royal typewriter he had bought upon leaving Hollywood in 1931, Drago continued writing until 1974. His last book, *Legend Makers: Tales of the Old Peace Officers and Desperados of the Frontier*, was published the following year. He lived in quiet retirement for another four years, passing away peacefully in his hometown of White Plains, New York, in October 1979.

In 1973, when asked by a local reporter if he had any advice for aspiring writers, Drago offered: "Keep the seat of your pants to the seat of the chair." During the same interview, he was asked about his most memorable moment during his long career. He said that it was the day he heard that President Dwight D. Eisenhower, upon being asked to name his favorite authors, replied "Bliss Lomax and Will Ermine."

Both Lomax and Ermine were pen names used by Drago for his many western novels.

Acknowledgments

MUCH OF THE MATERIAL presented in this book has been gathered over the years—many years—going back, in fact, to the early 1920's, when I was beginning to write Western fiction, without, I must admit, any loftier purpose in mind than to equip myself with authentic backgrounds and characters for my short stories and novels. It has served me well and owes me nothing. Most of those with whom I scraped acquaintance in those long-ago days have passed on. But their memory remains green with me. I am not going to attempt to name them; the list is too long. But I am grateful to them, as I am to the many who, more recently, have aided me with their advice and criticism, particularly to those kindly people who have helped me with my research: among them, the staff of the Oklahoma Historical Society, Mrs. Rella Looney, archivist; Nyle H. Miller and the Kansas State Historical Society; the California State Library, Sacramento; the State Historical Society, Columbia, Missouri; Bill Burchardt, editor of *Oklahoma Today;* Homer Croy, writer and historian; Peter Decker, writer and authority on Western Americana; Mrs. Shirley L. Spranger of the American History Room of the New York Public Library; Angus

Cameron, the well-known editor; Sol Lewis, publisher of Western history; Jefferson C. Dykes, collector, historian and esteemed bibliographer of the West; Melvin J. Nichols, of Summit, New Jersey, who has again given me the courtesy of his extensive library.

Introduction: Behind the Myths and Legends

୧୭

W HEN "progress" caught up with the old double-decked Fifth Avenue buses and sent them to the junkyard, one of the friendliest and most enjoyable pleasures incident to living in New York City disappeared forever.

On a May morning, brilliant with sunshine, back in 1919, I climbed the circular stairs to the upper deck of one of those old buses. No other seat being vacant, I sat down with an elderly, gray-haired man who might have been in his mid-fifties, but who, I learned later, was older than that. He had a strong, handsome, forthright face, and though there was nothing in his attire to suggest it, I had the feeling that his leathery tan was not recently acquired or one that would ever wear off, and that his life had been lived in the open. There was a neatness about him that was appealing. I noticed particularly how carefully his closely cropped gray mustache was trimmed. Naturally, I wondered who he might be.

We fell into conversation shortly, which was not uncommon in those days, riding the top deck of a Fifth Avenue bus. I cannot recall how Oklahoma was introduced into our conversation. Very likely it came from me, for at the time I was connected with a small publishing house and we had in preparation a book entitled *Through the Shadows With O. Henry* by Al Jennings, highly publicized as the last of the Oklahoma outlaws. A large part of the manuscript was devoted to Al's life in the Ohio State Penitentiary, at Columbus, to which he had been sentenced for life, and to a fellow inmate in the prison dispensary, William Sydney Porter by name, who was to become famous as the short-story writer O. Henry.

Al was in New York and I had been spending some time with him almost daily. (I shall have more to say of my connection with him later.) At the moment, Oklahoma meant Al Jennings to me, and to keep the conversation going, I said, "I suppose you've heard of Al Jennings, the outlaw."

"Yes, I've heard of him," the other replied, with a quiet, amused smile. "Al was never half as bad as he thought he was."

"You sound as though you were well-acquainted with him," I remarked, my curiosity aroused.

"You might say so," the stranger nodded reflectively. "One of my field marshals captured the Jennings gang singlehanded."

Understanding dawned in me suddenly, and I realized that the gray-haired man seated beside me must be Evett Nix, the famous U.S. marshal who smashed the outlaw gangs that were terrorizing Oklahoma Territory in the 1890's.

"You are Marshal Nix," I said, impressed at finding myself in such distinguished company.

"Yes," he acknowledged, "I am—or maybe I should say I was; that was a long time ago. I was pleased when President Roosevelt pardoned Al. He's led an upright life since he came out. He's told me more than once that I did him the greatest favor of his life in ending his career of outlawry."

I was familiar with Al's version of how he had been captured on Carr Creek Trail that October morning in 1897. Later, I was to learn how widely it differed from what actually occurred.

I have always treasured my chance meeting with Marshal Nix.

It quickened my interest in that controversial chapter of American history dealing with the horseback outlaws of Indian and Oklahoma territories and the little army of U.S. marshals and deputy marshals who hunted them down and finally eliminated them in the most prolonged and sanguinary game of cops and robbers this country or any other ever had known. Roughly speaking, it began soon after the forced removal of the Five Civilized Tribes from their homeland in the Carolinas, Georgia, Florida, Alabama and Mississippi to reservations in the uninhabited wilderness to the west of the state of Arkansas, comprising the eastern third of present-day Oklahoma, in addition to which the federal government held great areas of assigned or reserve lands in trust for them.

It was a land without law, other than the tribal law and courts of the Five Tribes. The only police were Indian police. There were a number of military posts between Fort Smith, Arkansas, and Red River, to the south and west, of which Fort Gibson, some sixty miles up the Arkansas River, at the confluence of the Grand and Verdigris, was the only one of real consequence. The military had no authority to interfere in criminal and civil cases arising among the Indians. In fact, they were expressly forbidden to do so, and this postscription covered mixed bloods of all degrees.

What had become Indian Territory had been known to the criminal element of a dozen Southern and Midwestern states for years. Though it offered a safe refuge for wanted men, few appear to have taken advantage of it. But now, with thousands of "civilized" Indians with their government allotments to prey on, they came from far and near, got themselves adopted into the tribes by marriage and not only proceeded to debauch their benefactors with the wildcat whisky they brewed in their illicit stills, but plundered and killed with a merciless abandon equaled elsewhere only by the pirates of the lower Mississippi and the white savages of the Natchez Trace. It was, of course, from those very depths of criminal viciousness that a substantial number of the lawless characters infesting the Territory had come.

The seeds of lawlessness had been planted, and it remained only for the passing years to bring them to flower. The half-breed sons of the white renegades grew to manhood with contempt for tribal laws, which among the Choctaws and Cherokees were strict and severe in their punishments. The invariable aftermath to a quarrel was murder. Usually the killings went unexplained, or, in the Cherokee Nation, were charged to the implacable feud between the No Treaty Party and the Treaty Party that took the lives of so many. There is no record to say what the number was, but it must have run into the hundreds. We do know that there were nights when four, even five, men were shot down within a few minutes.

The internecine strife that divided the Cherokees was waged up to and through the years of the Civil War, and it was responsible for the defeat of the adherents of the Confederacy among the Five Tribes. It also helped to provide the climate for the day of the horseback outlaws.

The strife that divided the Cherokee Nation went back to the treaty signed with the federal government that resulted in their removal from their ancestral homeland. Principal Chief John Ross, titular head of the tribe for almost forty years, had refused to sign it, and he and his faction held that those chiefs who had— Stand Watie; Elias Boudinot, his brother; and Major John Ridge —were traitors. Boudinot, Major Ridge and his son, John, were assassinated following the removal. Only death could heal that breach. It followed that when the conflict between North and South began, those two old enemies took sides, John Ross declaring for the Union, and Stand Watie taking the field for the Confederacy. The latter, a redoubtable man and something of a military genius, was made a brigadier general before the struggle was over, and when he surrendered at Fort Towson, in June 1865, he was the last of the Confederate commanders to lay down his arms.

I became acquainted with a number of "reformed" outlaws, among them Emmett Dalton, the last of the Dalton Gang, who had spent almost fifteen years in prison for his part in the spectacular and tragic Coffeyville, Kansas, fiasco before he was pardoned. I recall him as a well-preserved man, in his early fifties, still truculent and highly opinionated. He was looking for a writer to assist him in putting down on paper the "true" story of the Daltons, which he claimed had never been done, and which he alone was in a position to supply.

His need was the need without exception of all of the leftovers from the bygone days of the horseback outlaws, and the horseback marshals as well, who had achieved some claim on fame. Each was convinced that he had a "great" story to tell; all he needed was someone to write it. Eventually, most of them managed to get into print, with the aid of either a literary ghost or a collaborator. Unfortunately, the books they produced, including Emmett Dalton's *When the Daltons Rode,* had little to say that had not been said before. Most of the little that was new was either straight fiction or based on hearsay and alleged conversations, for which no substantiating evidence was, or could be, offered. That these so-called firsthand narratives are in violent disagreement with one another, even on what have come to be accepted as established facts, is not surprising, for among the score or more of professional writers of the first rank who have tried to break through the web of myth and legend surrounding a half-century of Oklahoma outlawry, there are endless contradictions, differences of opinion and an acrimonious readiness to charge with incompetence whoever might disagree.

I am thinking particularly of Burton Rascoe, the highly regarded and always caustic author of *Belle Starr the Bandit Queen,* which when published in 1941 was accepted widely as the definitive last word on Belle, Cole Younger (the father of her daughter Pearl), the Youngers' "cousins," Frank and Jesse James, Henry Starr (related only by Cherokee marriage of his cousin Sam Starr to Belle) and other characters who gained some prominence in the era of the horseback outlaws. Rascoe went out of his way to demolish the published accounts that had preceded his, and with evident relish points out the errors in them. He then proceeds to make many horrific errors of his own. He says, on page 281: "Train robbery 'invented' by Jesse James. First train robbery in the world, on July 21 (1873) when Frank and Jesse James, Cole and Jim Younger and three others held up the Chicago, Rock Island and Pacific passenger express near Adair, Iowa, getting $3,000 from the safe in the express car and several hundred dollars in cash and jewelry from the passengers."

He was very wide of the mark. It was generally known, and a writer of Burton Rascoe's prominence should have known, that the first robbery of a railroad train occurred on October 6, 1866, and was accomplished by "a crew of Hoosiers who thought it up, then put it into practice on the Ohio and Mississippi Railway near Seymour, in Jackson County, Indiana." I am quoting Stewart H. Holbrook, the dedicated historian of the steam cars. He continues:

"This first stickup was a simple job. A passenger train carrying an express and baggage car pulled out of Seymour in the early evening, heading east, and almost immediately two masked men came into the car from the coach just behind. In those days it hadn't occurred to expressmen to lock their car doors, so the entry was made without fuss. The two men secured the messenger's keys, opened the safe, took out some $13,000, then pulled the bellcord to signal the engineer to stop. Stop he did, and the robbers dumped another safe, unopened, from the car, and leaped after it into the darkness.

"This was something new. The train crew hardly knew what was expected of them. They discussed the event wonderingly, then took the train to the next station. Here an armed posse was recruited. They pumped their way on a handcar back to the scene of the crime, to find only the unopened safe, which had been too much for the robbers. Such was the holdup. A bit later, and doubtless with good reason, John and Simeon Reno, two brothers of questionable habits, and Frank Sparks, no better than he should be, were arrested, indicted for the crime, and admitted to bail. Their trial was postponed from time to time and was never held."

A year later, the same train was stopped and robbed, also near Seymour. Walker Hammond and Michael Collins, friends of the Reno brothers, were suspected, and it was believed that the Reno brothers, of whom there were four, had masterminded this second holdup. The Pinkertons got their hands on John Reno, and he was sent to prison for a long term. James D. Horan, in his *Desperate Men*, speculates, and wisely, I believe, that some member of the James Gang became acquainted with John Reno while both were serving time in the Missouri Penitentiary, and carried the idea of robbing trains to Jesse.

Since the days when that indispensable barbershop publication, the *National Police Gazette,* entertained its readers with its exciting, supermelodramatic and grossly fantastic and inaccurate "lives" of Frank and Jesse James and their outlaw contemporaries, so much has been written and so much documentation supplied that one is surprised to find Rascoe saying:

"You must remember that after Frank James got his release from prison (after having served twenty-one years) he had a tough time making a living. He was 60 years old and he had never worked a day in his life except while he was in the penitentiary, and about all he had done there was to sort gunny sacks."

This is wrong. If Frank James ever sorted gunny sacks it was not in prison, for he never served a day for his crimes. It is a matter of record. When he was brought to trial in Gallatin, the county seat of Daviess County, Missouri, it was the only time he ever faced a judge and jury. Paul Wellman, a writer for whom I have an enduring respect, says in his recent and excellent *A Dynasty of Western Outlaws:* "Except for the few weeks he [Frank James] spent in custody awaiting his trial he did not serve a single day in prison for his many crimes. No other charges were made against him, and he died peacefully in 1915, when he was seventy-two years old. Of all the gang, he alone escaped punishment."

Although in his introduction to *A Dynasty of Outlaws,* Wellman decries "the school of professional 'so-called' debunkers," he does not hesitate to point out numerous other errors in Rascoe (he misses some), and then says later, "It is almost impossible to avoid mistakes, particularly where there are many versions of a given event." He makes his share, honest mistakes of fact and opinion, which I shall have occasion to point out later, and without apology, knowing that mine will be pointed out to me. It is the surest way, I believe, to get at the truth and demolish the myths and legends that we have been duped into accepting as factual history.

In the more than forty years that have elapsed since my chance meeting with Evett Nix in New York, the course of my writing life has been such that I have seldom been beyond shouting distance of what I like to call the Horseback Outlaws of Indian Territory, Old Oklahoma and the state of Oklahoma, which emerged from those early beginnings. Digging through the musty files of old newspapers and examining such court records as were available was an enlightening and often confusing experience, made even more so by interviewing "eyewitnesses" (all but one or two of whom have passed away in my time). Under examination, those firsthand accounts seldom proved to be reliable. But the old-timers believed in the truth of what they had to say, even when they disagreed among themselves. Of course, most of them were going back half a lifetime to recall what they had seen and heard. What they failed to realize was that the imagination had been at work through the dim years they had put behind them, coloring whatever they chose to recall and leading more than one to appropriate something he had read and to palm it off as his own experience.

The absurd statement has been made that there were five thousand outlaws running wild in the two territories. There may have been as many as five thousand criminals unapprehended in the country between the Kansas line and Red River, at one time or another. I believe there were. That would include petty thieves, safe-crackers, murderers, a few rapists and the several thousand who were engaged in the manufacture and sale of whisky to the Indians, plus the fluctuating and ever-changing number of "wanted" men who regarded that lawless country as only a temporary refuge. Of the genuine horseback outlaws, who did their marauding in gangs, robbing banks and express offices and holding up trains, the acknowledged elite of their lawless world, the like of whom America had never seen before and was never to see again, I can account for fewer than two hundred.

No excuses can be offered for them. A few, Bill Doolin for one, were chivalrous, after a fashion. But with few exceptions, even the most hardened lived and died by a code that was not without honor, prizing bravery and loyalty above all other manly virtues. It is not glorifying their banditry to say that they are not to be confused or likened to the modern-day "hood" and gangster.

The argument has been advanced in their favor that they were cowboys, who found their occupation gone with the opening of the Territory to white settlement; that after the wild, free life of the open range, they rebelled at the thought of being cooped up on a quarter section of land and trying to scratch a living with a plow. This is sheer nonsense. As I have said elsewhere, cowboying as a way of life did not end with the opening of the unassigned lands of Old Oklahoma to white settlers in 1889; the northern ranges of Wyoming, Montana and Dakota were just entering the era of their greatest prosperity. The big outfits were hungry for men. To get them, they were paying higher wages and serving better grub than Texas and Oklahoma punchers had ever enjoyed. Any man who wanted a job could find one.

The truth is, of course, that very few of them were cowboys. I mean working cowboys, following that vocation from year to year. Frank and Jesse James and the members of their gang had never punched cattle for a living. That is equally true of Cole Younger and his brothers. The same can be said of the Dalton brothers, the Jennings boys, Cherokee Bill, Texas Jack and a host of others. Of all the major gangs of horseback outlaws, only Bill Doolin and his longriders can truthfully be identified as of cowboy origin. Doolin had been a top hand on Oscar Halsell's big H X Bar spread before he stepped into outlawry with the Daltons. Only a lame horse kept him out of the Coffeyville fiasco. Returning to the H X Bar, on the Cimarron, north of Guthrie, he began recruiting a gang of his own. When he was ready to take to the brush, the men who rode with him were, with one or two exceptions, H X Bar cowboys. They were rough, tough young men, reckless to the point of foolhardiness, who knew what they were doing. No one had pushed them into outlawry.

It has been said many times that it was the lure of easy money, the chance to make a big stake in a hurry, that took so many men into outlawry. Unquestionably the prospect of the rich pickings to be gleaned was of the first importance with them. But only in the beginning. After a few successful forays, the thrill and excitement of sweeping into a town and cowing it with their guns became almost as important to them as money. No one ever put it better than handsome Henry Starr, the most gentlemanly, and to me the most intelligent of all horseback outlaws, when he said, after thirty years of robbing banks and being in and out of prison: "Of course I'm interested in the money and the chance that I'll make a big haul that will make me rich, but I must admit that there's the lure of the life in the open, the rides at night, the spice of danger, the mastery over men, the pride of being able to hold a mob at bay—it tingles in my veins. I love it. It is wild adventure. I feel as I imagine the old buccaneers felt when they roved the seas with the black flag at the masthead."

Fred Sutton, the often unreliable author of *Hands Up,* says he jotted down the above (and a lot more) during one of Starr's visits to his (Sutton's) office in Oklahoma City. I accept it as authentic; it sounds like Starr, and it echoes sentiments he had expressed to others. I rather believe Sutton got it second hand from Marshal Bill Tilghman, who often befriended Starr and never completely lost faith in the man. But that does not matter; others had said much the same. It is important only because it partially explains why the confirmed outlaw stuck to his trade until his career ended in a blast of gunfire or the hangman's noose.

Only a very few had even the rudiments of an education; the rest were ignorant. Many, like Cherokee Bill, Bill Cook, Rufus Buck, could sign their name, and that was about all. But they were not fools. They had a native shrewdness and sagacity. If they knew anything, it was that none of their predecessors in the game they were playing had succeeded in piling up a fortune and getting away to Mexico or South America to enjoy it. (A few got away, but they always returned, and that was their undoing.) Knowing what the score was, why did they persist in their banditry until they arrived at the inevitable end?

For several reasons. Not only did they believe they were smart enough to avoid the mistakes that had been the downfall of others, but they held their lives cheaply, which is not difficult to understand. Many of them hailed from Missouri, the cradle of outlawry. Either as children or as grown men, they were products of the bitter cruel years of border warfare between the proslavery and antislavery factions of Kansas and Missouri, followed by the even bloodier years of guerrilla warfare between Union and Confederate forces, captained by such men as Kansas' mad Jim Lane and Charles Jennison, leader of the Red Legs, and the notorious William Clarke Quantrill of the Secessionists. Lee's surrender at Appomattox did not end the internecine strife in war-torn Kansas and Missouri. It went on for years, and a decade and more passed before it burned itself out. It is of the first importance to this narrative because it provided the climate which produced the horseback outlaws.

It is no longer possible to contact eyewitnesses to the raids and holdups or the surviving marshals and deputy marshals who made war on the outlaw gangs, as it was forty and more years ago when I was filling notebooks with firsthand interviews, very much as Frederick S. Barde, the Guthrie newspaperman, was doing as he traveled up and down and across Oklahoma by horse and buggy. The Barde Collection, a gift from his daughter, reposes in the archives of the Oklahoma Historical Society, immensely valuable.

But the facts have been there this long while, waiting for anyone with a discerning eye to see. And that is particularly true regarding the "Battle of Ingalls" and the hoary old myth about the legendary "Rose of the Cimarron" risking her life to save her outlaw sweetheart, Bitter Creek Newcomb. I know I am treading on dangerous ground in demolishing it, for the truth will be painful to some. However, the evidence I have marshaled is strong enough to withstand attack.

I am grateful to the Oklahoma Historical Society for the material in the Pickering diary and to Homer Croy for the privilege of reading his unpublished manuscript on the Ingalls–Rose of the Cimarron episode.

HARRY SINCLAIR DRAGO

1

Prince of Lawlessness

THERE CAN BE little question that in the long, unbroken chain
of outlawry which began in the Missouri-Kansas border warfare
of the late fifties and ended with the killing of Henry Starr, the
last of the authentic horseback outlaws, at Harrison, Arkansas,
on February 18, 1921, the link with the most far-reaching effect
was forged by William Clarke Quantrill.

Something must be said about Quantrill, the spectacular and
fearless guerrilla leader, if only because among the men who
rode with him were some who were to write their names large on
the pages of American outlawry long after he was shot down by
alleged "Union" guerrillas, no better than himself, at Bloomfield,
Kentucky, in 1865. At the end, he had scarcely a dozen followers
left, which was a far cry from the little army of approximately four
hundred and fifty gaunt, bearded, hate-ridden fanatics he had led
into Kansas and the sacking and burning of Lawrence in 1863.

Many of those four hundred and fifty were dead; others had
drifted away to form their own bands. But for years he had
dominated their thinking, molded them to a way of life that time
could not change; and they responded with a blind loyalty such

as no other man ever won from them. Schooled in reckless daring, their guns their only law, they were fit graduates of what has been called "Quantrill's Crime School." Among the foremost were Frank James; his cousins Cole and Jim Younger; Clell and Ed Miller, brothers; Wood and Clarence Hite, cousins; Charlie Pitts, Bill Ryan; and after the Lawrence raid, a newcomer, the youngest of them all, Jesse Woodson James. A dozen others could be named.[1]

Beyond doubt Quantrill welcomed the fall of Fort Sumter and the beginning of hostilities between the North and the South. His actions prove that he was quick to see that he was now presented with a golden opportunity for advancing himself and widening the scope of his operations. To scurry across the border with his freebooters to burn farmhouses, ambush an unwary group of Jim Lane's and Jim Montgomery's Jayhawkers or Charlie Jennison's Red Legs and make off with whatever was movable, meaning horses, was one thing. But for it he had no backing, other than his own might and the support of his sympathizers. Formal war was something else. By attaching himself to the Confederacy, he would be fighting for a "cause," and a very popular one in southwestern Missouri and parts of Kansas. Without losing any time, he disappeared from his haunts in Jackson County, Missouri, and next appeared in Indian Territory, where he joined up with Stand Watie's Irregulars, the Cherokee Mounted Rifles.

The record does not show whether he was accompanied on this excursion by any of his followers or was on his own. It is a matter of record that he fought in the battles of Wilson's Creek and Lexington, Missouri, in which he appears to have given a good account of himself. That he importuned General Sterling Price, the Confederate commander, to assist him in getting a commission as an officer is easy to believe. That Price, a good man, was not favorably impressed by Quantrill's record is best attested by the fact that when he retreated southward with his Rebel force, Quantrill slipped away and returned to Jackson County, where he reorganized his band, still small, perhaps no more than a score, and began attacking small parties of Jayhawkers and Red Legs, now incorporated in the Kansas militia, who had got possession of several Missouri hamlets. He became such a thorn in the side of the Union forces, all volunteer militia, that General James Totten, their commander, issued an order declaring that Quantrill and his men were in open opposition to the laws and legitimate authorities of the United States, and "will be shot down by the military upon the spot where they are found perpetrating their foul acts."

They were thus declared, officially, to be outlaws and denied all the legal processes. Death without quarter was what it meant. Totten's order had the opposite effect of that intended. Instead of scattering like a covey of frightened quail and seeking cover either in Missouri or across the line in Indian Territory, bewhiskered, hard-faced men in butternut jeans flocked to Quantrill's black flag. Presently he had several hundred recruits, anxious and ready to follow his leadership, with unquestioning faith in his judgment. Their raiding continued, and as their number grew, they roamed far and wide, scattering concentrations of green Union militia, mostly inexperienced farm boys, practically driving them out of Jackson, Bates and Cass counties.

Quantrill, on the way to the peak of his power, was still determined to win a colonel's commission in the Army of the Confederacy. The old reasons for wanting it still held good. General Totten's order naming him an outlaw, which gave all men the right to kill him on sight, without fear of redress, added a new one. Certainly Quantrill had some reason to believe that as an officer of the Confederacy he would have to be treated as a prisoner of war, if captured, and that the status of his men would likewise be so affected.

Late in 1862, when approaching winter served notice of its coming by covering roads and fields with a skift of snow that made it impossible for mounted men to move wthout leaving a trail that any greenhorn could follow, the activities of both Rebel guerrillas and Unionists came to a halt. Quantrill led his band into the caves and hills of friendly Bates County, where they were safe for the winter. Late in November, he informed his trusted lieutenants, Bloody Bill Anderson, George Todd, Fletch Taylor and Cole Younger, that he was going to Richmond, Virginia, the capital of the Confederacy, to see James A. Seldon, Confederate Secretary of War, and demand that his services for the South be recognized with a colonel's commission. They were agreeable, realizing as he did the advantage of continuing their depredations as a recognized military unit of the C.S.A. rather than as branded outlaws.

Anderson and Todd had another reason for speeding him on his way. Both were ambitious men, and those writers who have spelled out Quantrill's story in detail hold that during the winter of 1862/1863 both Anderson and Todd were becoming jealous of Quantrill's authority and envied him the rich pickings he was gathering unto himself. Certainly if anything befell him on his long journey, one or the other could reasonably hope to succeed him.

Quantrill's trip to Richmond was long, and possibly tedious, but it was not particularly hazardous. Once he had slipped across the Missouri border into Arkansas, he was in Confederate-held territory. The war was going well for the South, which was still in possession of Tennessee and its railroads. Without mishap, he arrived in Richmond. He seems to have had no difficulty in getting an interview with Secretary Seldon. From what little is known, it was a stormy one. Quantrill's reputation had preceded him, and his truculent manner did not further his cause. The bloodletting and barbarism, which passed for legitimate warfare with him, were, if we can believe the staff officers who were present, roundly condemned by the Secretary. With a finality that left him no hope, Quantrill's request for a commission was denied, and he headed back to Missouri smarting with rage.[2]

But he was not easily discouraged, at least not for long. Somewhere along the way he seems to have convinced himself that he could bring Secretary Seldon off his high perch and down to earth with some bold, spectacular stroke that would rock the country. The burning and destruction of Lawrence, Kansas, was the answer. Lawrence was the focus of everything he and his followers and all Southern sympathizers in Missouri hated.[3] It was believed that most of the loot torn out of Missouri by the Jayhawkers and Red Legs (a term of contempt coined in Missouri for those Kansans who, if they could afford them, wore red-topped boots) was stored there.

Lawrence was also the home of Jim Lane, who had been

elected to the United States Senate with the admission of Kansas into the Union in 1861. Jim Lane, as infamous as Quantrill himself, more so in some ways, was a sadistic fanatic, condemned by his own governor and excoriated by General George B. McClellan as having done more to injure the Union cause than a full division of seasoned Confederate troops.[4]

Quantrill was back in Missouri early in '63. Bill Anderson, Todd, Cole Younger, Dick Maddox and his other leaders were first aghast when he mentioned raiding into Lawrence. It was deep in enemy territory, a Jayhawker stronghold, reputedly heavily garrisoned—but it offered them everything, loot, revenge and best of all the chance that Jim Lane could be taken alive and brought back to Missouri to be publicly hanged. When they considered all the possibilities of what the magnetic Quantrill was offering them they cheered and whipped themselves into a frenzy that was strange in such hard-bitten men.

Word of what was afoot was leaked to men who could be trusted. By the end of May, they began riding into Quantrill's camp to join up. They came well armed and brought their own ammunition, but were poorly mounted by Quantrill's standards. Day after day they came, until the outlaw leader had almost four hundred and fifty men ready to follow him into Kansas. The laxness and do-as-you-please life that had characterized previous Quantrill camps disappeared; the recruits were forced to undergo a course of training as rigorous as they would have encountered in a military post. It was hardly what they had expected, but they submitted willingly; and when Bill Anderson and George Todd saw the near idolatry with which they regarded Quantrill, they caught fire themselves and forgot their envy and jealousy. The truth was that he understood them better than they understood themselves, and he exercised his authority over them by being stern when sterness was called for, mingling it with a measure of forthrightness and camaraderie that called forth their subservient loyalty.

Summer was wearing on, but he was not ready to move on Lawrence. Instead, he led his men across the line into Indian Territory. This was more or less just a pleasant excursion, its only purpose being to raid the villages of the Upper Cherokees (the Ross faction) and help themselves to the best horseflesh they could find. Preferably that meant tough, wiry animals of pure *mesteño* strain, and next best, crossbred mustangs which could go and go and go, and which, due to the incessant raiding among the tribes, had changed owners many times since originally being stolen out of Texas. A generation of Cherokees, born in the Territory, had become as adept at stealing horses as the so-called Wild Indians of the Plains. They tried to secrete their extensive herds, but the white invaders from Missouri found them and, in the process of taking what they wanted, left a trail of dead Indians in their wake, a business in which young Thomas Coleman (Cole) Younger distinguished himself.

Quantrill and his men had little to fear from Union reprisals. The War Department had withdrawn its troops from the posts in Texas and Indian Territory soon after the outbreak of hostilities, the announced reason being that it would be impossible to supply them. It was a mistake; among the Five Civilized Tribes, the faction loyal to the Union felt they had been abandoned. Stand Watie and his Rebel army moved into Fort Gibson and wrought havoc up and down the Texas Road, the main north-south route through the Nations, parts of which were variously known as the Osage Trace, the Shawnee Trail and the Sedalia Trail, until Secretary of War Stanton reversed himself and gathered a force of several regiments of Kansas volunteers and a Missouri battery, accompanied by several hundred Osage tribesmen, at Fort Scott, under the command of General James G. Blunt, and ordered them to retake Fort Gibson.

Stand Watie, in the face of superior numbers, retired from Gibson without a struggle, but for the rest of the war years, he raided up and down the Texas Road, waylaying wagon trains from Fort Scott, Kansas, from which Fort Gibson had to be supplied. On one occasion, at a spot where he had previously met defeat, he captured a supply train valued at $1,500,000. Of its 295 wagons, 4 ambulances and a number of ox-drawn ricks carrying three thousand tons of hay, escorted by 260 troops, not more than a hundred wagons and half that number of men managed to break through the line of fire, supported by a hidden battery, and reach Fort Gibson.

The scorched-earth policy Stand Watie pursued devastated the country and resulted in starvation and near-starvation for thousands of Indians. The Confederacy strengthened the Cherokee Mounted Rifles, renaming it the Indian Brigade by reinforcing it with several regiments of white Texan volunteers.

But it is not with the four bitter years of the war itself that this narrative is principally concerned; it is with the poverty, the starvation, the memory of the wanton killings and cruelty it left behind, all of which unmistakably made the ground fertile for the generation of outlaws who were to follow, such as Henry Starr, Sam Starr, Rufus Buck, Cherokee Bill, his brother Clarence and a score of others.

It was the middle of August when Quantrill and his band returned to Missouri and dispersed to various hideouts as had been their custom. They were superbly mounted now, which was of the greatest importance; so much was to depend on the stamina of their horses. As for the men, they were lean, hard, inured to danger. Even the greenest of them was no longer completely inexperienced.

On August 18, Quantrill notified his lieutenants that they and their contingents were to rendezvous with him at a previously agreed upon meeting place. They came in that evening—George Todd from the Grenshaw Farm, about seven miles from Independence; Bill Cunningham from the Little Blue River; Cap Cole from the Martin Jones Farm, eight miles out of Kansas City. Cole Younger and Bloody Bill Anderson were already with Quantrill. As the latter looked over the assembled riders he was satisfied with what he saw.

Nothing remained to be discussed; he was ready to move at last. When black night fell, they climbed into the saddle and headed for the Kansas line. Quantrill had not minimized the dangerous nature of this enterprise. To a man, they appreciated what they were courting. If they ran into trouble, there would be nowhere they could turn for support. Once on Kansas soil, every hand would be raised against them. As the crow flies, it was something less than seventy miles to Lawrence. But they had to avoid the main-traveled roads and move with what secrecy they could. Surprise was their best weapon. Without it, they could not hope to succeed. The long column, moving as stealthily as it could, lost its way in the ravines and among the little creeks and gullies it encountered. They needed a guide. They routed a farmer out of bed and impressed him to show them the way. They became suspicious of him when he became confused, and when they learned that he was a former Missourian, turned Jayhawker, they killed him on the spot.

How often that performance was repeated that night and the following day depends on whose account you are reading. Homer Croy, a meticulous workman, who goes to the grass roots for his information, puts the number at eight, in his *Last of the Great Outlaws*. (He is following William Elsey Connelley's *Quantrill and the Border Wars* here.) Paul Wellman trims the number down to three, which I find easier to believe. But Wellman goes astray in other details in his vivid and highly dramatic account of the march on Lawrence. To quote him: "Quantrill's men had been on the march almost without rest for two days and were showing signs of weariness," and "They had been continuously on the road for so long that many of them had to strap themselves in the saddle to keep from falling."

This I find difficult to believe. They were weary, no doubt, but it was more the weariness that tension induces than just saddle weariness. The miles they had come could hardly have reduced hardened horsebackers to extremity. If they had left their rendezvous in Missouri on the night of the eighteenth, as Wellman has it, and did not get their first glimpse of Lawrence until the early morning of the twenty-first (the acknowledged date of the massacre), they certainly had been moving slowly. It must be assumed therefore that they did no riding by daylight. Proof of this is found in the established fact that it was after midnight of the twentieth before they turned north at Gardner, still some twenty miles from their destination.

Quantrill had thrown out scouts ahead of the column. In the hour before dawn, they ran into Union pickets. A few shots were exchanged. Knowing his presence had been discovered, Quantrill called in his scouts. This was the moment of decision—to turn back or go on. Some say he conferred briefly with his lieutenants, others that the decision to go on was his alone and that it was made without hesitation. The Rebel yell was raised, and where the going would permit, the long column broke into a trot. The sun was up when they reached the low bluffs east of town and looked down on Lawrence, basking peacefully in the morning light, still strangely unalarmed and little knowing what the next four hours were to bring.

2

Quantrill's Fledglings

ALTHOUGH Quantrill had greatly overestimated the strength of the military guarding the town, there were, when his scouts ran into the Union vedettes, militiamen enough in the environs of Lawrence to put up a stout defense and possibly to have turned him back had they been courageously commanded—which was not the case. By their apologists, the conduct of the Union officers has been called "inexplicable." Cowardice was the word for it. When the vedettes raced into the lines with word that a large guerrilla force was moving on the town, all was panic, and orders were shouted to evacuate their positions at once and, without wasting time, to inform the citizens of Lawrence that they were being deserted. One column that left town on the double-quick did not stop running until it reached Paola, thirty-odd miles to the south.

Fire-eating Senator Jim Lane, who was directly responsible for the Lawrence raid, fled no less shamelessly.[1] He was in bed when the first shots sounded. As the raiders thundered into town, in columns of four, splitting the morning air with their fierce Rebel yells, he realized in a flash what it meant. In his nightshirt, he ran to his front door, ripped off the identifying silver name plate and bolted like a scared rabbit out the back way into a cornfield. Behind him, he heard sounds to put wings on his feet. In borrowed pants, astride a farm horse, he clubbed the heavy animal into a run and disappeared into Shawnee County, leaving his wife to face the guerrillas.[2] They did not harm her, but fired the house. The record says that no woman was harmed or violated.

The man Quantrill wanted most had escaped him, but he and his crew had Lawrence at their mercy. The slaughter began. Men who had never harmed Missouri went down with those who had. Boys in their teens were killed as they tried to run away. Houses and stores were searched. Money, jewelry, anything that was valuable and could be carried off, was snatched out of the hands of its owners. Liquor stores were broken into. Soon the whisky-crazed rabble put the torch to the town, howling with glee as it burned. The wonder was that Quantrill did not completely lose control of them. That he did not is attested by the fact that many men were spared through his intercession.

In four hours the town was thoroughly gutted, the damage in property destroyed or stolen being estimated at $2,000,000. Dead men littered the streets. The number killed? Connelley says 185. Croy and others say the same. *Kansas, a Guide to the Sunflower State* makes it 150, a convenient round number. Wellman makes it 142. It is a conservative figure, and I accept it.[3]

With his men weighted down with loot, surfeited with killing, the town in flames, Quantrill led his sodden army out of Lawrence and back to Missouri. Behind them they left one of their number, Larkin Skaggs, their only casualty. They had been gone for hours when Jim Lane returned to Lawrence and in an attempt to save face got a pursuit of sorts organized, making sure, however, to keep a safe distance between his posse and the retiring guerrillas.

The Lawrence massacre produced some hardy myths, several of which appear and reappear year after year. One has it that Quantrill "escorted" the guests out of the Eldridge House before his men rushed in to plunder and set the building afire, and gave them safe conduct to the City Hotel, where he sat down and enjoyed a hearty breakfast as Lawrence burned. Equally popular is the tale that he commandeered a horse and buggy and drove up and down Massachusetts Street, the town's main thoroughfare, enjoying his victory. These stories trace back to Connelley's *Quantrill and the Border Wars*. More truthful is the story of the two printers who were caught in the press room of the Lawrence *Tribune,* the radical Abolitionist newspaper and one of Quantrill's main targets. When the shooting started, the two men beat a hasty retreat to the wooden shack adjoining the building which housed the *Tribune* privy. They lowered themselves into that fetid retreat and remained there until the invaders left. One of the two was Marsh Murdock, later the founder and editor-owner of the Wichita *Eagle,* today, as it has been for decades, one of the great newspapers of Kansas. Marsh never bothered to deny or confirm the incident, and his silence gave it a permanent niche in Kansas folklore.

Quantrill had more than made good his sworn resolve to do something spectacular. All across the North newspapers blazed forth with the story of the Lawrence massacre. In the wave of revulsion that swept the land, he became the fiend incarnate, the butcher, the murderer and symbol of all that was evil. Because he still labeled himself a Confederate guerrilla, the South now both condemned and repudiated him. Instead of his winning the pseudo respectability that would have been his on being recognized as an officer of the Army of the Confederacy, the Lawrence holocaust had cost him his last chance. He could not understand it, nor would the sleek, dashing, blond Apollo, as vain of his good looks as ever, believe it even now.

In droves, his men left him. The infamous Order No. 11 issued by General Thomas Ewing, in command of all Union forces on the Missouri border, informing the inhabitants of Cass, Bates, Jackson and the northern half of Vernon counties that they had fifteen days in which to gather up what belongings they could carry with them and evacuate the proscribed area, in which all houses, buildings and crops were to be burned, was largely responsible for the disintegration of the guerrilla force. But not altogether. Order No. 11 was in retaliation for the Lawrence massacre, and Quantrill's men realized it. In fact, it was an open secret that Jim Lane had compelled General Ewing to issue the order, which applied to all men in the area, irrespective of whether they were Secessionist sympathizers or Unionists.

It was cruel, inhuman, and if Missouri soil needed further fertilizing for the crop of outlaws it was to produce, Order No. 11 provided it.[4]

Quantrill got out of the Burnt District with perhaps as many as fifty men and headed for Indian Territory. Riding with him for the first time was a boy just turned sixteen. His name was Jesse Woodson James, he of the piercing steel-blue eyes that were never still. According to those who knew him at the time, he had a "smooth, boyish, innocent face and liked to laugh." Early photographs show him entirely unlike his brother (or half-brother, as you may decide later) Frank, who was tall and had a long, "horse face," as they used to say. It did not take young Jesse long to convince his companions that he was not to be trifled with on account of his age.

On the morning of October 6, Quantrill attacked the small Federal garrison at Baxter Springs, Kansas, close to the Indian Territory line. Part of the garrison was off on a foraging expedition. There was a brisk fight, in which Quantrill lost two men and killed nine Federals. He was withdrawing after the brief engagement, when General James G. Blunt, accompanied by his staff, a regimental band and a troop of cavalry, neared Baxter Springs on his way from Fort Scott to his new post at Fort Gibson. Mistaking the departing guerrillas for a welcoming committee, he permitted himself and his men to be surrounded. He escaped with a handful; the rest were killed on the spot, numbering eighty-seven in all, not counting the nine men belonging to the garrison.

It served no purpose and can be explained only as the work of a man gone mad. Quantrill was digging an ever-deeper hole for himself. Open dissension broke out in the ranks as he led the way down through the Nations and crossed Red River at Colbert's Ferry. For several months they raided back and forth across the Texas counties lying between Fort Worth and the Red, plundering, killing, and fighting among themselves over the division of the spoils. Back in Missouri and Kansas their excuse for their crimes was that they were making war on the enemies of the Confederacy. In Texas, they could not use that subterfuge to justify what they were doing; the people they were robbing, plundering and killing were stanch friends of the South. That Texans would not long submit to his depredations does not seem to have occurred to Quantrill; but Bloody Bill Anderson was keenly aware of the rising tide of wrath that was setting in against them, and he was ready to take what men he could with him and break with the guerrilla chief he had followed so long. George Todd, still afraid of Quantrill, was thinking along the same lines.

The handwriting that had been on the wall for a long time became legible even to Quantrill when he rode into Bonham late in March and was placed under arrest by General Henry Mc-Culloch, the Confederate commander of the district. Like his more famous brother Ben, who was killed when Earl Van Doren's Rebel army got a drubbing at Pea Ridge, Arkansas, Henry Mc-Culloch was a former Texas Ranger and a rugged individual.

Taking Quantrill into custody, and not the several men he had with him, and the careless manner in which the prisoner was held, after being disarmed, suggest that McCulloch was proceeding according to a previously agreed on plan with none other than Bloody Bill Anderson, which was to culminate in the slaying of Quantrill as he attempted to flee from Texas. Why else was one of Quantrill's men permitted to ride out of Bonham and carry word to George Todd's camp at Mineral Creek that the guerrilla leader had been arrested? Or how else explain why Quantrill's pistols were left lying so conveniently on a bed at the back of McCulloch's office, in which he was being held, guarded by only two men?

As could have been predicted, Quantrill retrieved his pistols, "surprised" his guards and made his escape. Pursuit was almost immediate, and foremost among the pursuers rode Bill Anderson and his followers. Quantrill reached Todd's camp, finding the men already in the saddle. Riding for their lives, they made it to Colbert's Ferry and crossed the Red into Indian Territory.

It was the beginning of the end of the Quantrill gang. More defections followed as other guerrilla notables, Cole Younger and Fletch Taylor among them, broke away with their personal groups to form gangs of their own. (Jesse James went with Cole.) When the man who for so long had been the scourge of the border got back to Missouri, less than a score of men remained loyal to him. Frank James was one and young Jim Younger another. But there was no sanctuary for him in Missouri; those days were gone. He was hated and despised. Desperate, he struck out across the state for Kentucky with the pitiful remnant of followers who were determined to stick with him to the end.

Presumably, Quantrill hoped to find safety in the Kentucky mountains and recruit a new following. This was another of his plans that went awry. From November 1864 to June 1865, he and his men fought a score of minor skirmishes with Federal troops and Union guerrillas and, between times, plundered and looted wherever four years of war had left anything worth stealing. But though ravaged Kentucky was by now safely in the hands of the North, diehard Southern sympathizers were to be found on every hand, and they befriended and concealed Quantrill's ragged band on numerous occasions.

The war's end brought no peace to Kentucky. Bands of Northern renegades, still claiming to be "Union" guerrillas, and an equal number of so-called Rebel Irregulars, alternately hunted and chased one another from farm to farm, killing and stealing with lawless abandon. Things took a turn for the worse with Quantrill, and he divided his small force. With no more than a dozen men he holed up at the farm of a man named Wakefield, twenty-eight miles southeast of Louisville. After hiding in Wakefield's barn for two days, they were discovered by the enemy. In the fight that followed, Quantrill fell, mortally wounded, and two of his men were killed, the others making their escape. Quantrill was taken to a military hospital in Louisville the following day. There he lingered in great torment, his spine shattered, and died on June 6. He was still some three hundred miles from his home in Canal Dover, Ohio, where he was born on July 31, 1837, and which he had not seen since he went to Kansas in 1857. He was not yet twenty-eight.

The ghoulish (and to me incredible) story is told that his mother, twenty-two years after his death, had her son's bones dug up and turned over to her, which she sold for exhibition. W. W. Scott, a neighbor of hers with whom the tale originated, claimed he had visited the grave with her and aided in having it opened. He remained suspiciously silent, however, until after Mrs. Quantrill's death. You can draw your own conclusions.

Any mention of William Quantrill's several mistresses and his fondness for women of easy virtue has been consciously avoided here. There is no place for it in this narrative, for this is not a "life" of Quantrill. My concern is not so much with the man himself as with the evils of which he was the chief architect, and which shaped the lives of various men for half a century.

Anyone reading Major John N. Edwards' *Noted Guerrillas* and then turning to William Elsey Connelley's *Quantrill and the Border Wars* might wonder if he was reading about the same man. Edwards stands as Quantrill's chief apologist. In his infatuation with his subject he often becomes ridiculous—but no more so than Connelley, on the other hand, in his prejudiced, vindictive account of all that happened before, during and after the Lawrence massacre, even to brushing aside the fact that in the two weeks prior to what happened at Lawrence at least two hundred Missourians were killed by the Jayhawker–Red Leg partisans.[5]

I agree with Paul Wellman that no excuse can be offered for Connelley. He was the secretary of the Kansas State Historical Society and had firsthand sources and personal contacts open to him that no later writer enjoyed. Had he risen above bias and prejudice and written dispassionately, he unquestionably could have produced a book that would have made many that followed it unnecessary. With its wealth of detail, and despite its rancor and fanatical determination to portray Quantrill as the blackest imp of hell, it is our best source of information on Missouri-Kansas partisan strife, occupying much the same position in this regard that S. W. Harman's informative but poorly written *Hell on the Border* holds in relation to Isaac Parker, the hanging Judge, and the U. S. District Court at Fort Smith, Arkansas. They are the accounts on which all writers and historians must lean, more or less.

Charles Robinson, the first governor of Kansas, was in Lawrence on the day of the Massacre, but he was not molested. Though an ardent Free Stater, he was an eminently fair-minded man, outspoken in his denunciation of Jim Lane and Charles Jennison and the atrocities they sponsored and committed. His *The Kansas*

Conflict is a far saner appraisal of the underlying causes of the border struggle than Connelley's. Unlike the latter, he acknowledges that few Missourians crossed that invisible line without a grievance to avenge.

It is easy to understand why those old grudges were kept alive, for in the aftermath of war it was the border counties of Missouri that stood ravaged and desolate, poverty and despair the companions of hunger and hopelessness. Once-prosperous families returning to the Burnt District found only a cemetery of fire-blackened chimneys—"Jennison's Monuments," they were called—to tell them where their homes had been. In contrast, Kansas, aside from Lawrence, had suffered very little damage, and such scars as it received were quickly healed.

If Missouri was to become the breeding ground of outlaws and outlawry, it hardly can be doubted that the blighted, impoverished homeland to which Quantrill's fledglings returned had something to do with it. They were lean, bearded veterans, but judged by their ages, they were still fledglings. Connelley says "Quantrill commanded men twice his age." No doubt he did. But they are not the men whose names are remembered, not the ones who were to leave a red trail of murder and robbery behind them in the years that followed. Of the twenty-eight whom I have been able to check, the average age was twenty-three years. On the day that Quantrill died he was almost two months short of twenty-eight. Bloody Bill Anderson was his senior by a few weeks; Fletch Taylor was twenty-six; Cole Younger, twenty-one; Jim Younger, eighteen; Bob Younger, seventeen; John Younger only sixteen. Frank James was twenty and Jesse going on seventeen. What a brood!

They had to keep on the dodge, because the general amnesty given all who had worn Confederate gray did not apply to ex-guerrillas who had been officially branded outlaws. Union cavalry units (hated Kansas Volunteers) were scouring the country for them. Young Jesse and five others came in under a white flag, only to be fired on. Jesse was seriously wounded but made his escape, as did the others. After that there was no talk of giving themselves up. They appear never to have been far from Liberty, the seat of Clay County, and not far from Jesse's home. Just for amusement, it seemed, they would ride into Liberty and "hurrah" the town. They were just marking time, waiting to find a leader. They found one, second to none, in Jesse Woodson James. Out of the men available to him, he picked ten, Quantrill's ablest pupils, and cut away from the others. This was the beginning of the famous James-Younger Gang, and on February 13, 1866, the day before St. Valentine's Day, under the lowering skies of an impending blizzard, they cracked their first bank.

3

Springboard into Outlawry

THOUGH FOR considerably more than half a century the outlaw on horseback has been the subject of countless books, magazine articles, motion pictures and television dramas, he is little more than a name to millions. Among that vast audience, perhaps the most widely held misconception is that the more prominent gangs of horseback bank and train robbers continued their depredations for years before the law finally caught up with them. With one exception, that is not true. That exception is the James-Younger Gang.

Over the years in which they operated successfully there were changes in its personnel; if a man was killed or incapacitated, he was replaced. But the top men, the leaders, did not change. They seemed to bear charmed lives until disaster overtook them in Northfield, Minnesota, on September 7, 1876. Beginning with the robbing of the Clay County Savings Bank and Loan Association, of Liberty, Missouri, on February 13, 1866 (not February 14, as some would have it), until "the dirty little coward (Bob Ford) laid poor Jesse in his grave," on the morning of April 3, 1882, in St. Joseph, Missouri, sixteen years and two months elapsed—a period in which the James-Younger Gang, and what was left of it after Northfield, robbed, pillaged and killed with reckless abandon, defying sheriffs, marshals and the Pinkertons, money their only object, wanted dead or alive, with rewards on their heads running into the thousands.

Aside from expert leadership and complete ruthlessness, there was another reason for their longevity as an outlaw organization, and it became apparent early in their career. In the counties of western Missouri they had a refuge and "friends" such as Quantrill had never enjoyed. As the years ran on, the feeling for and against them became so bitter that they became a political matter, championed by those who had no banks to be robbed or trains to be held up, and denounced by those who demanded that they be hunted down and exterminated.

Their survival for a decade and a half, and better, set a record that no other outlaw organization ever came close to approaching. Henry Starr ran with the Bill Cook Gang briefly, but as the head of his own gang, his career began with the looting of the People's Bank, in Bentonville, Arkansas, on June 5, 1893, and ended with his death in the attempted robbery of the bank at Harrison, Arkansas, on February 18, 1921. His life of banditry covered a period of twenty-seven years and eight months, but unlike the James boys and the Youngers, many of those years were spent in prison. Properly speaking, he was among the first of the old-time horseback outlaws of Indian Territory, and he was the last.

Sutton is in error in saying: "He worked at the bandit trade off and on for thirty-five years." Henry Starr was only forty-eight when he died. All the other gangs were short-lived, and that included the "famous" Dalton brothers. Aside from the alleged participation of Grat and Emmett "and possibly Bob" (no one seems to be sure about it, and there is some doubt that any of them were involved in the robbery of a Southern Pacific train at Alila, California), the authentic record of the Daltons begins with the holdup of a Santa Fe train and the robbery of the express car at Wharton (now Perry), Oklahoma, on May 9, 1891, and it ends with the disaster that overtook them at Coffeyville, Kansas, on October 5, 1892; which adds up to one year and seven months.

Bill Doolin did a little better. After Coffeyville, which he missed only because his horse went lame, he organized his own gang.[1] His first strike was a bank at Spearville, Kansas, east of Dodge City, early in November 1892, four weeks after Coffeyville; and he led his gang high, wide and handsome until he was killed by marshals near Lawson P. O., Payne County, Oklahoma, on the night of August 25, 1896. His score was five years and three months.

The other, and not so well-known, gangs of Indian Territory–Oklahoma outlaws had a brief existence. They were constantly changing, disintegrating under attack and then reforming with new leaders. The Bill Cook–Cherokee Bill Gang was typical, new faces appearing and old ones disappearing every few months. The deadly little Rufus Buck Gang of Creek killers and rapists went the same way, shot down or hanged. A year or two did for the luckiest of them. The career of the comic-opera Jennings Gang was of even shorter duration. Texas Jack (his honest name was Nathaniel Reed, no relation to the Belle Starr Reeds) operated outside the law for ten years. But he was a lone wolf and seldom rode with an organized gang. Of his major crimes, only one was committed within the boundaries of present-day Oklahoma, the rest occurring in Colorado, Texas and Missouri.

While the banditry of Frank and Jesse James and the Youngers was not indigenous to Indian Territory, it was only one step removed, and by their exploits they handed down to generations of receptive minds the legacy of lawlessness which they had inherited from Quantrill. Then, too, they were not strangers to the Territory. On at least three occasions they crossed it on their way to Texas, and Jesse, at least once and very likely twice, idled some time away at Belle Starr's outlaw rendezvous in Younger's Bend, on the South Canadian, fifty-odd miles west of Fort Smith, Arkansas. Both Cole Younger and the James boys, in their days with Quantrill, had fought back and forth across this Cherokee country in their horse-stealing expeditions. There is no evidence to support the story that they engaged in other criminal activities within the boundaries of the Territory.[2]

In telling the story of Western outlawry, no one, not even Billy the Kid, has received the attention lavished on the leaders of the James-Younger Gang by historians, biographers and writers in general. This has been going on for years, and so many literary microscopes having been turned on them, it would be pointless to attempt another blow-by-blow account of their astounding career of crime. Their story was written a long time ago, and it is unlikely that anything new can be added now. But some of the legends that once surrounded them have survived. Thankless as the effort may be, it would seem to be pertinent to attempt to break them down at this late date, as well as to correct some of the errors that have been repeated so often that even the informed have come to accept them as fact.

Perhaps none of the legends is more widely believed than the one that has a blood relationship between the Jameses and the Youngers. On this, I regretfully have to part company with Wellman. In his *A Dynasty of Western Outlaws* he repeatedly states that such a tie existed, though he offers no proof of it. He uses it as evidence of a criminal strain being passed on, thereby keeping the "chain" of outlaw succession unbroken. I can find nothing to support his contention that the James and Younger families were even distantly related. Homer Croy, the Missourian and native historian of the James-Younger era says, "A hard-to-down legend was that the Youngers were related to the Jameses, but this is not true."

That the tale is given credence undoubtedly stems from the fact that the Younger boys and the Daltons were second cousins, not first cousins, which is a common mistake. The mother of the Daltons was Adeline Younger, the daughter of Charles F. Younger, the brother of "Colonel" Henry Washington Younger, father of Cole, Bob, Jim and John Younger. To quote Croy a bit further: "There is no evidence that he [Cole Younger] ever saw them [the Dalton boys]. The Dalton boys were younger and did not come into prominence until Cole was paling in prison [after Northfield, of course]."

The exploits of the Dalton boys can be dealt with at length a bit later, but the charge that they came into the world with inherited criminal tendencies having been raised, this would seem to be the time to explore it a bit further. When Louis Dalton, a Clay County farmer and veteran of the Mexican War, married Adeline Younger, his record was clean, and it stayed clean until his death. At the beginning of the Civil War, he moved with his growing family to an unimproved farm he had purchased north of Coffeyville, Kansas. Eventually thirteen children were born to Louis and Adeline Dalton—nine sons and four daughters. Of the boys, eight reached manhood. Of the eight, only four tarred themselves with the outlaw brand. The others lived honest, upright lives. If there was a criminal strain in the family blood, why didn't it show up in them? Their sisters were universally respected, so much so that no odium fell on them even after the Dalton name had become synonymous with banditry.

Burton Rascoe was another writer who succumbed to the tale of blood relationship between the James family and the Youngers. In his *Belle Starr* he says: "The Youngers, the Jameses and the Daltons of Missouri all appear, from legend at least [legend, he says] to have been related, either as blood kin or by marriage. And from this it would also appear that there was something as imponderably wrong with the family as there was with the descendants of Laius, in Greek legend. The Youngers, with whom the James brothers were associated by consanguinity as well as banditry, have certainly done their share to provide an American variant to the Oedipus story."

This is sheer literary nonsense, and no one should have known it better than Rascoe, for it was he who made game of Professor Caesar Lombroso, the famous Italian criminologist, and his theory of criminal impulse through heredity. It was Rascoe who invented the wholly false story of Frank James' return to society after spending twenty-one years in the Missouri State Penitentiary.

Let us take a look at the parents of the James boys and the Youngers. In October 1842, the Reverend Robert James, a backwoods preacher-farmer, and Zerelda Cole James, his wife, arrived in Missouri from Kentucky. Frank James claimed they came from Tennessee. It was to Tennessee that he and Jesse made their way after their escape from Northfield and were so befriended and screened from public attention that they were not heard of again for three years. It inclines me to believe that Frank was correct in saying that the family came from that state. Being desperately hunted men, it stands to reason that it must have been to distant clan connections they turned, not to new friends. It was during his stay in Tennessee that Jesse first used the alias "J. D. Howard," by which he was known in St. Joseph prior to the time of his death.

On January 10, 1843, Zerelda James gave birth to a son, who was named Alexander Franklin James, whom we know as Frank James. A second child, Jesse Woodson James, was born September 5, 1847.

Jesse was only an infant and Frank not yet five when the Reverend Robert James joined the stampede to the California gold fields, where he died of a brief illness in or near Marysville. In 1851, their mother was married a second time, to a man by the name of Simms, of whom little is known. Fifteen months later, Zerelda divorced him for nonsupport. She was a comely young woman, still in her twenties, and it was not long before she took a third husband, Dr. Reuben Samuel, a Kentuckian, a kindly, intelligent man, who, through the trying years to come, was devoted to her, as she was to him. They were a law-abiding Christian couple, strongly pro-Southern in their sympathies. Two children blessed their union; little Archie, eight years old when he was killed in the bombing of the Samuel home, and sister Fannie, much younger.

The criminal tendencies that made Frank and Jesse the most notorious outlaws of their time were self-imposed, fostered by the times and atmosphere in which they grew to manhood. It can not be traced back to their forebears. It began with them and ended with them. Is more proof needed than that Jesse's son and grandson, despite the load he left them to carry, led examplary lives and became outstanding men in their community?

The parents of the Younger boys were people of some consequence in Jackson County, Missouri. The father, "Colonel" Henry Washington Younger, was a rich man, by the standards of the community. The title "Colonel" was purely honorary, for he was not a military man and had never served in war or battle. "Colonels," says Croy, "were as thick as blackbirds on a barbed-wire fence; anybody so far down the line as to be called 'Major' was sensitive about it."

Like so many in the border counties of Missouri, he came from Kentucky, a tall, handsome man, with a flowing mustache and goatee. Settling near Kansas City, he soon acquired several thousand acres of farmland and won the contract to transport mail through that section of Missouri. He has been called "Judge" as well as "Colonel." He was, in fact, what was known as a "court judge," whose responsibility it was to lay out roads, supervise the building of bridges and oversee the voting of road bonds. Today, he would be called a county commissioner. He was never a judge of legal matters, sitting in court.

His mail contracts covered about five hundred miles, an operation that necessitated a considerable investment in wagons, horses and stables. As an agent of the United States government, he was important enough to be summoned to Washington on frequent occasions. As a result of his prominence and popularity, he was three times elected to the Missouri state legislature. In 1859, he was elected mayor of Harrisonville, the principal town of Cass County.

Though he hailed from Kentucky and was the owner of two slaves, he was a Union sympathizer, believing it should be preserved and that slavery should be abolished—not a popular position to take in a hotbed of Secessionists.

While he was away on business in the spring of 1862, a band of Jennison's Red Legs swept down on his stables in Harrisonville and made off with a number of horses and wagons, also destroying considerable property. The raiders came for plunder, and they got it. Younger's political leanings had nothing to do with it. To the day he died, Cole Younger claimed that it was this raid by Jennison that swung him over to the cause of the Confederacy for all time. If true, then the bushwhacking he had been doing was just an exciting adventure that called for no deep convictions on his part. If Cole Younger needed an excuse to justify his years of outlawry, I preper to believe it was the tragic end that overtook his father two months later rather than the Red Leg raid.

On returning to Missouri and assessing the damages he had suffered, Henry Younger drove to Independence and demanded reimbursement from the district Federal commander. As a mail contractor doing business with the United States government, his equipment, horses, wagons, barns, had been guaranteed against loss by the military. Though the claim he made was officially filed, it is not of record that it was ever satisfied.

On July 20, 1862, as he was driving to his home in Harrisonville, thirty miles away, alone in his one-horse buggy, he was murdered and robbed of a considerable sum of money which it has been said he derived from the sale of a herd of cattle made that day. This is not true. He had no cattle in Independence. But robbery was the purpose of the crime. Revenge for a personal slight could have supplied additional motivation. Henry Younger was known to carry large sums of money on his person. That was reason enough for killing him. Union sympathizers claimed it was the work of Rebel bushwhackers. There was enough evidence to the contrary to refute that story. The war raging between the states and the local bitterness between proslavery and antislavery elements had nothing to do with the slaying of Henry Younger.

Because the killing of the father of the Younger boys was to set the tone of much that was to follow, it is important enough to be examined in some detail. Remember that Cole was going on eighteen at the time and, unknown to his father, had been riding off and on with Quantrill for six months. During the winter of 1861, Cuthbert Mockbee, a Southerner, gave a dance in honor of his daughter, at his home near Harrisonville. Cole and his sister were invited. The festivities were in full sway, as they used to say, when Captain Irvin Walley, commander of a company of Federal militia stationed in nearby Independence, made his unwelcome appearance. To his embarrassment, the girls, including Sheba Younger, refused to dance with him.

Walley, with what justice I do not know, accused Cole of being responsible for the slight put on him. Losing his head completely, he called Cole a Quantrill spy and demanded to know where the still relatively unknown guerrilla leader could be found. When Cole said he did not know, Walley called him a liar. The fight was on. Cole knocked him down. Lying on the floor, Walley tried to draw his pistol. One of the partisan onlookers wrenched it away from him. Walley left a few minutes later, and so did Cole and his sister. On his father's advice, he took to the brush the following morning. That afternoon, Walley and six of his men dashed up to the Younger home and searched the premises. Not finding Cole, they rode away, threatening to return.

While formal war was being waged between the North and the South, the old border warfare took on new dimensions, blazing up like a forest fire out of control as opposing bands of bush-whackers and guerrillas spread terror, death and destruction wherever they rode. As 1862 opened, a man could go to his door after nightfall only at the risk of being shot down. Every night, in one direction or another, the sky was red as some farmer's home went up in flames. It was murder, arson and robbery without hope of redress. The opposing factions pretended to have a quasi-military status. Actually, they had none. The flag under which they rode might be the stars and stripes of the North, or the stars and bars of the Confederacy, but their real emblem would have been emblazoned with the skull and crossbones of piracy.

Northern sympathizers were no safer from Red Legs and Jay-hawkers than Southerners were and vice versa. The Kansans had an advantage which Quantrill and his cohorts did not enjoy; Senator Jim Lane had used his influence with the War Depart-ment, and where a Missouri border town was garrisoned, it was with Kansas militia, and in dealing with their own partisans, they saw no evil and heard no evil.

It can not be denied that the captains of some of the militia companies passed on information to Jennison and shared in the loot. That was the reputation of Captain Irvin Walley. If the Younger family entertained the suspicion that Walley had a finger in the theft of the Younger horses and wagon, and con-sidering the bad blood existing between the man and themselves they quite likely did, they said nothing. But when Henry Wash-ington Younger was murdered and robbed and the body dumped out on the Harrisonville road, the storm broke, and they loudly accused him of following their father out of Independence with a half dozen of his men and jumping him. The charge was taken up by all of the Younger faction and grew so heated that Walley was arrested, but he produced witnesses who swore he was else-where at the time of the murder, and the charge was dropped.

The Younger boys refused to believe Walley was innocent, an opinion shared by all Southern adherents. Cole Younger swore that he would attend to Walley—a threat that he never fulfilled. His explanation of this appears in a letter to J. W. Buel, author of *The Border Outlaws*, written while he was still confined in the Minnesota State Penitentiary at Stillwater. In part, it says: "I could have killed Walley nearly any time, but only by assassination—slipping up to his house and shooting him through a window. . . . I could not pollute my soul with such a crime." This is pretty hard to believe, coming from a man who had sent seventeen others to their death. Cole's years in prison had mellowed him, no doubt.

It is ironic that Henry Younger was found by Mrs. Washington Wells and her son Sam, on the way to their home in Lee's Summit, a few minutes after he was killed. The son, a hairy, crude, semiliterate farm boy, was to carve a niche for himself in the annals of outlawry as an important member of the James-Younger Gang. He was with them at Northfield and was killed by a sheriff's posse a few days later as he and the three Younger boys made their desperate attempt to escape from Minnesota. History does not know him as Sam Wells, but remembers him well as "Charlie Pitts."

While Mrs. Wells remained at the roadside with the murdered man, her son turned his team and galloped back to town with the news. Captain Everett Peabody and a militia detail soon arrived. Peabody had the body placed in the buggy and delivered it to the grief-stricken widow in Harrisonville. It was Peabody who discovered that Henry Younger was wearing a money belt containing $2,200, which the murderers had overlooked in their haste. His wallet was missing. How much it contained, no one could say. The $2,200 was turned over to the widow.

If there was a criminal streak in Henry Washington Younger, I can not find it. He was a rich man for his time and environment, and he was in politics, two counts on which many men have been accused of skulduggery. The integrity of the man seems to have lifted him above the usual calumnies fostered by the disgruntled. He died as he had lived, honored and respected.

4

Mothers of the James Boys and the Youngers

WHAT ABOUT THE MOTHER of the Younger boys? Was there a weakness of moral fiber in her, an evil strain, that made outlaws of her sons? Judged by all that is known of Bersheba Fristoe Younger, the answer must be no. The courage and fortitude with which she met the adversities and tragedy that confronted her for most of her life are no mean indication of her strong, resolute character.

The Fristoes were an old, established family when Henry Younger first appeared in Jackson County. Bersheba Fristoe's father, Richard Martin Fristoe, had been instrumental in organizing the county and in having it named Jackson County in honor of General Andrew Jackson, under whom he had fought in the War of 1812. In 1827, he became its first judge. On her mother's side, Bersheba came from equally good stock.

She was barely eighteen when she married Henry Younger. She bore him fourteen children, eight boys and six girls. Cole (Thomas

Coleman Younger) was the seventh child. He had three younger brothers—Bob, Jim and John. With him, they are the only ones known to history.

Cole Younger was not at home at the time his father was killed. It was known that he had been scouting for Quantrill. The Federal militia (spurred on by Walley, no doubt) could not wait to get their hands on him. Some sources say that he often risked capture by visiting his mother. It is another tale that has no corroboration and need not be taken seriously.

Confederate records, still available, prove that he enlisted in Captain John Jarette's company, Colonel Upton B. Hayes' regiment, which was part of General Jo Shelby's brigade, and given the rank of first lieutenant. His years considered, it sounds incredible, even if he had demonstrated some qualities of leadership. Shelby's brigade was recognized by Southern supporters as a unit of the Army of the Confederacy with official status. Actually, it was but once removed from Quantrill's guerrillas. The personnel seemed to be interchangeable; a man rode with Quantrill one month and with Shelby's brigade the next.

Cole took part in a second attack on Independence on August 11, which routed the Union troops. Five days later, he distinguished himself in the Rebel victory at Lone Jack, a few miles from Kansas City. Coupled with the part he played in capturing a rich cotton train in Louisiana, this seems to have been the provable extent of what, in his old age, he referred to as his "war record." He was seventy-two when he passed away peacefully, and was buried beside his mother and his brothers Bob, Jim and John. In addition to the imposing marble monument erected by his relatives, there is a much smaller one, incribed to "Captain Cole Younger, C.S.A." It is misleading, for it is not an official marker placed there by the Graves and Monuments Committee of the National Confederate Veterans Association. Surviving friends of his guerrilla days subscribed for it.

A week after the battle at Lone Jack, Cole risked coming to see his mother. He was caught in the house by Union militiamen (some say Captain Walley was in charge of them, but it is debatable) and escaped only through the connivance of Suse (short for Susan), who had grown old as a Younger slave.

Two months later, Union troops came to the house again in the middle of the night and searched it from cellar to garret for Cole. Infuriated by not finding him, they ordered Mrs. Younger to set fire to the place. She had her four youngest children with her. An early fall storm had put a few inches of snow on the ground. She pleaded that if the intruders were determined to make her burn her own home they wait until morning.

The men drew aside to talk it over. The danger that they might be caught there if they waited was, presumably, real enough, but it was well after midnight, and they were not averse to remaining indoors, where it was warm, until daylight. When she offered to cook them something to eat, they agreed to wait. At the crack of dawn, however, they hitched a horse to a wagon, tossed a mattress and some blankets into it. Some furniture having been gathered into a pile, they forced her to set it afire. They galloped off then, and Sheba Younger and her children stood huddled together in the chill morning air, watching as the flames devoured their home.

In his autobiography, *The Story of Cole Younger, by Himself,* published in 1903, he makes much of the burning of his old home and the treatment his mother and brothers and sisters received, though hundreds of other families were burned out in that fashion. In freezing weather, he has it, they had to make their way through two feet of snow to Harrisonville, eight miles away. (Oldtimers tell me that in their memory two feet of snow never fell on Jackson County in October.)

But Cole's bitterness can be understood, and it would have been surprising if he had not insisted that the burning of the Younger home was done at the instigation of his old enemy Captain Irvin Walley.

It has been claimed that depicting Irvin Walley as the ever-present menace whose machinations helped to drive the Youngers into outlawry was only a device to win sympathy for the latter and that it has little substance in fact. That may be; but it can not be denied that many similar crimes, and worse, were committed that served no purpose other than an individual's thirst for vengeance. The following from *Kansas, a Guide to the Sunflower*

State is pertinent here. It is as fair and unbiased as anything I have read:

"For two years a state of open warfare existed. Armed bands of border ruffians from Missouri made forays into Kansas and were answered by retaliatory companies of Jayhawkers. Men were called out into the night and shot down for no other reason than they supported or were suspected of supporting the opposite cause. Women and children, regardless of age or condition, were driven from their homes with only the clothing on their backs. Fields were laid waste and towns were sacked, all in the name of the cause, but *more often to gratify personal revenge or avarice.*"

The writer is speaking of what happened before war was declared between North and South, but the motivation did not change when Fort Sumter fell; revenge and avarice still ruled the minds of men.

Friends took Sheba Younger and her children in, but she did not remain long in Harrisonville. The Youngers had a house in Waverly that was available. If she expected to be safe there, she was mistaken. The men who had forced her to burn her old home came again. Word of the $2,200 that had been turned over to her had got around. In blunt words they informed her that they had come for the money. It was about all she had left, other than farmlands, for which there was no market. When she told them she did not have the money, they ransacked the house and threatened to hang old Suse in an attempt to make the black woman divulge the hiding place. Though they beat and abused her, Suse stuck to her story that she knew nothing about the money. They had been going through the house an hour before they went out to their horses and galloped away into the night. The money was sewed in Suse's skirt, the most unlikely place to look for it.

Again the Younger faction claimed this was some more of Captain Walley's work. Later, when the Waverly house was burned, they were convinced of it. Cole Younger had taken a prominent part in Quantrill's third attempt to capture Independence. He had been recognized. Burning his mother out again was said to have been done in retaliation. If this is only conjecture, so be it. But it would appear that the continued harassment of

Sheba Younger—I have touched only the high spots—went far beyond what other women with sons in the guerrillas had to endure. Maybe it was Captain Irvin Walley of the Missouri state militia that bedeviled her, maybe not; no one can say for sure.

Gathering her brood about her, she moved across the Missouri River to Missouri City, in Clay County, to live out her remaining days with her sister, Mrs. T. W. Twyman. Broken in health, she became an invalid and died in 1870, bowed down by the shame of having four of her sons, Cole, Bob, Jim and young John, numbered among the country's most notorious outlaws.

Zerelda Samuel, mother of the James boys, drained a cup of misery also, and it was brewed of reasons not wholly dissimilar. All the two women had in common was that their sons were first guerrillas and then outlaws. Zerelda had no Captain Walley, whether mythical or real, dogging her; with Zerelda it was to be the Pinkertons, and they were very real.

Unquestionably she was deeply distressed by the crimes attributed to her sons, but she made no excuses for them. Instead, she simply refused to believe they were as black as they were painted. To the very end, she remained loyal to them, and her affection for Frank and Jesse never wavered. Few, if any, among the many writers who have addressed themselves to the story of Frank and Jesse James have denied her their sympathy, even a measure of heroism. That she was a forceful, determined woman, there can be no doubt.

She and her third husband, Dr. Reuben Samuel, were driven from their first home by the infamous Order No. 11 and found shelter in the tiny Missouri River settlement of Rulo, just over the line in what was then Nebraska Territory.

In August, 1865, Dr. Samuel and Zerelda returned to Kearney, in Clay County, Missouri, to see if anything remained of their former home. They were surprised to find it still standing. As has been noted, Jesse was seriously wounded by a detachment of drunken Union cavalrymen when he rode in under a white flag to surrender. He had made his way to Rulo and was still an invalid when the doctor and Zerelda returned to Clay County. They left him in Kansas City with the family of John Mimms to regain his health. Mimms had married the sister of the Reverend Robert

James and was Jesse's uncle. It was there that he met Zerelda Mimms (named after his mother), whom he later married.

With the end of the war, families had begun streaming back to the Burnt District to begin life anew. Labor was cheap. Dr. Samuel had the old home repaired and made livable. It is often referred to as a "log cabin." It was built of logs, but it was commodious enough to deserve the name of house. Between doctoring and farming, he was making a humble living, when Jesse catapulted the family into prominence by robbing the bank at nearby Liberty. After that, life was never the same for Zerelda and the doctor. Other robberies and train holdups followed, all attributed to the James-Younger Gang. The hunt for them was intensified, but dangerous as it was, they often slipped in out of the brush and spent the night at the Samuel house. It was not long before information to that effect was in the hands of the Pinkertons. What they did about it ended in stark tragedy.

The Pinkerton National Detective Agency, the foremost sleuthing organization in the United States, had been retained by the Missouri Bankers' Association in an effort to protect its member banks by running down the James-Younger Gang. For months, a score of the agency's best operatives had been crisscrossing Missouri, peering through windows and looking into old barns; the results were distinctly embarrassing to the Pinkerton Agency. As the year of 1874 drew to a close, the score read: three detectives and only one outlaw, John Younger, killed. (We will return to these.) And trains continued to be held up and banks robbed with annoying frequency.

However, on January 5, 1876, the agency got a break. Jack Ladd, one of their best operatives, who had been working as a psuedo farmhand within several miles of the Samuel home, wired the Kansas City office that Frank and Jesse were visiting their mother. Arrangements to capture or kill the two men were completed within the hour. That evening, a special train running over the Cameron branch of the Hannibal and St. Joe, took a group of Pinkerton men into the heart of Clay County. Their horses filled the baggage car. Perhaps the train crew knew the purpose of the "special." Certainly the conductor, William Westphal, did. His orders were to signal the engineer to stop several miles before reaching Kearney. As soon as the detectives and their horses were unloaded, the train went on. This was a device to prevent word reaching Frank and Jesse that a party of mounted men were riding through the night, headed for the Samuel home.

There is some disagreement as to what followed, but it concerns only what one of the Pinkertons tossed through the window that he had opened. The only light within came from the fireplace. It was a bitter night, the temperature hovering around zero. The doctor, Zelda, their two young children—Archie, aged eight, and Fannie, aged five—and a Negro servant woman, who had come west from Kentucky with Zelda and her husband, had retired for the night. Whatever it was that came sailing into the room, it exploded, and the effect was ghastly. Zelda's right arm was torn off at the elbow. Archie was disemboweled and died almost at once. Dr. Samuel and the Negro woman were seriously injured. Little Fannie was only scratched and slightly burned. The irony of it was that Frank and Jesse were a hundred miles away.

A feeling of revulsion against the Pinkertons swept the state. But from Allan Pinkerton down, his agency swore that the object tossed through the window was nothing more than a lighted iron oil-pot, to enable the men to see better when it blazed up. Though they protested long and vehemently, very few accepted their story. Explosive experts scouted the idea that an exploding oil-pot could have wreaked such havoc. Missourians said it was a lighted grenade, and most writers agree with them.

Wellman is one of the few who do not, and for a reason that I can not accept. He says: "I simply do not think that responsible and law-respecting people would knowingly throw a grenade into a room where they were not even sure who was there."

I can only ask: why not? I recall the part played by Pinkerton men in the bloody strike at the McCormick Reaper Company Works, in Chicago, and again in the revolt of the steelworkers at the Homestead Mills, in Pittsburgh. The Pinkertons of that era are not sacrosanct with me. I am skeptical of the tale that has Jesse stalking Allan Pinkerton in Chicago, determined to kill him if they met face to face—which never came off.

Zerelda had been dead for years and Frank James for twelve, when a small paperback book entitled *The Only True History of the Life of Frank James, Written by Himself* was published by a job printer in Pine Bluff, Arkansas. It is a collector's item today, but like so many that are, it is trash, and so filled with errors of fact, with which the alleged author would have been well-acquainted, that it is to be doubted that Frank James wrote it. It attracted no attention until Burton Rascoe came across it. He says: "I at first tossed it aside as one of those horrible examples of meretricious trash, fabricated by some hack to capitalize on the notoriety of the James brothers."

But he came back to it, for it contained a titillating tidbit that he could not forego pouncing on. "Upon rereading it, something told me that this piece of shoddy, for a wonder, was just what it was alleged to be. It is maudlin, illiterate, vague, confused, pathetic. It is just the sort of thing that Frank James, in his distressful, diabetic, last days might write, when sufficiently urged to do so by the down payment of a few dollars and the promise of some more to come."

This is the item on which the all-knowing Rascoe based some startling conjectures, which have been repeated and enlarged on by subsequent writers:

"I was a base begotten child. It was never known to the world. My parents came from Tennessee to Missouri. I was born a short time after they arrived in Clay County, Missouri, and the people there never knew or thought anything about the child that was called Frank James.

"My mother was promised to be married secretly to a man named Edd Reed. He was killed before I was born, and to save the disgrace my mother married Robert James and then moved to Missouri. So the people of this old world did not know that Frank and Jesse James were only half brothers."

"Looking back, it somehow rings true," comments Paul Wellman. "It would account for many things: the sudden arrival of Robert James and his wife from their home in Kentucky [sic], interrupting his theological studies; the birth of the first son to Zerelda shortly after; the utter difference in appearance, personality, disposition, even thinking of Frank and Jesse."

We have some specious reasoning here. Did the Reverend Robert James and his wife arrive "suddenly" in Missouri? And what were those "theological studies" that had to be interrupted? Robert James was a back-country, horseback preacher. As for the dissimilarity between two brothers, it would be exceedingly rash to say it was something peculiar to the sons of Zerelda James. It would be equally rash to brand this tale a myth, but before I accept it, some substantiating evidence will have to be presented.

I have mentioned Jesse's son and grandson, who made names for themselves as honest, upright men. Frank James had a son, Robert F. James. He, too, was untainted by any hint of criminality. And there was Roosevelt Starr, Henry Starr's son. He did not grow up to follow the trail his father had blazed. If the criminal impulse is in the blood, something that is handed down from father to son, we should have had a second generation of such outlaws as the James boys, the Daltons, the Youngers, and a third and so on. But that did not happen. Not many had sons. Among those who did, I do not know of a single instance in which it could be said: like father, like son.

In a day when large families were the rule, ten to fifteen children, the James clan, by blood and by marriage, must have numbered a hundred or more. Of all of them, in addition to Frank and Jesse, only two were tarred with the brush of outlawry. They were brothers, Wood and Clarence Hite. They were ex-guerrillas, crude, ignorant men, second cousins to the James brothers. Of the score or more who at one time or another rode with the James Gang, they were the most unimportant. Jesse tolerated them, but he did not trust them. Wood Hite was killed over a woman, a sister of Bob and Charley Ford. Clarence Hite contracted pneumonia while in prison and died soon after being released. It was good riddance. Both were worthless.

Because they were distantly related to Frank and Jesse, some writers give it as proof of the "bad" blood in the James clan. That only four out of a possible hundred went wrong could be considered a much stronger argument to the contrary. The truth is that it proves exactly nothing; every family has its black sheep.

For a last word on the theory that the outlaws with whom we are dealing were born criminals, that their lawless impulses were due to heredity, let me quote from an interview Henry Starr gave a feature writer for the *St. Louis Republic* while he was incar-

cerated in the Chandler, Oklahoma, jail, following the bank robbery at nearby Stroud. This interview almost in its entirety appears
in *Hands Up,* with the author of the book asserting that it was
made to him:

"There is no such thing as a born criminal, as heredity badness,
unless the person is insane. I think I ought to know criminals.
They have been my companions for forty years, in prison and out.
I have eaten and slept with them, helped them plan crimes, led
them into crimes, knelt beside them when they died . . . if the bad
criminal mind is hereditary, then the good honest mind is hereditary, too; and all the sons of preachers and doctors and honest
bankers would be good, like their parents. But nearly all the
bandits and outlaws and criminals I have known were the sons
of good fathers and mothers.

"If the criminal tendency was hereditary the sons of every criminal would be criminals, too. I never knew the son of an outlaw
to be a criminal.

"The criminal tendency is not transmitted from father to son,
any more than the tendency to be religious is transmitted. Getting
religion depends upon environment and circumstance. Religion
is not born in a fellow . . . he catches it in the same way he catches
measles or whooping cough, by coming in contact with it, just as
criminals are made by environment and circumstance."

Starr's argument would have more merit if he had excluded the
Cherokee Bills, Rufus Bucks and lesser fry among the sadistic
Indian and mixblood killers of early Indian Territory outlawry.
Limit it to the men whose thinking and way of life were channeled
by the evil influence of Quantrill, and it makes sense. Had the
Jameses and the Youngers grown to maturity in another place
and in another time, they very likely would have lived dull and
blameless lives. It was the environment in which they grew up,
saturated with the hatreds and bloodletting of border war, that
turned them to outlawry; not inherited criminality.

5

Their Guns Their Only Law

AMONG THOSE whose knowledge of the James-Younger Gang (and other bands of horseback outlaws) is slight, the idea flourishes that robberies and train holdups followed one another at intervals of only two or three weeks. The record reveals how far from true that is. After the robbery at Liberty, in February, the James-Younger Gang did not strike again until October 30, more than eight months later, when they looted the bank at Lexington, Missouri.

They were accused, very likely unjustly, of robbing an Austin–San Antonio stagecoach at Blanco, Texas, although three, possibly four, stagecoach robberies can be rightly charged up to them over the decade and a half of their spectacular banditry. In all that time, however, they entered only a dozen banks (counting their misadventure at Northfield) and held up only seven trains. Add to that the Kansas City Fairgrounds robbery and you have the complete score of their major undertakings—twenty in all, which averages out at no better than one every nine months.

Needless to say, they were accused of many crimes of which they were not guilty—sometimes of two on the same day, hundreds of miles apart.

In the course of their forays, they killed ten men—eleven if you include John Rafferty, an engineer who was scalded to death in the derailment of the Rock Island train at Adair, Iowa, July 21, 1873. Undoubtedly there were others of whom there is no record. The list of trainmen, bank employees and plain citizens who got in the way and were injured by their gunfire is staggering.

Many estimates have been made of how much money they got away with. The popular reckoning is half a million dollars. Cole Younger, who was the only one of the bandits to say anything about it, claimed that they never got half of what they were supposed to have taken. It was believed by scores of men that the fortune stolen by the gang had been buried somewhere, and for years a great deal of secret digging for it went on all over Clay and Jackson counties. No one ever found a dollar. The best answer as to what became of the money is that it was spent. A little simple arithmetic is all that is required to arrive at that conclusion. If in fifteen years the loot totaled half a million dollars, the yearly take was less than $35,000. Divided among eight to ten men, all it amounted to was handsome wages. Cole Younger says they got nothing like half a million dollars. He was in a position to know, and he had no reason to lie about it, for the statement was made in his old age; long after he had squared the grudges the law had against him.

Turn back to the robbing of the bank at Liberty. Greenup Bird, the cashier, in a sworn statement, says the outlaws rode off with $57,072, of which $40,000 was in bonds, $15,000 in gold coin and the balance, scarcely more than $2,000, in silver and greenbacks. The bonds were nonnegotiable, hence worthless to the bandits. The gold was an even more tantalizing problem, since there was so little of it in circulation that to start spending it was certain to fasten suspicion on whoever possessed it as a member of the robber gang. The only way out of the dilemma was to dispose of the gold to a "fence," at a usurious discount.

Croy says that Cole Younger knew of such a man, a Mexican named Gonzales, in San Antonio, Texas, and speculates that Cole had head about him through a guerrilla acquaintance, who hailed from Tensas Parish, in Louisiana. Even for men who were at home in the saddle, it was a long journey to San Antonio. The incentive being what it was, the four leading spirits of the gang agreed to go. There is bountiful evidence that Cole Younger was one, and little doubt that Jim Younger and Frank and Jesse were the others. I do not know how the figure was arrived at, but all commentators agree that they got $9,000 for their $15,000 in gold.

If, as claimed, twelve men took part in the Liberty bank robbery, a little more arithmetic reveals that each man netted only a little over a thousand dollars. Doubtless some of the loot from other robberies was in gold or nonnegotiable paper. No figures are available, but if it happened often enough, their net take was, as Cole claimed, considerably less than half a million dollars.

The bank robberies and train holdups of the James-Younger Gang were not confined to Missouri. Including those that were attempted and ended in disaster, seven states—Missouri, Texas, Arkansas, Iowa, West Virginia, Kentucky and Minnesota—suffered from their depredations. Over the years, the number of men who, at one time or another, rode with the Youngers and the Jameses totals at least twenty-seven. Seven—Charlie Pitts, Clell Miller, Bill Chadwell, Tom McDaniels, Payne Jones, Bud Daniels and John Younger—were killed by gunfire; three—Arch Clements, Andy McGuire and Dick Burns—were lynched; another three—Jesse James, Wood Hite and Ed Miller—were assassinated by their companions in outlawry; two—Jim Younger and Charley Ford—committed suicide. Of the rest, at least nine served long prison terms. This did not include Frank James and Jim Cummins. Bob Ford, "the dirty little coward," was gunned to death in his own saloon in Creede, Colorado, in July 1892.

Because the sojurn in Texas of Frank and Jesse James after they had concluded their business with the slippery Señor Gonzales was to introduce to the history of horseback outlawry one of its principal characters, it must be examined. Ten miles east of Dallas, a small town at the time, was a much smaller settlement named Sycene. A number of emigrants from Kentucky, Tennessee and Missouri had settled there, among them John Shirley, the erstwhile tavernkeeper of Carthage, in Jasper County, Missouri. His eldest son, Preston, had preceded him to the Sycene neighborhood and was farming. But Preston Shirley and his younger brother Ed (known as Bud), who was killed by Federal guerrillas at Sarcoxie, Missouri, in 1863, are only incidental figures as far as this narrative is concerned. The reverse is true of their sister, Myra Belle, who was to blaze across the firmament of Western outlawry as Belle Starr, the Bandit Queen, about whom a vast amount of utter nonsense has been written. But of that, later. For the present, let it suffice to say that Myra Belle was eighteen when Cole Younger and his companions stopped over in Sycene to visit old firends. They found things so pleasant that they remained there several months. The Shirleys and other old Missouri acquaintances knew them only as boys who had ridden with Quantrill and had no reason to suspect that they had recently turned their talents to banditry, though they were well supplied with money.

Cole Younger, as he was then, was a big, handsome, generous young man, with a pleasing, friendly personality. Myra Belle seems to have appealed to him at once, and he to her. His romantic dalliance with her was serious enough to cause him to buy a small farm near Sycene, which could have been prompted only by his intention to settle there permanently at some future date. Even at eighteen, Myra Belle was not pretty, but she had an attractive figure and an abundance of feminine allure that appealed to men, and she was wild and reckless enough to be doubly desirable in Cole's eyes.

His brother Jim and the Jameses were not similarly enamored of Texas. They had exhausted the pleasures of Sycene and nearby Dallas and wanted to get back north. Who suggested that they hold up the army paymaster on his way from Fort Johnson to Fort Belknap is not known. Very likely it was Jesse. Cole threw in with the others, and they disappeared from Sycene for a few days. They made their stand, but having no experience as highwaymen, they bungled the job. Their intimidating shots brought the paymaster's lagging escort around a bend in the road at a driving gallop, and they were forced to flee. They returned to Sycene knowing they were being sought. It gave them an excellent reason for quitting Texas at once.

When Cole informed Myra Belle that some mysterious business had come up that made his return to Missouri necessary immediately, it may be presumed that he softened his parting by promising her he would soon be back. She was not to see him again for five years.

Eight months later, she gave birth to a daughter. Beyond reasonable doubt, Cole was the child's father. It was only hinted at first, but as the years passed, evidence to that effect became so overwhelming as to leave no room for speculation. It was a pretty baby, and through its childhood years the litttle tot became increasingly lovely. At sixteen, she was a truly beautiful young woman, resembling the father she had never known, but possessing her mother's fire and spirit to a marked degree.

Throughout the tempestuous ups and downs of her life, and they were many, Myra Belle Shirley never wavered in her love and devotion for her daughter, who she was determined, come what might, should grow up to be a "lady"—a dream that was not to be realized. Myra Belle named her Pearl Younger. It was by that name, and none other, that she was known until she married William Harrison, late in life.

Cole had been behind the walls at Northfield for thirteen years when reporters brought him word that Belle Starr (nee Myra Belle Shirley) had been murdered. Since the news dispatch from Fort Smith, Arkansas, stated that she had once been married to him, he was asked if it were true that she was or had been his wife. His answer was guarded but truthful, I believe. "I have never been married, so it can't be true that the lady who has been murdered was my wife." When pressed, he added: "I knew the lady slightly some years ago; but it has been many years since I have seen her."

After their return to Missouri in the fall of 1866, the James-Younger Gang looted the bank at Lexington, Missouri, in October. On March 2 of the following year, they failed in the attempted robbery of the private bank of Judge William McLain, at Savannah, Missouri. This was followed on May 23 by the bloody looting of the Hughes and Mason Bank, at Richmond, Missouri, in which the mayor of the town and the local jailer and his son were slain.

The whole state was now aroused against the outlaw gang. They dispersed at once—an old Quantrill trick—but three of them, Dick Burns, Andy McGuire and Tom Little, were dug out of their hiding places and lynched by the irate citizens of Richmond. A fourth bandit, Payne Jones, was cornered, but he shot his way out of trouble, killing a doctor and the little girl who had led the posse to his hiding place.

The Jameses and the Youngers lay low for a year. They had only to read the newspaper to learn that in addition to an army of deputy sheriffs and marshals, the Pinkertons had been engaged to hunt them down. When the gang struck again, it was far afield, at Russellville, Kentucky, on May 20, 1868. Cole Younger and Jesse walked into the Long and Norton Bank and, shoving a pistol in Nimrod Long's face, ordered him to open the vault. Instead of obeying, the cashier bolted for the rear door and, though slightly wounded, leaped outside and sounded the alarm. Two men on horseback, members of the gang, fired at him without bringing him down. Inside the bank, Cole and Jesse cowed a clerk and a customer and stuffed $14,000 into the ever-serviceable grain sack that was an indispensable part of their equipment.

As they emerged from the bank, a man named Owens opened fire on them. One or the other snapped a shot at him and put him out of action. A moment or two later, the two men were in the saddle, and the whole gang was pounding out of town, with a score of excited citizens shooting at them but doing no damage. They got away without a man lost or wounded. But the Pinkertons took up the trail. One of their operatives named Bligh got an identification on George Shepherd, an ex-guerrilla and a James-Younger man since the first raid on Liberty, and began looking for him in Clay and Jackson counties. He soon learned that Shepherd was living with the buxom widow of Dick Maddox, another noted Quantrill guerrilla and friend of Cole Younger, who had been killed in a personal quarrel with a drunken Cherokee. Bligh caught him there and surrounded the house with a posse.

Shepherd held them off all night. When he tried to make a break by jumping from a window at dawn, a slug caught him in the right leg and he was captured. On being returned to Kentucky, he received an indeterminate two-to-five-year sentence, though he stoutly denied participating in the robbery and refused, of course, to admit being acquainted with those who had taken part in it.

Following the Russellville affair, the James-Younger Gang dropped from sight for better than a year and a half. Some commentators have it that they went as far as California to hide out until the heat was off them. However, evidence to that effect has never been presented. Wherever they were, they were conducting themselves so circumspectly that Missouri peace officers began to relax their vigilance. According to the old cliche, the public has a short memory. It was true in their case. Just when bank presidents were beginning to breathe easily again, the dreaded names of the Jameses and the Youngers hit the headlines with a bang.

On December 7, 1869, two men, positively identified as Jesse James and Cole Younger, walked into the Daviess County Savings Bank, at Gallatin, Missouri. A third man, Frank James, remained outside in the saddle, holding the horses. John W. Sheets, the cashier, was filling out a deposit slip for a farmer named McDowell. When he looked up, he found Cole Younger's pistol staring him in the face. Jesse covered the farmer. Neither man offered any resistance. Jesse exchanged a nod with Cole, and the latter hurried behind the counter to rifle the safe and the cash drawer. Very little went into the grain sack this morning—less than a thousand dollars. Perhaps their rage at getting so little was responsible for what followed, or maybe it was, as has been said repeatedly, that they believed cashier Sheets to be in reality none other than Lieutenant S. P. Cox, the Union officer whose militia detachment had ambushed and killed Bloody Bill Anderson, Jesse's commander when he first rode with Quantrill.

However it was, Jesse, without saying a word, cold-bloodedly put a bullet through the cashier's head, killing him instantly. "The shot was heard, and citizens began looking for guns," says Wellman. "Frank James, outside the bank, cried a warning, and Cole and Jesse emerged."

It is hard to believe that a single shot could have so quickly aroused a town that had been caught off-guard. The bandits got away, but not without a trying few moments, for as Jesse started to swing into the saddle, his horse bolted. He was dragged a few feet before he got his foot out of the stirrup and was thrown clear. With the ice-cold nerve he often exhibited, Frank James, seeing his brother was unhorsed, swung back. Jesse climbed up behind him and off they went. They encountered a horseman astride a fine animal and relieved him of it. Pursuit was quickly organized, but, as usual, it kept at a respectful distance.

If one cares to speculate on the Gallatin robbery, the possibility exists that Jesse was convinced before he embarked on it with only Frank and Cole—not the usual James-Younger complement—that the man known in Gallatin as John Sheets was Lieutenant Cox and that from the first it was revenge, not the hope of making a big haul, that supplied the motivation. Certainly he knew that the Daviess County Bank was not a rich one. That would be a more convincing tale than the one we are asked to accept, which has nothing to recommend it but its repeated retelling.

I prefer to believe that Frank, Jesse and Cole had been inactive so long that they had run out of money and that the Gallatin job looked like an easy touch. That revenge had anything to do with it hangs on the very tenuous thread that the bandits compelled a country preacher to "guide" them around the tiny settlement of Kidder, on the main line of the Hannibal and St. Joe Railroad, and that Jesse remarked to him: "I've killed S. P. Cox, if I haven't mistaken the man."

They were not more than thirty miles from home at the time. Why they should have needed a "guide" to get them through country with which they had been familiar for years passes belief. We are told that Jesse's horse was recognized when captured as belonging to him and that "Deputy Sheriff Tomlinson and three others caught the James brothers hiding in the barn; and that the wanted men escaped." The Gallatin bank was robbed and John Sheets cruelly and needlessly murdered. The rest, I am convinced, is just folklore.

Though the proceeds of the Gallatin robbery added up to very little, it unleashed a veritable hornet's nest of trouble on the James-Younger Gang. For the first time, peace officers attempted to coordinate their efforts in a state-wide hunt to run them down. It was high time to get out of Missouri again. By twos and threes, they crossed the line into Indian Territory and holed up in old Tom Starr's domain, east of Eufala. They knew old Tom from guerrilla days. He had ten brothers, several sons and daughters.

With all of his progeny and kinsfolk, he was the head of perhaps the largest of all Cherokee clans, and he ruled it with a cruel, iron hand. The "Starr country" was wild, desolate, without roads, and no one attempted to cross it who was not known to be friendly with its overlord. Its limestone caves were a perfect refuge for men on the scout. Then, too, a man could turn a dollar by stealing horses and cattle for Tom Starr.

Other Starrs will enter this narrative. But mark old Tom, for he is important.

On June 3, 1871, the world heard from the James-Younger Gang again. This time it was the prosperous town of Corydon, Iowa, twelve miles north of the Missouri line, in Wayne County. They rode in quietly for a change and discovered they had arrived at a most propitious moment. Several blocks from the Ocobock Brothers Bank, their objective, a political rally was in full swing. As they walked into the bank, they could hear the Honorable Henry Clay Dean spellbinding the crowd. Inside, they found only the cashier. He opened the safe, as ordered. When they walked out, the grain sack was bulging with $45,000 in assorted bonds, gold and paper currency.

It was one of the gang's richest hauls. Jesse felt so good about it that as they passed the meeting on their way out of town, he stopped and interrupted the speaker.

"What is it?" the Great Man demanded with understandable annoyance. Looking Jesse over, he made the mistake of taking him for just another heckler. "If you have anything to say that's so important that it can't wait till I finish my speech, let's hear it!"

"I'm sorry to interrupt," Jesse called back, "but there's something wrong down at the bank. In fact, it's just been robbed. Maybe you better look into it, sir."

With a mocking laugh, he and his fellow conspirators put spurs to their horses and dashed away in a cloud of dust.

The story is still told in Corydon.

6

Robbery on the Rails

K EEPING TRACK of the whereabouts of Jesse through the years of his outlawry is no great problem, since he took part in every major robbery committed by the James-Younger Gang. Almost the same can be said of his brother Frank. It is when the attempt is made to follow the movements of the Younger brothers that confusion steps in. In Cole's case it is largely because of his connection with Belle Shirley. You will read that because of his infatuation with her he repeatedly tore himself away from his trade of banditry and made the long journey to Texas—five hundred miles as the crow flies—expressly to see her and their daughter Pearl. You will be treated to page after page of romantic dialogue between them, all of which is sheer fiction.

Cole and Belle met on two occasions in Sycene, but no eavesdroppers were listening in on what passed between them. Putting words into their mouths is pure humbug, born in the writers imagination, and mostly a rewrite of the trash first coined by the anonymous hack who was responsible for the lurid tale "Bella Starr, the Bandit Queen, or the Female Jesse James," published in the *National Police Gazette.* Though Belle named her daughter Pearl

Younger, and later named her place on the South Canadian "Younger's Bend," she never gave any evidence, by either letter or word of mouth, that she entertained any lingering affection for Cole. Nor he for her.

It has been said repeatedly that she named her place on the South Canadian in honor of him. She never said so. It seems far more likely that she named it for Pearl, to whom she was devoted. Likewise, the story that she spent large sums of money in an effort to effect Cole's release from prison need not be taken seriously, no evidence to support it having been discovered.

Up to and including the Corydon robbery, only two of the four Younger brothers, Cole and Jim, had been identified as members of the outlaw gang, but it was generally believed that Bob and the even younger John were riding with them, inasmuch as they were no longer seen in their old haunts in Jackson County. It was this erroneous conclusion that was to mystify writers and readers alike years later when the story of the Jameses and the Youngers began to be told.

As a matter of fact, both boys were living in Dallas County, Texas, and not engaging in outlawry. Bob had a job in a Dallas store. His brother John had joined him after the Gallatin robbery and put in the winter of 1869/1870 as a deputy sheriff of Dallas County.

In 1871, however, young John got into trouble. He made his home on the farm Cole had bought near Sycene but spent most of his time in the saloons of Dallas. In a bit of drunken nonsense, late in January, he tried to shoot the pipe out of a man's mouth and the slug clipped off the tip of the target's nose. A warrant was sworn out for his arrest, and Deputy Sheriff Charles H. Nichols went out to Sycene to serve it. According to the *Dallas Weekly Herald,* Nichols took a posse with him. He found John Younger and a friend recently arrived from Missouri named Porter (unquestionably an alias for one of the James-Younger Gang) as they were about to sit down to breakfast in the little hotel at Sycene. Younger asked permission to finish breakfast before riding to Dallas, which Reynolds granted.

It should be interjected here that the apparent laxity with which law enforcement officers in the north Texas counties treated renegades from Missouri sprang from the fact that many of them were ex-guerrillas themselves who had fought with either Quantrill or Jo Shelby and were personally acquainted with the leading members of the James-Younger Gang.

It seems that when Nichols left the two men eating their breakfast, he stepped into a store next door. They seized this opportunity to run to the barn where their horses were quartered. Finding Nichols' possemen guarding the barn, they turned and ran into the store, their pistols blazing as they came in. Nichols was killed instantly. The proprietor, identity unknown, returned their fire, a slug from his revolver striking John Younger in the right leg. Younger and the mysterious "Porter" ran out, helped themselves to Nichols' horse and one belonging to a member of the posse. They were chased, but by nightfall they were across Red River and safe in the Territory. The state of Texas offered a reward of $500 for the arrest of John Younger. It was an empty gesture. After spending a few days at Robbers' Cave, the famous owlhoot hangout in the San Boise Mountains, north of present-day Wilburton, where he received the necessary buckshot surgery for his leg, he went on north to old Tom Starr's place.

Of course, after the Corydon robbery the gang had to scatter once more and lie low for a few months. If Cole Younger entertained any great hankering to renew his relations with Belle Shirley, this was his opportunity. It would not have interfered with his "business," and Texas was reasonably safe. Instead, Frank James and he made a scout into Kentucky and Tennessee. He was particularly fond of Frank, a feeling he never had for Jesse. Perhaps by now they were beginning to resent the airs and authority Jesse gave himself. He was their leader; he could plan and carry out a raid. But they knew their worth; without them, and possibly Clell Miller, he could not get very far.

Heading for the Cumberlands, they crossed Adair County and came to the pleasant little town of Columbia, the county seat. Having a professional interest in banks, the one in Columbia caught their eye. It stood on the corner, in a red brick building of its own. The entrance was on the street level, no steps to climb, which was always important in their scheme of things. The possibilities from their point of view were so enticing that they circled around Columbia and acquainted themselves with the roads leading out of town. The one to the south led into the hills. The Tennessee line was less than forty miles away. They filed these facts away in their minds, and on April 29, 1872, they were back. Five of them this time: Jesse and Frank James, Clell Miller, Cole and Jim Younger.

They were still flush from the proceeds of the Corydon robbery, and they had come a long way to reach Columbia, which made what followed doubly humiliating. They entered the bank without difficulty but found a tartar in R. C. Martin, the cashier. When ordered to open the safe on pain of death, he refused to be intimidated. They killed him and took what they found in the till—a matter of only several hundred dollars. If they had got very little at Gallatin, this was even worse. They got away safely, but the business of robbing banks had hit an all-time low. It must have given them food for thought.

It may explain why they turned their talents in a new direction on September 26 of that year. The Kansas City Fair had been in progress for several days, long enough for anyone who was interested to ascertain how the box office was handling the money, which averaged about $10,000 a day. By arrangement with the First National Bank of Kansas City, the Fair Association was able to send their money into town for deposit after regular banking hours. One afternoon, sometime after four o'clock, a messenger (not a boy as some say) stepped out of the fairgrounds office carrying a tin box that contained the deposit for the day. He had taken only a few steps when he was accosted by three mounted men with drawn pistols. They relieved him of the box and, after firing several shots to overawe the score or more startled witnesses, dashed out of the fairgrounds at a driving gallop.

The "Fairgrounds Robbery," as it came to be called, is ignored by some commentators and regarded with extreme skepticism by others, among them, Horan and Rascoe. They say among other things that the money (much of it in silver, according to them) would have been too heavy to be carried in a tin box; that a sum of that size would hardly have been entrusted to a boy (sic); that a deposit could not have been made that late in the afternoon. If they had read J. W. Buel's *The Border Outlaws*, published in

St. Louis in 1882, their doubts would have been answered. Buel was a reporter on the Kansas City *Journal* at the time of the robbery, and in his book he uses the story he wrote for that newspaper the following day. It is the best source material we have.

By relying on it and interlarding his own logic, Wellman demolishes the doubters. He makes one statement, however, that goes beyond my knowledge, in saying: "Actual participants in the holdup at the Fair Grounds were believed to be Frank and Jesse James and Bob Younger. Bob Younger, only twenty years old, had just recently joined the gang, and this must have been his first robbery."

Wellman may be correct about Bob, but I would place him in Texas. Certainly he was in Sycene a month later. So were Cole and Jim Younger. So were other members of the gang, possibly Jesse himself. They had more business to transact with Señor Gonzales in San Antonio, and it seems reasonable to surmise that Jesse would have been on hand to see what the deal was.

Over the years, the romanticists who, with little regard for facts, have fashioned the beautiful, glamorous image that they call "Belle Starr" grow lyrical about Cole's presence in Sycene in October of 1872 and his meeting with Belle after an absence of five years. "His affection for her had never wavered," we are told. "He knew her parents had no use for him and that her brother Preston hated him, but he could remain away no longer. Braving everything, he had come to Sycene just to see Belle and his daughter Pearl, now just past her fifth birthday. At last he rode up to John Shirley's house, the very house where he had met Belle that day that now seemed so long ago. A very tender scene follows, one that pulls at the heartstrings when Cole takes his daughter in his arms."

The trouble with the foregoing is that it is all wrong. Belle was no longer living with her parents. For more than a year she had been running wild with a bunch of two-bit desperadoes and ne'er-do-wells. Her father had locked her in her room for a time, but her friends had "rescued" her, and in a mock marriage she had become the "wife" of Jim Reed, a young bandit from Rich Hill, Missouri, not far from Carthage, where she was brought up. As children they had known each other. Reed had killed a neighbor who accused him of stealing a blooded mare and had been forced to get out of Missouri on the double.

For several months prior to Cole Younger's arrival in Sycene in 1872, Belle had been living with Reed as man and wife on his farm south of town. Pearl was with her grandparents. And here the "love idyll" of the romance writers collapses completely. Cole was acquainted with the man who had taken Belle away from him. But he did not go gunning for him, which he most certainly would have done if he felt that his "rights" had been invaded. To the contrary, they met several times with no apparent ill-will on the part of either.

It was Ed Reed who led Belle into outlawry. We will have to get back to him.

When Cole and whoever was with him in Texas had finished their business with Gonzales, they settled down on Cole's farm outside of Sycene. There were enough of them gathered there to make the cooking a chore. Rascoe says that Cole tried to induce Belle to take over, an absurdity on the face of it. Far more believable is Croy's statement that Cole tried to induce his long-suffering sister Amelia to join them. There is no evidence that she ever did. But a man they had not seen for four years rode into Texas and put his feet under their table at Sycene. He was none other than George Shepherd, fresh from the stretch he had served behind bars for his part in the Russellville robbery. He was a Cole Younger man, and his coming strengthened the latter's hand in the growing rivalry for leadership between Cole and Jesse.

Jesse was both proud and jealous of his leadership, as he had a right to be. His reputation as a successful outlaw leader was fairly well established. That he was aware that it was being challenged can be authenticated. Croy got the story from Harry Younger Hall, Cole's nephew, in whose home the old outlaw lived out the last years of his life, and I thank him for permitting me to use it.

Though Jesse needed Cole as he needed no one else, including his brother Frank, he treacherously tried to turn Cole and Shepherd against each other. According to Harry Younger Hall, Jesse took Cole aside and informed him that in some way Shepherd held him (Cole) responsible for his capture at the home of Dick Maddox' widow and meant to kill him at the first good opportu-

nity he got. He then poisoned Shepherd's mind with the story that
Cole no longer trusted him (Shepherd) and intended to rub him
out. The stratagem almost succeeded. Cole and Shepherd shared
the same bed and went to sleep with their hands on their guns.
When one stirred, the other was instantly alert. It was a long night
for both. When they went out to feed their horses in the morning,
Shepherd said, "Cole, why do you want to kill me?"

"Because you want to kill me," Cole answered.

"Why, I never had it in my mind to kill you till Jesse told me
you was goin' to kill me," was the astonished answer.

Cole laughed. He saw through Jesse's game to get rid of one
or both of them, and so did Shepherd. They shook hands, and that
was the last of it.

One wonders if during the big get-together at Sycene it was
suggested that they could outwit the authorities and Pinkertons,
whose attention was concentrated on banks, by forgetting about
bank robbery for a time and trying their hand at holding up a
train. It would be less dangerous, very likely just as profitable and
certainly more spectacular and exciting. If so, it must have been
Jesse who did the talking. Looting banks had become pretty dull
stuff to him. As with Quantrill, the spectacular appealed to him.

No doubt the suggestion would have interested the gang, but no
decision could have been reached, for they were back in Missouri
in the spring, and on May 23 crossed the state to the district known
locally as "Swampeast" and stuck up the Sainte Genevieve Savings
Association.

Sainte Genevieve was a sleepy little town, hard by the Mississippi River. It had been settled by the French, and more French
than English was spoken there. That the gang regarded it as an
easy touch is attested by the fact that only five men took part; two
riding in from one direction and three from another, timing their
coming so that they met in front of the bank.

According to Robertus Love, in his *The Rise and Fall of Jesse
James*, which has withstood all the attacks leveled at it and remains
the most accurate life of the great bandit leader that we have, the
five were Cole Younger, Bob Younger, Clell Miller, Bill Chadwell
and Jesse. Cole, Jesse and Clell Miller went into the bank. Cole
had the grain sack. Into it went about $4,000.

They had no trouble inside. Not a shot was fired. But when they came out, Cole's horse broke away. It was embarrassing because the grain sack with its $4,000 was tied to the saddle horn. Sainte Genevieve was not yet aware of what had happened. A Frenchman riding into town obligingly caught the animal and turned it over to Cole. The five bandits then thundered out of town in the usual cloud of dust.

Six weeks later, on July 21, Jesse had his way about it and they did the "spectacular"—their first train robbery. It was well-known that the Chicago, Rock Island and Pacific was transporting rich consignments of gold from faraway California to the East. With no more detailed information on how to proceed, he led his men by easy stages to Adair, Iowa, a few miles east of Council Bluffs. They arrived at their destination about nine in the evening and broke into a shed in which track workers kept their tools. Securing a spike bar and a sledge hammer, they went east of town a short distance, to a curve, pried off a fishplate, removed the spikes and attached a rope to the loosened rail so that it could be pulled out of alignment. Hiding behind an embankment, they had nothing to do but wait until the express came panting around the bend.

It was after midnight, when it hove into view. Years later, Cole Younger said that they expected the train would stop when the locomotive left the tracks. Instead, it plowed ahead a few feet and toppled over, breaking the steam pipe. John Rafferty, the engineer was caught in the cab and scalded to death. His fireman was badly burned.

The express car yielded less than $3,000. Very little more was garnered when the bandits went down the aisle of the passenger cars with their greedy grain sack. "Railroad records show," says Croy, "that $75,000 went through the following night." The gang had missed the jackpot by only twenty-four hours. The James-Youngers had not had a man wounded or killed, and there were no subsequent arrests. Viewed in that light, they could call the Adair holdup a success. But in no other way.

They had undertaken the holdup without adequate information, which they might have secured, and they bungled the job in sending Rafferty to a cruel death. The Pinkerton Agency, basing its findings on descriptions given by passengers, charged the James-

Youngers with the crime. Newspapers the country over headlined their stories with "The Horrible Death of a Brave Engineer." Jesse James, the "merciless outlaw," was reviled from coast to coast.

Fearful of what was to come, the railroad companies banded together and did what the bankers had done. They turned to Allen Pinkerton and his sons to protect their trains and, in an all-out effort, expense no item, to put the James-Younger bandits behind bars.

If Jesse had wanted the attention of the country focused on him, he achieved his goal. He was now a national figure, the acknowledged leader of the greatest gang of outlaws the country had ever known. He responded to his newly found notoriety by leading his gang out of Indian Territory, where he had been "resting," into Arkansas, where they waylaid the Hot Springs–Malvern stage on January 15. How much they got is unknown. But this was a distinctly offbeat job. Jesse's eye was on the St. Louis, Iron Mountain and Southern Railroad, whose main line ran up through southeastern Missouri to the Mound City. In another two weeks he had his "research" completed, and on the evening of January 31, 1874, he and five others appeared out of nowhere, took over the depot at Gads Hill Station (the Pinkertons were looking for them far across the state) and tied up the Iron Mountain agent and half a dozen rustics who were waiting to see the express go through. When the train appeared out of the blackness of the night, it was flagged down. The train crew was marched into the depot, one of the bandits riding herd on them. The rest of the gang went through the express safe and the passenger cars. Again they got very little—not more than $3,000—but this was a professional job, neatly handled. Jesse was proud of it.

"When you see the reporters," he said to the engineer, "tell 'em you was talking to Jesse James!"

After firing a few shots into the air, "just for the hell of it," says Stewart Holbrook, they swung into the saddle and raced away, with a wild halloo for the bewildered villagers.

This was a new and different Jesse James. He had always been vain, but never a show-off. Obviously he was reading his own press notices now.

7

The One and Only Jesse

Iₙ ᴛʜᴇ ꜰᴏᴜʀ ᴡᴇᴇᴋꜱ following the Gads Hill holdup, the Pinkertons sent their best men into Missouri. But no arrests were made. They complained to their superiors that they could get no cooperation from the inhabitants of the border counties of western Missouri, where the outlaws had a number of hiding places, that the James-Younger Gang had friends in every crossroads village and on every farm. It is true that there were many who, for one reason or another, were sympathetic to Jesse and his men, but the overwhelming majority kept silent because they were afraid to inform on them.

What was more to the point, Jesse had perfected a secret intelligence system that worked so well that whenever a stranger appeared in Clay County word of his presence was quickly conveyed to him by his hangers-on.

Detective John W. Whicher, brave to the point of foolhardiness, came out from Chicago to enter Clay County, the heart of the outlaw country, to track the Jameses to their lair. He was warned that he was taking his life into his own hands. His story, as he moved about, was to be that he was a farmhand looking for work.

He was "spotted" almost as soon as he got off the train at Liberty. He made his first mistake in arriving in Liberty wearing "city" clothes and made a second in conferring with Pete Moss, ex-sheriff of Clay County and a hater of the James brothers.

Moss had told him where he would find the Samuel farm, and he walked to Kearney, reaching there the following evening. After supper he went on, though the night was cold for a wayfarer on foot. It was March 10. He was only four miles from his destination. Needless to say, he had been followed all the way from Liberty. As he was passing a patch of scrub timber, three armed men stepped out of concealment and confronted him. The three were Jesse and Frank James and Clell Miller. Jesse did the talking.

Whicher was wearing butternut jeans, a blue flannel shirt and a sheepskin coat. He looked like the farmhand he said he was, but Jesse was not fooled.

"Those ain't the duds you were wearing when you stepped off the train the other day, mister. If you're a farm worker, as you claim to be, let's have a look at your hands."

Whicher's death sentence was written when he held out his hands, palms up. There were no calluses on them. When they searched him and found a revolver, that did it; they were satisfied that the man was a Pinkerton.

They tried to force him to divulge information about the plans of the detectives. Whether or not they got anything out of him is unknown, of course. They killed him, put the body on a horse and Jesse carted it across the line into Jackson County—the Younger stronghold—and dumped it at the roadside. When found, there was a bullet hole in Whicher's head and three or four in his chest. Just who killed him is as much a mystery today as it was then. Perhaps all three sped him into eternity.

It is worthy of note that Cole did not appreciate Jesse's effort to cast suspicion on him and his brothers for a murder they had not committed. It widened the growing breach between them that was to end in Cole's bitter hatred of Jesse.

Five days after the killing of John Whicher, two other Pinkerton detectives, Louis J. Lull and James Wright, acting on a tip that the Youngers were holed up somewhere in St. Clair County, along the Osage River, rode into that sparsely settled section of the

Ozarks posing as cattle buyers. With them went E. B. Daniels, a former deputy sheriff who was acquainted with the country around Osceola, the county seat, a clannish, backwoods town of fewer than eight hundred people, but the only settlement of any size in all St. Clair County.

When the three men put up for the night at Monegaw Springs, eight miles west of Osceola, Daniels, the former deputy, now a paid Pinkerton employee, was recognized. To ride through that region of mountains, hills, sharp bluffs and rushing streams—the wooded hills still wore their winter brown—in the company of strangers made any man suspect. When they left Monegaw Springs and continued west, suspicion ran ahead of them.

The farms were far apart, and they were primitive. If a man had a few acres of rich bottom land put to corn, he did not have much else but his hogs and a cow or two that might be for sale. The Pinkertons stopped whenever they found a house. They were shown some cattle, but the price they offered was not satisfactory, as they knew it would not be—they did not want to be burdened with livestock. In the course of a conversation they tried to elicit some information about the men they were seeking. That they got any is doubtful, for in some instances they were talking to men who were kinsfolk of the Youngers.

One early afternoon, the detectives stopped at the farm of a man named Snuffer. It was the wrong place to stop, Snuffer being distantly related to the Youngers. Jim and John Younger were hiding upstairs and heard every word the strangers had to say. It convinced them that the three men were Pinkertons. They could have killed them there, but they allowed them to leave, not wanting to make trouble for Snuffer, and then took after them, John carrying a shotgun and Jim armed with his pistols.

When the detectives heard horsemen pounding after them and coming up fast, Wright raked his horse with his spurs and fled. Jim Younger snapped a shot at him that carried away his hat. He escaped unmarked, however. The other two were lined up at the side of the road and dropped their revolvers as they were ordered to do. But Detective Lull had a second pistol concealed in his clothes. When he saw that Daniels and he were mired in their story of being cattle buyers and that their death was imminent, he drew his hidden pistol and sent a bullet crashing into John Younger.

The shot was fatal, but before Younger fell from the saddle, he pressed the trigger of his shotgun and the blast tore a gaping hole in Lull's throat. The detective's horse bolted, and Lull was thrown to the ground. In a frenzy of rage, Jim Younger killed Daniels with a single shot and then pumped several shots into Lull. Draping the body of his slain brother over the saddle, he bore him away and, with assistance, buried him in a small apple orchard.

Louis Lull was not dead, though he was mortally wounded. He was found by a farmer and taken to the village of Roscoe, where he lingered for some weeks before dying. In the interval, he was able to make an affidavit telling what had happened. Horan, who had access to the Pinkerton archives, found the story, and we are indebted to him for it.

Nothing was heard of the other members of the James-Younger Gang for months. If Cole can be believed, they were in California. Attempts have been made to locate them in and around San Diego, close to the Mexican border. It sounds reasonable, but I have found no evidence to support it.

Jesse and Frank were back in Missouri in April. It was marriage, not robbery, they had on their minds this time. Not too much is known about Frank's marriage in 1874 to Annie Ralston, the daughter of a respectable Clay County family, other than that her people objected so strenuously to her marrying Frank that she had to elope with him. On April 24, 1874, Jesse married Zerelda Mimms, who had been waiting for him for eight years. No elopement for him. Dressed in the finest raiment money could buy, he boldly came into Kansas City and was married by a minister.

What kind of women were these who married famous outlaws, men with a price on their heads, wanted dead or alive? They were a far cry from what today we call "gun molls." They lived on "outlaw" money, but on no other count can they be faulted. They took no part in the lawless deeds of their husbands, not even as spies or go-betweens. They were loyal to the men they married, and Frank and Jesse were true and loyal to them. If there is one untarnished page in the life of the James brothers, it is to be found in their marital relations with Annie and Zerelda.

What the lives of these two women, married to the most notorious bandits in America, must have been can easily be imagined. The very nature of their position cut them off from old friends and made the making of new ones too hazardous to be risked. Whenever they said good-by to their husbands, who could be leaving them for weeks or months, it must have been ever present in their minds that they might never again see them alive.

They followed Frank and Jesse to strange towns and secret hiding places whenever they could, living in outlaw caves, lonely cabins or obscurely in cheap hotels. They must have had some ray of hope held out to them that things would change one day. Very likely it was the seldom realized dream of most outlaws that they would make a big strike and then leave the country and begin life anew in some foreign land. If so, Annie and Zerelda James were doomed to disappointment.

Jesse and Frank disappeared from Missouri, taking their wives with them, and were not heard of again for eleven months. That they "lost" themselves in Tennessee has been pretty well established. It was at this time that Jesse adopted the alias of J. B. Howard and Frank, not so imaginative, became plain Frank Woods—not Woodson, as some have it.

Frank and Annie became the parents of a son, Robert, who grew up to be a highly respected farmer in Clay County, Missouri. Jesse and Zerelda had two children—Jesse, Jr., who studied law and became a member of the Kansas City bar, and Mary, who married a well-to-do farmer named Henry Barr. Mary's three sons became leaders in the Methodist church at Excelsior Springs. Later, one of them was ordained a minister.

The long inactivity of the James-Younger Gang ended dramatically on the night of December 13, at the tiny villiage of Muncie, Kansas. The Kansas Pacific's Denver–Kansas City night express was their target this time. They used the same tactics that had been so successful at Gads Hill. They literally took possession of the tiny hamlet, herding into the small depot a score of people, along with the railroad agent, and holding them there at gunpoint.

The express, on being flagged, came to a stop. The train crew, taken by surprise, had to do as they were bid. The express car was uncoupled, and the engineer was ordered to pull it up the tracks several hundred yards. Frank Webster, the messenger, opened the car door when he was given the choice of doing so or being blown to bits with a blast of dynamite. They repaid his cooperation by slugging him unconscious.

On opening the safe they found they had hit the jackpot. Between what it held and what they got by going through the coaches, they rode off with upward of $60,000.

Again there were no arrests. Not immediately, that is. But a few days later, Bud McDaniels, a long-time member of the James-Younger Gang, was picked up by the police in Kansas City on a drunk and disorderly charge. When searched, he was found to have a thousand dollars on him, for which he could not account. Under police grilling, he confessed to taking part in the Muncie robbery. He was brought to trial in Topeka and sentenced to ten years in Leavenworth. He escaped his guards as he was being taken to the penitentiary. A posse of prison officers and sheriff's deputies tracked him down before the week was out and wasted no time blasting the life out of him.

The arrest, conviction and killing of Bud McDaniels was not a feather in the Pinkertons' cap, for they had had nothing to do with it. They were becoming desperate in their embarrassment. Three of their operatives had been killed, and the only success they could point to was the rubbing out of John Younger. They opened a secret headquarters in Kansas City. The only thing secret about it was that the name of the Pinkerton National Detective Agency did not appear on the office door. It hardly can be doubted that the loss of face they had suffered to date in their war on the James-Younger Gang put them in the mood to try anything and culminated in the tragic bombing of the Samuel house on the night of January 5, 1875. The mutilation of Zerelda Samuel, the injuries suffered by Dr. Samuel and the killing of little Archie cost them what little support and sympathy they had had and, for practical purposes, ended their usefulness in Missouri.

Men and women waited for the boys to strike back, confident that Jesse and Frank would not let the bombing go unatoned, a feeling that the Pinkertons shared. It weighed on them, and wherever they went, a ghostly death rode at their side.

But nothing happened. Weeks passed without bringing the expected retribution. As usual after a big strike, the gang had separated, each man going his own way. That Frank and Jesse again found the Tom Starr country in Indian Territory a safe and comfortable refuge seems likely. But they were back in Missouri by mid-March. Clell Miller was with them. They busied themselves ferreting out information concerning the men who had taken part in the attack on the Samuel place.

Jesse's underground intelligence system was unable to identify the man who had tossed the grenade, but it gave him the names of William Westphal, the conductor in charge of the special train that brought the detectives and other officers to Kearney, and of Dan Askew, the neighbor on whose farm Jack Ladd, the Pinkerton detective, had worked; and, of course, enough about Ladd to convince Jesse that Ladd was the one who had set the tragic business in motion with his misleading telegram to the Pinkerton office in Kansas City.

An intensive search for Ladd now became the first order of business for the avengers. After it had been prosecuted for ten days, Jesse became convinced that the man had left Missouri (which he had). But the James boys knew where to find Dan Askew. He was not a Pinkerton accomplice, but Jesse would not have it that way. On April 12, he rode to the Askew farm, called him out and shot him down without listening to an explanation.

The Pinkertons had made it necessary, said Jesse. He made sure they heard about it. It was expected that more reprisals would follow. When they failed to materialize, people wondered why Jesse was holding off, but they refused to believe that he was finished; he was not a man to forget his grudges.

Other bandit outfits, delighted to be mistaken for the James-Youngers, were looting banks in the states of the Middle Border.

When a group of second- and third-raters rode into a town and the word spread that the redoubtable Jesse James and his boys were at hand, it made things considerably easier for them. On the other hand, to be charged with a robbery in Iowa, when they were scattered in their hideouts in Missouri and the Territory, confused the lawmen and worked to the advantage of Jesse and his gang.

They were safe enough and lying low. The year 1875 was three-quarters gone before they made what Croy facetiously calls "a courtesy call on the bank in Huntington, West Virginia."

It was more than that. The did not get more than several thousand dollars. When they came out of the bank, they ran into gunfire. They got away, crossed the Big Sandy and disappeared into the safety of the Kentucky hills. Back in town, however, they left an unidentified member of the gang lying dead in front of the Huntington National. It very likely was Art McCoy.

Whatever gave them the notion that they would find the Huntington bank a fat goose, waiting to be plucked, will never be known. They not only had got very little but lost a man. The whole business had to be put down as a failure. It kept them idle for months. Cole and Jim Younger went to Texas, to Dallas, to pinpoint it. And again the romanticists doggedly pursuing their course, would have us believe that he went to Dallas because Belle was there—Belle, who had been Mrs. Jim Reed and was now a widow. They fail to produce a single peg on which this fantasy can be hung.

How Belle came to be "widowed" and the robbery of the Austin–San Antonio stage can be dealt with in their proper place. In passing, I would like to ask why Cole Younger was using Dallas as a hideout if he was, and many contend so, involved in the stagecoach robbery? Surely he could have found a safer place, knowing that the authorities had the description of a heavy-set man who was a participant, which fitted him.

The law did not bother Cole or his brother Jim. When Jesse sent word along the grapevine calling the gang together in mid-summer, both responded promptly. Jesse had his plans all made. It was to be the Missouri Pacific's Kansas City–St. Louis Flyer (forty miles an hour) this time; the place, the little town of Otterville, twelve mile seast of Sedalia. What appealed to all was that the surrounding country, broken and well-wooded, was favorable for a quick and safe getaway.

At a spot around a curve which the engineer would not be able to see until he was almost upon it, they piled wooden ties on the track and set them afire. The train screeched to a stop. Using their regular technique, they cowed the crew and got into the express car. On demand, the messenger tossed his keys to Jesse and backed away from the safe, hands raised. It chanced to be a "through" safe, in transit from Denver to Chicago, and could not be opened until it reached its destination.

They were not to be stopped, however. One of them found a combination pick and ax hanging in brackets on the wall of the express car, the usual tool carried for use in case of a wreck or other emergency. This was an emergency. Cole Younger, the brawniest man in the gang, took the pick and, after some mighty swinging, managed to break a hole through the top of the safe, just large enough for a man with a small hand to reach inside. Jesse was the man.

Any guess as to how much they took out is as good as any other. The estimates run all the way from a few hundred dollars to $14,000. Counting what they collected from the passengers, it could hardly have amounted to more than several thousand dollars.

They got away without difficulty, but several weeks later, due to some loose talk, one of them, Hobbs Kerry, was arrested by the St. Louis Police Department—not the Pinkertons—and got four years in the Missouri Penitentiary for his part in the robbery.

But immeasurably more important to the James-Youngers than losing Hobbs Kerry, who had never been regarded as overly bright and who for that reason had played a minor role in the gang's business, was the recruit who had wormed his way into the outfit prior to the Otterville robbery. He was a swarthy-faced little man, with a mouthful of flashing white teeth, and a very persuasive talker. He is known to history as Bill Chadwell, an alias for his honest name of William Stiles.

Jesse and his stalwarts should have run from him as from the black plague, for it was he who sold them the idea that they should try their luck up north in prosperous Minnesota, where the country banks were bulging with money. Bank robbery in the Gopher State being practically unheard of, they could hit almost any small town and grab a "bundle." The people were foreigners, hayseeds, Swedes and the like, too stupid to make trouble for anybody.

He made it sound good. His credentials were satsifactory: horse thief, highwayman and all-around desperado. He had given a good account of himself in the Otterville robbery. Even so, the wonder is that Jesse, Frank and Cole, the brains of the gang, took him seriously. But they did. In the days that followed, Chadwell never stopped talking. They began to catch fire and make plans.

The first thing they agreed on was that they would go by rail to St. Paul, where they would split up into pairs and live at different hotels, so situated that they could keep in touch with one another. They would buy horses up there and do some riding to make themselves familiar with the country, posing as farm buyers, well-heeled with cash.

They would need eight men, eight good men, the best they had. Jesse made out the list: Jesse and Frank James, Cole and Bob Younger, Clell Miller, Charlie Pitts, Bill Chadwell. That was seven. Jesse turned to Cole. The latter understood the unasked question. Jim Younger was ranching in San Luis Obispo County, California, and through with outlawry. Cole agreed to write Jim. "He'll come." And Jim did, for one more "last" ride.

Late in August, their elaborate plans completed for what they believed was to be the greatest coup of their careers, they entrained for the north by twos and threes. For horseback outlaws of their renown, it was a strange way to be setting out on such important business. Never before had they deserted the saddle for the smoke and cinders of a railroad coach. If it was a strange beginning, it was to have an even stranger ending. For five of them it was to be a one-way journey. Of the three who came back, one was not to see Missouri again for twenty-seven years.

8

Calamity at Northfield

Historians of outlawry have lavished a vast amount of attention on the eight to ten minutes in Northfield which spelled disaster for the James-Younger Gang. Not counting preliminaries, it took no longer than that. Seemingly, every shot has been counted, every wound described. Strangely enough, the various accounts of what happened there, early in the sunny afternoon of September 7, 1876, are in remarkable agreement.

The sources are many: beginning with those old stand-bys, *The Rise and Fall of Jesse James,* by Robertus Love and Buel's *The Border Outlaws; The Autobiography of Theodore C. Potter* (one of the guards placed over the Youngers when they were captured); Croy's *Last of the Great Outlaws;* and his *Jesse James Was My Neighbor;* Horan's *Desperate Men;* Wellman's *A Dynasty of Western Outlaws;* the files of the *St. Paul Pioneer Press,* the *Faribault Republican,* and the small but important weekly published at Mankato, *The Review.*

When you have digested them carefully, you know what happened; you can visualize it. But they do not tell why it happened, why things went as they did. Neither can I. The bandits had taken the town by surprise; Northfield was not waiting for them. They "hurrahed" it as they had done elsewhere almost a score of times, driving the surprised citizenry to cover. They were veterans at their trade, no weaklings like Hobbs Kerry and Wood and Clarence Hite riding with them that afternoon. What tipped the scales against them? I believe Wellman comes close to the correct answer when he says: "The Minnesotans did not cow as easily as had at first appeared. They lived in deer country, and most of them were deer hunters. Many of them were also veterans of the Civil War, and others had fought the Sioux in Little Crow's bloody uprising of 1862. They were not gun-shy." And not the "hayseeds" that Bill Chadwell had led Jesse and the others to believe.

Things had gone well with them when they first arrived in St. Paul, some of them staying at the Merchants' Hotel and the rest at the European Hotel. They rented livery rigs, and in pairs they began driving about the country, looking for horses and pretending to be interested in buying good farmland. The long linen "dusters" with which they had equipped themselves (the usual attire of farm and livestock buyers) concealed the weapons they wore. They found the horses they needed, good animals, and took to the saddle. As they rode about the country, they accustomed the horses to the sound of gunfire, asked questions, studied the lay of the land and the roads in particular. They looked over Red Wing, Faribault, Mankato. The First National Bank in Mankato looked ripe for the plucking; Northfield was an afterthought with them.

Mankato, they agreed, was their target. At high noon on September 3, Jesse and Charlie Pitts cantered into town for a final look. Whatever it was they saw or ran into, it was enough to convince Jesse that they would have to forget about Mankato.

There is a choice of explanations. Some say that a man on the sidewalk recognized Jesse; others have it that a crowd of fifty people had gathered in front of the bank to watch workmen putting a new oramental metal cornice on the building, a job that would not be finished for hours.

When Jesse returned to the outlaw camp, several miles north of town, and announced that they would have to forget about Mankato, Bill Chadwell was not thrown for a loss. He suggested at once that they cut back east for fifty miles and have a go at Northfield. It was a smaller town than Mankato, but it too had a First National Bank, rated as one of the richest country banks in the state. In addition to being located in the very heart of a prosperous and closely settled farming community, it had the payroll of the Ames and Company flour mill to add to its prosperity.

As they listened to him, the disappointment over Mankato disappeared, and they struck out for Northfield. They camped on the Cannon River, a few miles south of the town the following evening. Again it was necessary to reconnoiter the surrounding country, special attention being given to the roads, rivers and bridges. They were satisfied with what they found, and on the morning of September 7, Cole and Clell Miller rode into Northfield for a close look at the bank and its environs.

It must have been to their liking. The business district of the town centered in Bridge Square, so named because of the iron bridge that spanned the Cannon River, which, flowing from west to east, cut Northfield in two. The day was hot for September, the sun bright in a cloudless sky. Up on the bluff overlooking the town, the several buildings of young Carleton College, only ten years old, could be seen among the drooping maples that were beginning to put on their fall coloring. Around Bridge Square, Northfield seemed to drowse in quiet contentment.

The Scriver Block, a two-story brick and stone building on the southwest corner, dominated the square. Scriver's general store and the establishment of Lee and Hitchcock, furniture dealers, occupied the lower floor. The First National Bank was located at the rear end of the building, a few feet from the corner. There were offices on the second floor that were reached by an outside iron stairway.

Directly across the street from the bank entrance, Wheeler & Blackman conducted a drugstore, and next to it was a small hotel, the Dampier House. The bank had a back door which opened on an alley that gave access to Bridge Square. The Scriver Block formed one side of this alley; on the other, standing cheek by jowl, were located Northfield's two hardware stores. All were to play a part in what followed.

Cole and Clell took a leisurely turn around the square before leaving. The word they carried back to Jesse and the others was so favorable that it was only a matter of minutes before the final touches were put on their plans. After their business at the bank was finished, they would stop at the railroad station on their way out of town and cut the telegraph wire. That would slow up pursuit.

The three "inside" men for the bank job were named: Jesse, Frank and Charlie Pitts. The three of them, Jesse announced, would jog into town at once, have lunch there and be waiting at the corner of the Scriver Block when the others came racing into Northfield, guns popping and screeching the old Rebel yell. Three of them, Bob Younger, Bill Chadwell and Clell Miller were to come in from the south; Cole and Jim Younger to charge in from the west.

The five of them were to move up to the outskirts of town and wait there until the clock in the belfry of the Lutheran church struck one. That was to be the signal for the wild dash into North-field, both groups timing themselves so they would reach Bridge Square within a few minutes of each other.

It lacked a few minutes of twelve o'clock when Jesse, his brother Frank and Charlie Pitts cantered into Northfield. Unhurried, they walked their horses across the Division Street bridge and tethered them at the hitchrack in front of the Scriver Block. Their apparently good-natured casualness was so deceiving that no one gave them a second look. One of them—later identified as Charlie Pitts—asked a passer-by where they could find a good place to eat. They were directed to Jefft's Restaurant, a few doors up the street.

They unbuttoned their linen "dusters" as they entered the restaurant but did not remove them. The proprietor, little suspect-ing that he was entertaining three of the most desperate outlaws in America, hovered about their table. They were heading west to look at some farms out Mankato way, Jesse told him.

After enjoying a hearty lunch, they strolled back down the street and sat down on a wooden packing case in front of Man-ning's hardware store, Charlie Pitts puffing a cheroot. They had some nine to ten minutes to wait. Everything was going fine. They were confident, self-possessed. They had been through such moments as this too many times to be troubled by any misgivings now.

The church bell struck the hour. Charlie Pitts tossed away his cigar, and they walked leisurely, three abreast, to the corner. To have something to do as they waited, they pretended to examine the riding gear of their horses. Then, suddenly, it happened. Bob Younger, Bill Chadwell and Clell Miller roared into town, yelling like savages, their guns barking. As they thundered across the bridge, Cole and Jim Younger swept in from the west, their .45's cracking.

Around Bridge Square, the startled citizenry made a wild dash for cover. For a few moments, it looked as though Northfield had been thoroughly cowed. Jesse, Frank and Charlie Pitts hurried into the bank. Out in the middle of the street, Cole dismounted, a pistol in each hand and "looking four ways at once." A boy, Nicholas Gustavson, a seventeen-year-old six-footer, recently arrived from Sweden, who knew no English, started across the street. Cole yelled at him to get back inside. When young Gustavson failed to heed the warning, Cole killed him. Bob, Jim and the others were shooting right and left to keep the street clear.[1]

It is time to introduce Henry M. Wheeler, a young medical student home on vacation from the University of Michigan, where he was a senior. As much as anyone, he turned the tide of battle against the bandit gang that afternoon in Northfield. He stated, when interviewed later, that from a window of his father's drug store he saw young Gustavson felled.

"I knew the bank was being robbed. I knew how to handle a rifle; I had done a considerable amount of hunting, from fourteen on. But my rifle was at home, blocks away. I remembered suddenly that there was an Army rifle and a sack of cartridges behind the desk in the Dampier House. I figured if I could get my hands on it that I could run upstairs to one of the front rooms of the hotel and start shooting from the window. When I stepped out of the drug store, a bullet whizzed by so close it drove me back. I made it the next time. I snatched up the rifle and cartridges behind the desk and raced upstairs. Across the street, a man on horseback saw me and snapped a shot at me. He was using a pistol. I took dead aim on him, and he tumbled out of the saddle and lay still. I knew I had killed him."

It was Clell Miller.

Across the way from an open window on the second floor of the Scriver Block, a man named Stacey began blasting away with a shotgun, the only weapon he could find. His shells were loaded with No. 6 shot, too light to do much damage to a man at thirty yards. But the pellets stung. Bill Chadwell was half-blinded by them. Two of the Youngers were struck.

There was a great deal of shooting by now. Manning and Allen, the proprietors of the two hardware stores, had been handing out loaded rifles to whoever showed a disposition to use them. Manning went into action himself. Stepping around the corner of the building, in full sight of the bandits, he sent a slug ripping through Cole Younger's shoulder. Cole charged him, but a second slug lifted his hat from his head, and he turned back. A few yards away, Bill Chadwell was weaving drunkenly in the saddle. Manning brought him down with a bullet through the heart.

Bob Younger's horse was brought down. Bob leaped clear as the animal fell and ran to the foot of the iron stairway that led up to the second floor of the Scriver Block. He found little cover there. Young Wheeler could see him. His aim was good enough to shatter Bob's right elbow.

Seeing how things were going, Cole rode up to the bank door and yelled, "Come on! They're killing us!"

It was not only in the street that luck had deserted them. When Jesse, Frank and Charlie Pitts walked into the First National they found three men facing them: Joseph Lee Heywood, the cashier, Frank Wilcox and A. E. Bunker, tellers. The outer door of the vault stood open. Jesse, stepping through the swinging gate in the counter, confronted Heywood, demanding that he open the inner door. This Heywood refused to do. Jesse entered the vault. Heywood reached out to lock him inside. Charlie Pitts knocked the cashier's hand down and felled him with a blow on the head from his pistol barrel.

Bunker chose that moment to make a break for the back door. The door was latched, but he hit it hard enough to go crashing through. Charlie Pitts fired at him and missed. Jim Younger had ridden around the corner of the bank and reached the alley. He drilled a shot at Bunker that struck him in the shoulder. It spun him around, and though he went to his knees, he regained his feet and disappeared through the side entrance of Manning's hardware store. Wilcox, the other teller, stood facing the wall, his hands raised. He was not harmed.[2]

Irony creeps in here. The inner door of the vault was closed but not locked. If Jesse had given it a tug it would have swung open. If he missed a trick, perhaps it was because he was troubled about the amount of shooting he heard on the street. He was experienced enough to know that his men, armed only with six-guns, were not doing all of it. Rifles were cracking out there.

There was money in the counter tills. They scooped it up and stuffed it into their pockets. The grain sack was not needed today. They started for the door. Jesse glanced back and saw Heywood reaching under the counter, as though for a gun. With deadly aim, he sent a slug crashing into the man's brain, killing him instantly.

They knew they had run into trouble, but they did not know until they stepped out of the bank how serious it really was: Clell Miller and Bill Chadwell lay dead in the street; Cole, struck half a dozen times, his face pocked with birdshot, was a bloody smear; part of Jim Younger's jaw was shot away and both shoulders pierced; Bob was under the stairs, trying to work his pistol with his left hand, his right arm hanging uselessly at his side.

As he was swinging into the saddle, a bullet tore through Frank's right leg between the knee and thigh. Miraculously, Jesse did not receive a scratch.

The story that Bob Younger thought the others were about to leave him behind, when they made their dash from town, has been told so often that few people question it today. He is supposed to have run out from the stairs, when he saw the others were all mounted, and shouted: "Don't desert me, boys, I'm shot!" He had no horse, of course. Cole is said to have turned back and got Bob up behind him and raced after the rest.

This story traces back to the *National Police Gazette,* where so many myths originated. It may have been lifted from one of the Minnesota newspapers, which gave the Northfield raid extended coverage. I would find it easier to believe if Cole had put Bob up ahead of himself, not behind, where he could have kept him from falling. How Bob, with only one arm, could cling to his brother on the back of a horse running at breakneck speed is difficult to understand.[3]

Though some of them were desperately wounded, what was left of the gang got out of Northfield and headed west. They had no time to stop and cut telegraph wires. They should have risked it at all costs. When the Northfield operator began putting news of the raid on the wire, he did not leave his key until the entire state was aroused. By nightfall, as many as three hundred men had taken up the trail of the fugitives. The following day the number soared to a thousand. Posses were everywhere, and in the confusion they often caught themselves hunting one another in the mistaken idea that they were closing in on bandits.

To keep the ardor of the searchers at fever heat, the state of Minnesota posted a reward of a thousand dollars a man, dead or alive, on the bank robbers. The First National Bank chipped in with seven hundred more and the Winona and St. Peter Railroad added another five hundred. The greatest manhunt in history was on.

The weather turned sour. Rain fell in torrents, day after day. Dirt roads became almost impassable. In the swamps and sloughs water rose and turned them into treacherous morasses in which both horses and men mired and had to turn back. The surrounding forests, wet, dripping, became dark and gloomy caverns, clogged with underbrush, with trails washed out. After a day or two of fruitless searching, many men returned home, bedraggled, soaked to the skin. Others took their place, and the great hunt went on.

The results were discouraging. The possemen found the camps the outlaws had made, identified by the blood-stained rags the fleeing men left behind after caring for their wounded. Soon after pulling out of Northfield they had relieved a farmer of a horse and saddle for Bob. It was now Jim who gave them the most concern. He had been wounded in several places, but it was the hemorrhaging of his shattered jaw that was pulling him down. By the fourth day he was so weak from loss of blood that he had to be lifted into the saddle. Soon, he could not ride without being supported.

They were moving in the general direction of Mankato, traveling only by night. Their progress was slow; never more than three or four miles a night. They had no food, other than what they could steal from a farmer's truck patch. Time after time they were surrounded, but they always managed to slip through the net that was closing in on them. Their situation was becoming increasingly desperate—six men, one of them almost helpless, against a thousand. Only their indomitable will drove them on.

They were still to the east of Mankato when Jesse is alleged to have told the others that something would have to be done about Jim, who was holding them up, if they were to have any chance of escaping.

To which Cole is said to have replied: "If you shoot him, I'll kill you."

"We're not going to kill Jim, or anyone else," Frank declared. "What we can do is split up."

The Youngers stuck together, and Charlie Pitts elected to take his chances with them; Frank and Jesse struck off by themselves.

There are several reasons for accepting the foregoing as factual. Buell claimed to have received an undated letter from Cole confirming it. In his old age Cole Younger never mentioned Jesse's name without bitterness. He never said what had turned him against the younger of the James brothers. It could have been this. Most convincing of all is that the cold-blooded, practical suggestion to do away with Jim sounds like Jesse.[4]

Frank and Jesse made their way through Minnesota and crossed the line into Dakota Territory eight days later, after three or four brushes with the posses that were scouring the country for them. In one encounter they were put afoot and painfully wounded by a bullet that ripped across Frank's right knee and embedded itself in Jesse's thigh. They soon stole horses and continued to dodge their pursuers.

The last information regarding them came from a country doctor by the name of Mosher, who encountered them some miles north of Sioux Falls while driving along in his buggy. They stopped him and made him remove the slug from Jesse's thigh and dress their wounds. When he was finished, he was forced to change clothes with Jesse, to make identification more difficult. He was not harmed.[5]

No more was heard of the Jameses for three years. The popular supposition was that they were somewhere in Mexico and that the crushing defeat at Northfield had spelled the end of the James-Younger Gang.

When Frank and Jesse escaped from Minnesota, the three Younger brothers and Charlie Pitts were still floundering around in Hanska Slough, a few miles west of the little town of Medelia. Their horses had played out and they proceeded on foot, a mile or two a night. Jim was barely able to walk. Cole had been wounded again and was so weak he had cut a staff to support himself as he walked. Bob was in terrible shape. Only tough Charlie Pitts had any fight left in him. In broad daylight he made his way to a farmhouse and bought eggs, bread and a slab of bacon. He was followed when he returned to camp. An hour later, it was surrounded by a posse of a hundred men.

Nothing could be seen of the outlaws, but the posse, led by Sheriff Jim Glispin of Watonwan County, fired round after round into the patch of timber in the hope of driving them out. When that failed to accomplish anything, Glispin and half a dozen others, at risk of their lives, began moving through the underbrush. They had not gone far when Glispin glimpsed one of the fugitives. It was Charlie Pitts. He and the sheriff fired almost as one. It was rifle versus pistol again, as it had been in Northfield. Pitts took a dying step before he pitched forward on his face and lay still.

The Youngers fell back, fighting until they found themselves under attack from both front and rear. Cole and Jim went down. Only Bob was left standing. With his pistol clutched in his left hand, he continued firing until it was empty. There was no going on. "Hold your fire!" he cried. "We're all down except me."

"Throw your gun away!" Glispin called back. Bob obeyed, and in a few minutes the three men were prisoners. The great manhunt was over.

A wagon was secured. Charlie Pitts was tossed into it. The Youngers were placed on the wagon floor with him, under guard.

Medalia was the nearest town. News of the capture was sent there at once, and there was great excitement when the wagon carrying the prisoners arrived. "The streets were filled with people who wanted to see the dangerous men," reported the *St. Paul Pioneer Press*. The excitement in Medalia became state-wide as the telegraph spread the news. The date was September 21, an even two weeks from the day the James-Youngers had descended on Northfield.

When doctors had done what was immediately possible for the wounded men, they were hustled by train to Faribault, the county seat of Rice County, in which Northfield is located.

Though there seemed to be little question but that the two men who had escaped from Minnesota were Jesse and Frank James, the Youngers, thinking to help themselves, refused to be trapped into admitting it. They claimed that the two men who had got away were known to them only as Howard and Woods (the aliases Jesse and Frank had used in Tennessee) and were newcomers to the gang.

It did not make much difference. When the brothers came to trial, they faced four indictments:

The murder of cashier Joseph L. Heywood.
The murder of Nicholas Gustavson.
Assault with deadly weapon on A. E. Bunker, bank teller.
Robbery of the First National Bank of Northfield, Minnesota.

They stood in grave jeopardy of being sentenced to hang. They had no grounds on which to base a defense. They were informed, however, that under Minnesota law a man charged with murder could not be hanged if he pleaded guilty. The Youngers decided so to plead. When the verdict was read, they listened with bowed heads: they were to be confined in the Minnesota State Penitentiary at Stillwater for the rest of their natural lives.

9

The Jameses and the Youngers
Fade into History

❦

ON THE NIGHT of October 7, 1879, a Chicago and Alton train was held up at Glendale station, twenty-two miles from Kansas City. This was "the Glendale Train" of the famous ballad. The railroad company said $35,000 was taken from the express car.

The method used was the one made familiar over the years by the old James-Younger Gang: a tiny hamlet was chosen as the site of the robbery; the handful of citizens were herded into the depot and the station agent forced to flag the train; the express messenger was beaten and relieved of his keys. When finished in the express car, the bandits moved down the aisle of the coaches with the old familiar grain sack.

Missouri was inured to train robbery, but this one made people sit up and take stock of things. Frank and Jesse James were still at liberty. Was it possible they were back?

They were. They had recruited a new gang. In it were only two who had ridden with them in the old days: Dick Liddil and Bill

Ryan. Tucker Basham, a young farm boy, none too bright, and Ed Miller, Clell's younger brother, were embarking in outlawry for the first time. The others—Clarence and Wood Hite and the Ford brothers, Bob and Charley—were two-bit desperadoes with unsavory reputations.

It must have been a blow to Jesse's pride not to be able to do better than surround himself with such third-raters. He must have sensed also that the climate in which he had operated so successfully in the past was changing; Missourians were no longer willing to condone outlawry as a postwar symptom.

The first sign of trouble appeared when Tucker Basham, wellheeled with his share of the Glendale loot, did some foolish bragging that led to his arrest. William H. Wallace, the newly elected and vigorous prosecuting attorney of Jackson County, put the screws on young Basham and got a full confession from him.

Young Wallace was a shrewd, determined, fighting prosecutor. With Basham's confession in his hands, he believed he had the weapon that would enable him to bring the James Gang to justice. Accordingly, he did not make the confession public. The first dividend came when Bill Ryan was picked up near Nashville, Tennessee, in the course of a week-long carouse. He had several thousand dollars in his possession. His explanation of how he came by it was so unsatisfactory that Tennessee authorities held him on suspicion of robbery. The description of him that was sent out caught the eye of Deputy U.S. Marshal Whig Keshlaer. It fitted Bill Ryan. Keshlaer went to Wallace. The latter agreed that the man arrested in Tennessee was very likely Bill Ryan. Keshlaer went to Nashville and found that his surmise was correct. Ryan was brought back to face trial in Missouri.

People shook their heads in consternation—not over the outcome, which they regarded as certain, but at the prosecutor's audacity in pushing through an indictment of Ryan. Never before had a member of the gang been brought to trial in Jackson County. There was not a chance in a million, they said, that he could impanel a jury that would bring in a verdict of guilty.

Wallace's life was threatened. Sheriff Timberlake learned that Ryan's "friends" were gathering near town and were preparing to rush the jail and release the prisoner. Nothing came of it, but on the night of July 15, 1881, Jesse wrote another bloody page in the history of Missouri outlawry. At Cameron, forty miles north of Kansas City, three men boarded a Rock Island train bound for Davenport and Chicago and found seats in the smoking car. William Westphal was the conductor. They scrutinized him carefully as he collected their tickets and nodded to one another as he passed. They were sure he was the man they wanted.

The train stopped at Gallatin. As it started to pull away from the depot, two men leaped out of the shadows and swung aboard between the baggage car and the tender. Before the train gathered speed, they climbed over the coal and confronted the engineer and fireman with drawn revolvers. Just beyond Winston, they ordered the engineer to stop the train.

Several new passengers had got on at Gallatin. Conductor Westphal re-entered the smoker to collect their fares. As he came up the aisle, the three men who had boarded the train at Cameron jumped to their feet. The tallest of the three (Frank James) fired at Westphal and missed. The smallest of the trio (Jesse) snapped a shot at the conductor. His bullet found its mark. Mortally wounded, Westphal managed to reach the rear door of the coach and open it—this was still the day of open-platform cars. The train was moving when he plunged out onto the platform and rolled down the steps.

The terrified passengers leaped to their feet. One of them, a mason named Frank McMillan, started to run down the aisle in a frenzied attempt to escape. He went down with a bullet in his head.

The engineer applied the brakes as ordered, and the train limped to a stop. The bandits then ran forward to the express car. It was a hot July night. The messenger had left the door open for greater comfort. They subdued him and rifled the safe. How much they made off with is a matter of opinion. Buell puts the figure at between $8,000 and $10,000. It could have amounted to that.

Killing conductor Westphal was a matter of long-delayed vengeance. It was on January 5, 1875 that he had been in charge of the special that had brought the Pinkertons to Kearney and the bombing of the Samuels' home. This was 1881—six years and more later. Jesse had waited a long time. But he had a long memory.

The Winston robbery and the double killing of Westphal and McMillan were viewed by prosecutor Wallace and his supporters as an unmistakable attempt to intimidate him and the court. That was how Governor Thomas T. Crittenden also interpreted it. From his office came a proclamation offering a reward of $10,-000 each for the capture of Frank and Jesse James, together with a guarantee of executive clemency for any member of their gang who would give information leading to their arrest.

In Independence, Wallace proceeded with the trial of Bill Ryan. Basham's confession was introduced, and it created a sensation. Supporters of the James boys were stunned. That night Tucker Basham's home was burned to the ground. And now, unexpectedly, a remarkable thing happened. A score of men who had fought for the Confederacy, many under Quantrill, and who in their hearts were still as "unreconstructed" as on the day Lee surrendered at Appomattox, rallied behind Wallace. It came at the right time. The wavering jury took courage and stood firm. The evidence against Ryan piled up and he was sentenced to twenty-five years in the Missouri Penitentiary. For turning state's evidence, Tucker Basham got off with five years. He was glad to go. He stood exposed as a traitor, and his life was no longer safe in Jackson County.

Jesse had received a blow from which he was never to recover. Northfield had been a bitter defeat, but this was worse; he could no longer trust his own men or the so-called friends on whom he had relied for years. Another Chicago and Alton train was held up and a bank in Iowa robbed. But he was now a wolf running with wolves, no longer the peerless, unquestioned leader. Becoming suspicious of Ed Miller's loyalty, he shot him down with no more compunction than he would have shown a mad dog. The only ones he could trust were his brother Frank and Dick Liddil. Liddil repaid his faith by playing him false.

More than anyone who had ever ridden with Jesse, handsome Liddil was a ladies' man. He had a girl in Kansas City, but he tired of her and transferred his affections to Martha Bolton, the young and widowed sister of the Ford brothers. It led him into difficulties with Wood Hite, who felt that Martha was his property. He killed Hite. He began to regret it almost at once. He had violated the gang code in killing a fellow member. Fearful of what might happen to him, he induced Martha Bolton to visit the governor and sound him about what would happen to him if he surrendered. Crittenden assured her that Liddil would be given clemency if he gave himself up and supplied information leading to the capture of other members of the gang.

When Liddil got the message, he lost no time surrendering to prosecutor Wallace. The confession Wallace obtained from him led to the capture of Clarence Hite, who was convicted for his part in the Winston robbery and sentenced for the customary twenty-five years. The reader will recall that, as stated, he contracted what used to be known as "galloping consumption" in the Missouri Penitentiary and was released to go home to die. Liddil got five years for his misdeeds.

Frank was the only one Jesse had left (if you disregard the two Fords, and they could hardly be regarded as an asset). Of the men who had ridden with him since Northfield, four were in prison—Bill Ryan, Tucker Basham, Dick Liddil and Clarence Hite. Two were dead—Ed Miller and Wood Hite. Why he didn't call it a day and get out of Missouri, even out of the United States, no one will ever know.

Governor Crittenden was in Kansas City early in January and was stopping at the St. James Hotel. Bob Ford paid him a secret visit. Ford made the governor a proposition. If the $10,000 reward on Jesse would be for taking him dead or alive, he and his brother would go after him, provided the state would forgive the several grudges it had against them.

Though Crittenden always denied that he had made a "deal" with Bob Ford, he certainly must have agreed to something. In a statement made under oath at the coroner's inquest, Ford said: "Governor Crittenden asked me if I thought I could catch Jesse James, and I answered yes. . . . The governor therefore agreed to pay $10,000 apiece for the production of Jesse and Frank James, whether dead or alive."

It happened on the morning of April 3, in the modest house in St. Joe in which Jesse was living with his wife and children, under the alias of J. D. Howard. A single shot was heard by the neighbors. They ran in and found the bearded man, whom they knew as Mr. Howard, lying dead on the floor.

Bob Ford says in his sworn statement:

"I was with Jesse about ten days ago, when at his request I accompanied him to his mother's home and slept with him in the barn. We remained there for two days, then started on horseback for St. Joseph, stopping overnight in a church, and before reaching the town we hid in a patch of timber until night, so as to make our entrance unobserved. That was a week ago last night. Jesse and I had a talk yesterday about robbing the bank at Platte City, and which Charley and I both agreed to assist.

"Between eight and nine o'clock this morning while the three of us were in a room in Jesse's house, Jesse pulled off his coat and also his pistols, two of which he constantly wore, and then got up onto a chair for the purpose of brushing dust off a picture.

"While Jesse was thus engaged, Charley winked at me, so I knew he meant for me to shoot. So, as quickly as possible, I drew my pistol and aiming at Jesse's head, which was no more than four feet from the muzzle of my weapon, I fired, and Jesse tumbled headlong from the chair on which he was standing and fell on his face."

Bob Ford's moment of glory was brief. A wave of revulsion at the cowardly manner in which the treacherous assassination had been accomplished swept over Missouri. In the outburst of feeling Jesse's crimes were temporarily forgotten, and men and women spoke of him as "our Jesse." His avowed enemies, William Wallace and many others, were loudest in condemning the cowardly Ford brothers, who, in the words of one, had "put a blacker stain on the fair name of Missiouri than years of outlawry had ever done." [1] Bob Ford fled the state, only to be reviled wherever he went. The reward money brought him no happiness. As has been previously stated, he was killed in the boom town of Creede, Colorado, ten years later. He was operating a tent saloon at the time. Four years after the slaying of Jesse, Charley Ford, in ill health and worn down by the stigma attached to him, committed suicide with a pistol in a clump of underbrush near his home in Richmond, Missouri.

Jesse was buried in the yard of the Samuel place. Over his grave, his mother had a stone erected, the inscription reading:

Jesse W. James
Died April 3, 1882
Aged 34 years, 6 months,
28 days.
Murdered by a traitor and a
coward whose name is not worthy
to appear here.

On April 4, a guard conducted Cole Younger to the warden's office, where a reporter had come to inform him that Jesse had been murdered. Cole listened wooden-faced to the details. He had been a model prisoner and had never lost hope that his sentence might be commuted. He could not afford to acknowledge his close ties with Jesse. When pressed to give a statement, all he would say was: "I knew him when we were with Quantrill's Guerrillas. I have no sympathy for men engaged in the kind of things he is reported to have been in."

Such sanctimoniousness, coming from him, must have made the reporter smile. But it served its purpose, and he was taken back to the prison hospital, where he was now employed as a nurse, without having injured his case. It must have given him something to think about—Jesse, his onetime friend turned enemy, cut down like that.

Two women walked into prosecuting attorney Wallace's office one day. In his *Speeches and Writings,* published in 1914, part of which is autobiographical, Wallace says he recognized the younger of the two women as soon as she raised her veil. He had known her as Annie Ralston, the girl who married Frank James. The one-armed woman who accompanied her this day was Zerelda Samuel, mother of the James boys. They had come to tell him that Frank was anxious to give himself up if he could surrender to Wallace personally, that he was living in constant fear that he would be killed for the reward money on him, as Jesse had been. If he surrendered, would he be released on bond?

Wallace could not promise that. He knew there was an old

indictment, secured long before he came to office but still in effect, charging Frank James with murder in the death of John Whicher, the Pinkerton detective, whose body had been found in Jackson County. Though it was extremely doubtful that a conviction could be had, the indictment was for murder, which was not bailable. Wallace was also aware that there was a very "live" case against Frank in Daviess County growing out of the Winston robbery and the killing of conductor Westphal and the stone mason, Frank McMillan.

Once Frank James was in custody, the reward would be withdrawn. Beyond that, he would have to take his chances. Wallace could promise no more than that. It did not satisfy the two women, and they left without anything having been accomplished. A week later, Wallace received a wire from Crittenden saying that Frank James had surrendered to him and that he was being sent under guard to Independence. Wallace got in touch with William D. Hamilton, the prosecuting attorney of Daviess County. When Frank arrived in Independence he was taken immediately to Gallatin and lodged in the Daviess County jail.

The surrender of the last of the famous outlaw brothers created a sensation. Following so close on the slaying of Jesse, there was an outpouring of sympathy for him.

Hamilton secured an indictment against Frank James, charging him with murder in the death of Frank McMillan. Being young and inexperienced, and realizing that the trial would be the most sensational ever put to a jury in Daviess County, he induced Wallace to handle the prosecution.

Wallace recalls the tense atmosphere he encountered in Gallatin, the appeals by prominent men for him to drop the case, and the threats made against his life. He found witnesses reluctant to testify. Men who were in the smoking car the night of the crime and saw what happened suddenly developed hazy memories.

Colonel John F. Phillips, counsel for the defense was an able, even brilliant lawyer. The fact that he was an ex-Union officer defending an ex-Southern guerrilla lent piquancy to his words. He and Wallace wrangled for several days over the selection of a jury. The latter was so disgusted with the result that he threatened to step out of the case. He was convinced that the jury was packed and that a conviction was impossible. The demonstrations within the courtroom and out told him that he was battling something more potent than evidence.

He was persuaded to continue, but only after stating publicly: "We will simply try Frank James before the world. The verdict of the jury that is being selected is already written."

As he had predicted, Frank James was acquitted. Frank spent some time with his mother and Jesse's wife at the Samuel place in Clay County. Later he took various jobs. He became a special policeman at a St. Louis theatre, where he was more of an attraction than the actors on the stage. He found employment at various Missouri and Arkansas race tracks as an assistant starter and starter for several years. His health was not good. Rascoe calls him a diabetic. There is no evidence to support him. It was Frank's old bullet wounds that were pulling him down. As the years passed, he became bonier and thinner.

Rascoe, careless with his dates, has Jesse and the Younger boys visiting Belle Starr at Younger's Bend in 1880 after her "marriage" to Sam Starr. It is a ridiculous statement. Cole, Jim and Bob Younger were not doing any "riding" in 1880; they were behind the walls of Stillwater Penitentiary, serving out their life sentences. Four weary years had dragged by, all but extinguishing any hope that they might again be free men. And then in 1882 a man named Bronaugh—Warren Carter Bronaugh—came to Stillwater who was to devote twenty-one years of his life to winning a pardon for them.

Bronaugh was a selfless, indomitable, incredible man. He was attempting the impossible. In the face of a thousand rebuffs, avoided at first as an irrational fanatic, he never wavered, even though it meant impoverishing himself and his family. The battle he waged to free the Younger brothers is a story in itself. No one has told it so well as Homer Croy in his *Last of the Great Outlaws*.

Bronaugh's devotion to Cole Younger had a valid explanation. Cole took part in the battle of Lone Jack, Missouri. Just before noon, when the tide of battle had turned temporarily in favor of the Union forces, a young Confederate cavalryman came pounding up the road that Cole and a detachment of guerrillas were

guarding. The young soldier was Warren Bronaugh. His troop
was in full retreat and so badly scattered that in his confusion he
had got turned around and was riding straight into disaster. Surmising what had happened, Cole leaped out in the road, stopped
him and directed him to where Colonel Upton B. Hayes' regiment
was standing firm.

Bronaugh realized that but for the stranger who had stopped
him, he would have been picked off by Union snipers in another
few hundred yards. It was not until he recognized a photograph of
Cole Younger in a magazine article about the Northfield raid
that he knew who his benefactor was. To make certain, he left
for Minnesota at once.

The incident on the Lone Jack road had slipped from Cole's
memory. It came back to him as he sat in the warden's office talking with Bronaugh. A mighty resolve took possession of the latter
as the interview proceeded. He suddenly became a man with a
purpose, uplifted, dedicated. Cole Younger had saved his life, and
he would spend it getting him out of prison—no matter how long
it took.

It was to take twenty-one years. He pounced on every fact he
could that was favorable to the Youngers; wrote thousands of
letters; interviewed hundreds of men, governors, judges, religious
leaders; solicited contributions to finance the campaign he was
waging. Failure could not daunt him. But the years ground on,
and Cole and his brothers remained behind the walls of Stillwater Penitentiary.

Cole had been appraised of the killing of Jesse James in 1882. In
1889 he was informed that Belle had met a violent death. That
was early in the year, in February. Seven months later he was
to suffer a real loss. His brother Bob, who had been shot through
the lungs in the Northfield fight, had never completely recovered.
He was working in the prison library, the lightest work that could
be found for him. He came down with pneumonia on the tenth
of September and was dead six days later. Retta Younger, the
boys' sister, came up from Missouri for the body, which was taken
to Lee's Summit and buried in the family plot.

Cole and Jim knew that Bronaugh was working for their release. For a time they had had some faith in him, but they had

long since given up hope that he would be able to do anything. And then it happened. In an unexpected about-face, the Board of Pardons, due solely to Bronaugh's long campaign, granted the Youngers a conditional pardon. There were some very strong strings attached to it. The youngers were not to leave the state of Minnesota, nor were they to exhibit themselves in any dime museum, circus, theatre, opera house or any other place where a charge was made for admission. They were to observe the law and refrain from using intoxicating liquors. On the twentieth day of each month they were to write the warden of the state prison a report on themselves.

Bronaugh was on hand to greet them as they came out. After twenty-five years behind the walls they were too stunned to have much to say. Jobs had been provided for them—selling grave stones, of all things. They were to be paid sixty dollars a month, plus commissions. But there were no commissions. Wherever they went men and women were glad to be able to talk to such famous visitors. They were not interested in buying grave stones.

Cole and Jim stuck it out for a year. Jim became so discouraged that he gave it up and tried selling insurance for a St. Paul firm. That did not work out, either. The world had changed so much since he had been put away that he could not cope with it. He was living at the Reardon Hotel in St. Paul, so depressed that he seldom left his room. On Sunday afternoon, October 19, he put a pistol to his head and killed himself. He lies beside Bob in the family plot in Lee's Summit.

Only Cole was left. Bronaugh was still busy on his behalf. In February 1903 success crowned his efforts. Cole was given an unconditional pardon and told to leave the state. At last he was free to return to Missouri. Late on the night of February 16, he got off the westbound Missouri Pacific train at Lee's Summit. He was home after an absence of twenty-seven years. He was no longer the young, handsome, dashing guerrilla fighter and bandit leader. He was fifty-nine, fat, flabby, nearly bald, his once florid face stamped with the indelible prison pallor.

Frank James came over to see him a few days after he got back. Frank was farming the old Samuel place, forty miles away. The Wild West Show had become very popular. He was sure they could do well at that business if they teamed up and could get someone to finance them. He had been corresponding with a Chicago brewer with that in mind. Cole was agreeable. When the Chicago man put up the cash, the Cole Younger–Frank James Wild West Show took to the road, playing through Missouri, Arkansas, Louisiana and parts of Texas.

Business was good, but after several seasons Frank's failing health made it impossible for him to continue. Cole joined the Lew Nichols Carnival Company as a star attraction. He saved his money, and when he had enough put by to keep him in comfort for the rest of his days, he retired and bought the house in Lee's Summit that he gave to his niece Nora Hall, and in which he lived with her and his nephew Harry Younger Hall until he died.

After leaving the Wild West Show, Frank James had bought a small farm near Fletcher, Oklahoma. Again poor health would not permit him to work it. He sold out and returned to the old Samuel place. There, on February 18, 1915, he died.

Cole himself was so "poorly"—as they used to say—that he could not attend his old friend's funeral. He was alone now, the last of the James-Younger Gang. He was seventy-two, and the road he was traveling was all downhill. He took to his bed and did not leave it. On the night of February 21, 1916, he breathed his last.

The greatest saga in American outlawry had reached its end.

10

Mistress of Outlaws

IN OUTLAW-INFESTED Indian Territory, in the period between May 10, 1875, and February 3, 1889, two people dominated the never-ending struggle between the forces of good and evil: Judge Isaac C. Parker, the "Hanging Judge," on the one hand, and the woman history knows as Belle Starr, on the other.

It is time to do some catching up on Belle, who was born Myra Belle Shirley, either in or near Carthage, in Jasper County, Missouri, on February 3, 1848. Rascoe speculates that she may have been born on her parents' farm in Washington County several months before they moved to Carthage, where her father, John Shirley, operated a tavern and a livery stable. It does not seem to be important.

We know she spent her childhood in Carthage and received her schooling there, attending a one-room private school conducted by William Cravens, and later was enrolled (if some of her biographers are to be believed) in the Carthage Female Academy, which was not as elegant as it sounds, its enrollment being limited to the daughters of the ten to twelve well-to-do families of the town. It was there, according to the *National Police Gazette,* that "she became an accomplished pianist." Read whom you will, you will not get far before she is described as a "talented musician." Perhaps it would be more accurate to say she could play the piano, and let it go at that, which would cover the exhibition she gave one night in a Fort Smith saloon when she played to a crowd of hilarious, more or less inebriated male admirers.

The Shirleys had three children—Preston, the eldest; Ed (called Bud), the next in line; and Belle, the youngest.

Success seems to have attended John Shirley as the innkeeper of Carthage. He was a Southern sympathizer, as were the majority of people living in Jasper County. For some reason, not readily understandable, Carthage had escaped the ravages of the border warfare that preceded the War Between the States. That it could continue to go unmolested seemed so unlikely to Preston Shirley that he left Missouri for Texas. He wanted no part of the war if he could avoid it. His brother Bud got into it, fighting as a Confederate bushwhacker, and was killed by Union militia at Sarcoxie, Missouri, on June 20, 1863.

Belle was only fifteen at the time, but fiction began to swirl about her even at that early age. The favorite story (and there is no reason to believe it) has her out riding and being intercepted by a Major "Enos" and his troop of Union cavalry, who had sent a detachment to Carthage to capture her brother, information having come to him that Bud was at home visiting his parents. After questioning her, the major released her, confident that his men would reach Carthage ahead of her. Here is the way it is told in Harman's *Hell on the Border:*

"With eagerness, trembling in every lineament, she [Belle] sprang to the door, rushed down the stairway and out to a clump of cherry bushes, where she cut several long sprouts for use as riding whips.

" 'I'll beat them yet,' said the girl, as with tearful eyes she swallowed a great lump in her throat. Her horse stood just where her captors had left it; vaulting into the saddle, she sped away, plying her cherry sprouts with vigor. . . . She deserted the traveled road and, leaping fences and ditches without ceremony, struck a bee line in the direction of Carthage. She was a beautiful sight as she rode away through the fields; her lithe figure clad in a closely fitting jacket, erect as an arrow, her hair unconfined by her broad-brimmed, feather-decked sombrero, but falling free and flung to the breeze, and her right hand plying the whip at almost every leap of her fiery steed."

Harman was cribbing when he penned the foregoing. It is pure *Police Gazette.* Fifty years after it was written, people were believing it. But fiction is not to be lightly brushed aside when it occurs in narratives dealing with outlawry and the marshals who suppressed it, especially when it is decked out with all the trappings of pseudoreality and offered as history.

It is remarkable that of the many books devoted to the lives of Western outlaws and Western peace officers, only three (to my knowledge) achieved the distinction of first appearing in the pages of the *Saturday Evening Post.* They were immediately successful when they appeared in book form. For years their authenticity was not questioned. Today they stand riddled to shreds. The first was *Beating Back* by Al Jennings and Will Irwin. The brilliant Irwin did the writing. *Hands Up!* by Fred Sutton and A. B. MacDonald a Pulitzer award winner, followed in 1927. In 1931 came the most successful of the three, *Wyatt Earp Frontier Marshal,* a biography by the talented Stuart N. Lake. Though the extent of their fictional content has long since been recognized, they remain what they were in the days of their success—thrilling, fascinating accounts of supermen and largely mythical events, fashioned to satisfy the reader's passion for excitement.

The low estate to which *Hands Up!* has fallen is of more than passing personal interest to me. Over the years I have been one of Sutton's few defenders. I am sure he never knew Wild Bill Hickok, or Earp, Masterson and the other notables of the Dodge City crowd, as he claimed. But he was a man of some importance in Oklahoma and had a wide acquaintance among Captain Payne's "Boomers," of whom he was one, and the pioneers of Old Oklahoma and the Cherokee Strip. If the material he gathered first hand was only folklore, it was good folklore and deserved to be preserved. It was not necessary for him to indulge in the fantastic fabrications that compose a large part of the book. Of it, the sarcastic Burton Rascoe says:

"This book is a treasure, a literary curiosity—the most comical lot of brummagem ever put together with scissors and paste, and doubly comical because Sutton has himself figuring personally in nearly every episode, either as eye-witness or as one who got his information direct from the persons concerned."

For all of his biting criticism, he ends up by quoting from *Hands Up!* in his *Belle Starr* and neglects to give credit. That is true of its other detractors; they damn it, but they do not hesitate to pilfer from it. The pity is that when a book is so soundly damned, the good that is in it is lost along with the bad.

The incident telling how Belle, or Myra Belle, as she was known at the time, was "captured" by Major Edwin B. Eno (there was no Major Enos, as Harman had it) and raced back to Carthage to warn her "young" brother (Bud was five years older than she) is unadulterated hokum.

The killing of his son seems to have filled John Shirley with a burning desire to get out of Missouri as quickly as possible. He sold his inn and livery business, put the family belongings into two covered wagons and started for Texas, driving one wagon himself and Belle and her mother the other.

He was not getting away from Carthage any too soon. Confederate guerrillas burned the town in October, apparently for no better reason than to prevent the enemy from occupying it. Jennison's Red Legs destroyed the little that was left in the spring of 1864.

We do not know, but it seems likely that John Shirley would have gone down the old Sedalia Trail as far as the South Canadian, turned west there and followed the Briartown–Eufala Trail to Edwards' trading post on Little River. If so, Myra Belle got her first look at the wild country along the South Canadian to which she was to return years later and establish herself as the mistress of Younger's Bend.

From Edwards' trading post to Rock Bluff Crossing on Red River was approximately a hundred miles, all of it down through the Nations, wild country but not particularly dangerous for white wayfarers. Once across the Red, they had the surveyed Preston Road to take them the rest of their journey.

John Shirley had a brother living a few miles east of Sycene. His son Preston was farming south of McKinney, in Collin County, not far away. He and his family moved in with Preston temporarily, while he was building a clapboard house in Sycene. It was to this house that Cole Younger, his brothers Jim and Bob, and Frank and Jesse James came three years later. We are already acquainted with what resulted from that visit.

Myra Belle was eighteen. Her passion for fine horses, which was to run throughout her life, had already taken hold of her. She could ride like the wind. The more mettle an animal had the better she liked it. You never see a picture of her wearing breeches or a divided skirt. She said it was not ladylike; she rode sidesaddle.

According to the *Police Gazette* school of fictioneers, she wore a gunbelt and a brace of pistols even in those early days. She may have gone armed; north Texas was still frontier country, and she rode wherever fancy took her. Still, I doubt it; a young girl was safe in Texas where a man would not be. In her days in Indian Territory, it was a different story; she never went unarmed. Presumably she knew how to handle a revolver. Naturally, she has been described as an expert with the pistol. That was the peg on which her mythical reputation as "the female Jesse James" was hung. A perusal of the record does not reveal that she ever shot or killed anyone. The law never charged her with murder.

Though we have nothing better for it than the old wives' tales handed down by neighbors of the Shirleys in Sycene that Myra Belle's home life after the arrival of baby Pearl was a continuous round of bickering and quarreling, they would seem to have some substance. We can be sure that John Shirley and his wife did not relish being presented with an illegitimate granddaughter. To escape from their taunts and bitterness, Myra Belle began spending as little time at home as she could manage.

Cole had been gone for four years when she found the excitement her willful, high-spirited nature craved. Her brother Pres had been killed in a quarrel with a man named Lynn at Spring Creek, Texas, in 1867. Her father was the only one able to check on her. When he learned how she was spending her time in Dallas, and that she was consorting with men like John Fischer, Jim Dickens and Cal Carter, who lived without any visible means of support and were suspected of horse stealing and other crimes, he lost all patience with her. She had already disgraced her family, and the way she was going would bring even greater shame to it. They quarreled. It was a quarrel that was never to be wholly mended.

Breaking with her father had no effect on the headstrong girl. Her new friends were free-spenders. She liked to gamble, and they supplied her with money so she could. It was about this time, 1872, that she is said to have taken a job as dealer in the gaming room of a Dallas saloon. I am inclined to believe it.

The stage was set for Jim Reed to step into Belle's life—she had dropped the Myra by this time. He was a small-time bandit and no-good. About all he had to recommend him were his good looks and the airs he gave himself.

When he met Belle, and how, is told many ways. Some have it that he met and "married" her as early as 1869. That is not what the record says. The first authentic news of him in Texas goes back no further than 1872, when he bought forty acres of land in Bosque County. He sold it within a few months and moved to Sycene. It was then that he met Belle, and she became enamored of him. It was undoubtedly through her that Reed met John Fischer and his friends and made himself the leader of their gang of minor desperadoes.

John Shirley tried to break up the affair between Reed and his daughter. He was an innkeeper again, having enlarged his house and now conducting it as Shirley's Hotel. His best weapon to compel obedience from Belle was little Pearl. He sent her word that her conduct was such that he was going into court and have legal custody of the child given to him.

It brought Belle to Sycene in a hurry. She was wearing fine clothes now—a black velvet riding habit, with a tight-fitting, high-necked bodice that set off her figure to advantage, topped with a wide-brimmed fawn-colored beaver, turned up rakishly on one side and decorated with a curled black ostrich plume. It was the costume to which she was to be partial for the rest of her life.

Her father's threat was real enough. He gave her a few days in which to make up her mind about what she wanted to do about giving up the life she was leading. In the meantime he made her a virtual prisoner in an upstairs bedroom.

Reed came to see her. John Shirley ran him off the property

with a shotgun. Several nights later, he was back with a dozen friends. They put a ladder up to Belle's window and "rescued" her. Now occurred the famous "horseback marriage." A mile out of town the cavalcade drew up, and with John Fischer functioning as preacher, Belle was "married" to Jim Reed. It was a mock marriage, which all understood. It was good enough for Belle, and she went to Reed's farm to live with him as man and wife.

Belle was definitely one of the gang now. They supported themselves in the months that followed by thievery of one sort or another. No one goes so far as to say that she rode with them on their expeditions, but the gang rendezvoused at Reed's farm. That she knew what they were doing and was ready with helpful advice and suggestions can hardly be doubted. It was the role she was to play successfully years later, after she settled at Younger's Bend, in Indian Territory.

Texas was rapidly recovering from the poverty and prostration of years of carpetbag rule and the dislocations of the Civil War. I can not agree with Rascoe that "the war itself had left Texas prosperous and undisturbed." When peace came, there was no "hard" money in the state. In east Texas, the Negroes, no longer slaves, refused to work cotton. Out on the plains and down in the brush country of south Texas, millions of unbranded Longhorns were running wild. But they had no value except for the hides and tallow. It was not until Joseph G. McCoy opened his cattle market at Abilene, Kansas, and the great trail herds began moving north that the economy of Texas began to revive. By the early seventies, millions of dollars of Yankee money were flowing back into Texas. Banditry became more profitable.

Jim Reed, looking for bigger game than could be bagged on the cattle trails, left Texas with two men, Dan Evans and W. D. Wilder, for the cabin of Watt Grayson, in the Creek country, some miles west of Tom Starr's stronghold. Old Watt was one of the three subchiefs of the Creek Nation and had become rich by subverting United States government funds from the tribal treasury. Reed had spent so much time in the Territory, often disposing of stolen Cherokee horses in Kansas for Tom Starr, that he was familiar with the tale of Watt Grayson's hoard.

On the night of November 19, 1873, the three men broke into

the Grayson cabin, but neither old Watt nor his aged wife would reveal where the money was hidden. The bandits strung up the old couple by the thumbs, burned their feet and otherwise tortured them until they were willing to talk. A cache beneath the floor yielded $30,000 in gold and notes, some of it in Confederate currency.

Some would have it that a fourth person, "a smallish figure, possibly a woman wearing a man's clothing," took part in the robbery. This smallish figure they identify as Belle. In proof of it they point out that when members of the Grayson family, ten years later, sought reimbursement from the government, which guaranteed the Five Tribes against loss from the crimes of white men, Belle Starr appeared as a witness for the Graysons. They have her admitting she was in the house when the robbery occurred.

This is the old *Police Gazette* story, replete with all the details of the cruelty inflicted on old Watt and his wife, taken from her alleged diary. Belle kept no diary. I reject the story almost in its entirety. There is no record of the claim having been paid by the United States Treasury and no record of Belle being indicted for her part in the robbery. Jim Reed was dead, Dan Evans had been hanged for murder in another case, and Wilder was in prison for his confessed participation in the theft of the Watt Grayson hoard. Reasons suggest themselves as to why Belle would have wanted to help the Grayson heirs, but if she said anything, we can be sure it was not to her own disadvantage.

Reed returned to Texas with his share of the Grayson loot and remained on the scout. Belle moved into the Planters Hotel. The tales of her high-living, her costly apparel, her gambling losses and her private flunky to look after her horse agree too uniformly to be disregarded. If she wanted to see Reed, she met him at the farm beyond Sycene.

Shortly after December 1, he sent for her. Via the grapevine he had received news that his elder brother Scott Reed had been slain in a family feud. This was a summons home that he could not ignore. He was now the head of the Reed clan, and he knew what his duty was. Belle was seven months pregnant. It was his idea that she go to Rich Hill, Missouri, with him and have her baby there, with his mother and sisters to take care of her, to which Belle agreed.

Living in Vernon County, Missouri, were three brothers by the name of Shannon. Little is known about them. Why they had felt it incumbent on them to slay John Fischer, the outlaw who played preacher in the mock marriage of Belle and Jim Reed, is a mystery. However it was, they arranged an ambush and killed their man, or thought so. It turned out to be a case of mistaken identity. In their eagerness, they had committed the unforgiveable error of killing Scott Reed.

There can be little doubt that it was on this trip up through the Nations that Belle met the giant Tom Starr for the first time. She was well acquainted with him by reputation, of course. When they came face to face, it must have been a case of steel meeting steel, for one was as strong-willed as the other.

Though the blood-stained feud which the Starr clan had waged against the John Ross faction for several decades in retaliation for the murder of James Starr, Tom Starr's father, was now quiescent, the Starrs were still stealing horses from their fellow Cherokees. Jim Reed's coming seemed to be opportune, since they had a herd of horses on hand, ready to be driven north. But Reed was not there on business this time. After Belle had rested for a day or two, the two of them would have to go on. When the situation was explained to old Tom, he agreed that Reed would have to go on to Missouri. Being a feudist himself, family honor was a matter of the first importance with him.

Stories of Tom Starr's cruelty are legion. He stood six feet six in his socks, and despite his years was as straight as the proverbial arrow. His sons were like him, tall, handsome men, with slate-gray eyes that could be as vacant and unrevealing at a moment's notice as only an Indian's can. He had many brothers, perhaps as many as ten. But for twenty years he had been the clan leader, and the Starrs had slit the throats of countless followers of John Ross, the principal chief of the Cherokee Nation.

The Tribal Council, dominated by the Ross faction, had outlawed them and deprived them of all their tribal rights. But the killings had continued, and in desperation the council had offered to rescind its edict, grant them amnesty and restore their rights.

Tom Starr had said no; he wanted more than that—namely the allotment money the clan had not received for years—and he got it. Save for President Andrew Jackson, no other individual, red or white, had ever bent the Cherokee Nation to his will.

There is little doubt that it was on this occasion that Belle became acquainted with Sam Starr, old Tom's stalwart son, who was to play an important role in her life in the years to come. Remembering her condition, this first meeting could not have stirred any romantic lightning in either.

On reaching Rich Hill, Reed proceeded with the business that had brought him home. It took some looking to find the Shannons, but with some help from Fischer, he ran them down and killed two of them. The aftermath followed the pattern of Ozark clan feuds. When a killing occurred, someone always stepped forward to carry it on. Reed was suspected at once, and he was well aware of what he faced. To escape such unpleasantness, as well as to shake off the law, which was interested in him for other crimes, he slipped away to California with Belle.

In Los Angeles, their son Ed was born.

Some writers have them living there for two years, some for only a few months. It could not have been longer than two years. But here again we run into the bewildering confusion of dates and disagreements that cloud much of Belle Starr's career. In self-defense I prefer to disregard the guesswork and speculations and present a chronology based on the known and provable facts. They leave no doubt that Jim Reed and Belle were back in Texas with their son early in 1874.

Belle appears to have effected a reconciliation with her parents—at least with her mother. She and the children may even have moved in with them, for Jim Reed discovered that the law was snapping at his heels and he had to go on the scout once more. But as spring came along, he had his next move planned. Both he and Belle disappeared from Sycene and Dallas. Then, on Tuesday evening, April 7, 1874, the San Antonio–Austin stage was held up at the Blanco River crossing, four miles north of San Marcos. The passengers were robbed and the strongbox and mail bags rifled.

This is the robbery attributed by many to the James-Younger Gang. Others have it that only Cole Younger participated. These presumptions are not borne out by the evidence. This job has been definitely pinned on Jim Reed and two members of his gang.

I quote parts of the statement made by U.S. Marshal Purnell, who led the hunt for the three men, which appears in the files of San Antonio and Dallas newspapers:

"It is now definitely settled that the robbery was perpetrated by three men from Missouri, as follows: James H. Reed, alias 'Bill Jones,' from Bates County, Missouri, where all the family now live, consisting of mother, brother and two sisters.

"He came to Texas in 1872 and settled in Bosque County . . . and removed to Sycene, Dallas County, where he now lives. At this place he seduced a girl, named Rosa McComus."

A description of Reed follows. Purnell then names the second man: "Cal H. Carter, also from Bates County, Missouri," and then the third: "Nelson, alias Jack Rogers, a large young man, about six feet tall and very awkward."

Some writers have professed to believe that Nelson, "the large, very awkward" young man, was in reality Cole Younger. No corroborating evidence has ever been produced. But the myth endures.

Purnell states that Reed, the girl named Rosa McComus, Nelson, Carter and J. M. Dickens and his "wife" rented a house in San Antonio and lived together, that on April 1, the Dickenses and Rosa McComus went north and were joined that evening by Reed, Nelson and Carter, and all camped on the San Marcos River. The following evening the stage was robbed at the Blanco River crossing.

"The robbers are traveling in a northwest direction, keeping between the settlements and the Indian country," Purnell goes on to say. "Reed has a friend in the Territory (Tom Starr) to whose home he goes whenever he gets into trouble, and it may be that he is making for that place now, but he is said to be very fond of the girl he seduced, and it may be the lodestone that will bring him back to Texas."

Purnell was mistaken in thinking that Reed had crossed Red River into the Territory. The three men involved in the robbery of the stage had separated. All were still in Texas, Reed no farther away than McKinney, in Collin County, no more than thirty miles from Dallas. What is remarkable in Purnell's statement is the ignorance he displays regarding Belle. That he is unaware that the young girl Reed seduced at Sycene had been living with the outlaw for two years and was the mother of his son—knowledge he could have acquired on any Dallas street corner—might have led him to surmise that his "Rosa McComus" was an alias for Belle Reed, the bandit's common-law wife.

There was a Rosa McCommas (not McComus) living in Sycene, the respected daughter of Reverend Amon McCommas, a Campbellite preacher. Undoubtedly it was spite, or envy, coupled with the diabolic sense of humor she often displayed, that led Belle to use the innocent girl's name.

11

The Bandit Queen

ONE OF THE PASSENGERS aboard the stage that was held up at the Blanco River crossing was Bishop Gregg, of San Antonio. He was relieved of his watch and other valuables. His prominence in the state gave the newspapers an issue, and they kept pounding away at it, demanding that the robbers be apprehended without further delay. The mails had been plundered, making the case a federal matter which put it squarely in the lap of U.S. Marshal Purnell. That he set the wheels of a neat bit of police skulduggery to turning was doubtless due to the pressure being put on him.

On the evening of April 26, Sheriff James E. Barkley of Dallas County, in cooperation with Dallas City Marshal Peak and two policemen, jailed two men who gave their names as Wilder and Bidwell, admittedly aliases. Sheriff Barkley informed the press that papers found on the prisoners implicated them in the Blanco River robbery and that the one using the alias of Wilder was very likely Jim Reed.

U.S. Marshal Purnell was notified by wire, and he arrived in Dallas the following day. After questioning the two men, he ordered their release on the grounds that there was insufficient evidence to warrant holding them for grand jury action. Both Purnell and Sheriff Barkley were severely criticized for taking such swift action.

Wilder and Bidwell were released forthwith. Proof that trickery was being employed lies in the unnoticed fact that when Purnell left Dallas for Sycene, the man "Wilder" went with him. The real W. D. Wilder had long since been apprehended and sent to prison for his part in the Watt Grayson robbery. The "Wilder" who accompanied Marshal Purnell to Sycene was John T. Morris, a former member of the Jim Reed gang. The deal between Purnell and him, to put it bluntly, was that he was to pretend to be on the scout, find Reed and bring him in dead or alive, for which he could count on getting one-third of the total $4,500 reward posted for the capture of all three of the Blanco River bandits. He was sworn in as a deputy marshal and turned out on his dangerous mission.

Morris had no difficulty finding Reed. The latter does not appear to have been suspicious of him. For three months they ranged back and forth across the Red River counties of north Texas, with Morris waiting for an opportunity that never came. Both were armed, and as was to be expected of men on the scout, they never laid their guns aside.

At noon on August 6, they decided to turn in at a farmhouse fifteen miles northwest of Paris, Texas, to get dinner, for which they were in the habit of leaving a dollar on the table. As they approached the house, Morris suggested that they leave their gunbelts on their saddles to avoid suspicion. Reed foolishly agreed. They had been eating only a few minutes when Morris made some excuse for stepping outside. When he returned, Reed instantly realized his mistake. He tipped the table over and crouched down behind it. Morris had to fire only twice, the slugs from his pistol ripping through the pine table top with deadly effect.

It was murder that in cowardliness matched Bob Ford's killing of Jesse James.

The body was taken to McKinney. Legend has it that when Belle was brought there, she refused to identify it in order to prevent Morris from claiming the reward. Like so many of the Belle Starr legends, there is no truth in it. Belle did not go to McKinney.

The body was so badly decomposed that it had to be buried at once, but not before many who knew Jim Reed had identified it. Morris got the reward money and apparently lived to enjoy it.

Belle lived quietly in Dallas for a year. Her father had died. That may have had something to do with it, though there had been no affection between them for several years. There is general agreement that at this period in her life she devoted herself to her children. Pearl was the best-dressed little girl in Dallas. Belle lavished money on the child's finery and saw to it that she had singing and dancing lessons. Even at that early age, Belle may have envisioned a theatrical career for her daughter, which would not have been strange, for she was theatrical herself.

Mrs. Shirley sold the property in Sycene and moved to Dallas. Belle placed Pearl with her and took Eddie up to Rich Hill to be brought up by his Grandmother Reed. Getting to Missouri from Texas was no longer difficult; the Missouri, Kansas and Texas Railroad had bridged Red River and established itself in the new town of Denison; the Houston and Texas Central had built up from Houston. With one change of cars, you could leave Dallas early one day and be in Rich Hill the following evening.

Usually when a railroad was built into new country in the 1870's, new towns sprang up and civilization (at least of a kind) followed. Nothing of the sort happened when the rambunctious "Katy" Railroad, undeterred by hell and high water, slashed and slopped its way down through the Nations to Texas. Indian Territory remained a wilderness. Most of the scattered military posts had been deactivated. The only attempt at law enforcement came from the roving deputy marshals working out of the U.S. District Court at Fort Smith, Arkansas, and the Indian police and tribal courts. Thievery and crimes of violence continued to occur with grisly frequency.

Relieved of her children, Belle returned to Dallas and got back in character as a professional faro dealer. If she was not pretty, she had plenty of feminine allure. With her good clothes, ready wit and aggressive personality, she must have been an attraction. We are told that she often appeared in the saddle dressed in beaded buckskin, two ivory-handled pistols strapped about her waist, and raced through the streets in such fashion as to make Dallas sit up in disgust or admiration. With her flair for the theatrical, it is exactly what she may have done. Just for kicks, she and a girl named Emma Jones are said to have set fire to a small building on the outskirts of town, for which lark she was arrested on a charge of arson. Out of this arrest comes the story of the rich cattleman who went her bail and gave her several thousand dollars with which to defend herself. It must have been an expensive trial, for she did not return any of it.

These are amusing tales that may or may not be true. One that is not amusing concerns Pearl, when she was not yet fifteen. Belle is said to have arranged for the child's appearance in a Dallas variety theatre. Harman says the excitement of it caused Pearl to have "a brain hemorrhage." He speaks of it as an "accident."

The years between 1876 and 1880 are, to me, the great mystery in the life of Belle Starr. They are almost a complete blank. I am convinced that the writers who have preceded me were as unable to discover anything pertinent about Belle at this period as I have been, and that they dragged out such tales as the burning of the store and the rich cattleman only to gloss over the four-year gap. Remember that at this time Dallas was a town of only 3,000 inhabitants. Very little could have happened without someone recording it.

To keep Belle's criminal career marching on, we are told that she was engaged in some secret activity—to wit, that she was masterminding an organized gang of cattle thieves, who were cutting out longhorns from the trail herds and subsequently "marketing them at Abilene to cattle buyers who would ship them east by rail to the packing houses."

The trouble with this is that it is wrong. Abilene had ceased to function as a cattle market as far back as 1872. Ellsworth, Newton and Wichita had lost the trade in turn, due to legislation against the entry into Kansas of Texas cattle, which were held responsible for the epidemics of "tick" or "Texas fever" among native shorthorn stock. Caldwell was still shipping cattle, but Dodge City, lying far to the west of the proscribed area, was getting almost all of them.

With the opening of the Chisholm Trail, the herds that had been crossing the Red at Colbert's Ferry shifted to Red River Station, a hundred and twenty-five miles up the river. By 1879, the trail drivers had left Red River Station and were crossing the river at Doan's Store, another one hundred and twenty-five miles up-river, for the new Western Trail to Dodge.

In all the history of the Kansas cow towns no instance was ever recorded of a herd of stolen cattle being brought up from Texas and offered for sale. It would have been sheer folly to attempt it, for when a trail herd reached the market it was in such poor condition that it had to be held on the Kansas prairies from three to five weeks to recuperate before it could be sold. At such towns as Abilene, Wichita and Dodge City it was usual for ten to twenty herds to be held at the same time. That meant two to three hundred cowboys, plus trail bosses and owners. As the old saying had it, "They knew cow." Rustled longhorns would have been spotted immediately, no matter what road brand they wore.

If Belle was secretly engaged in some nefarious business, it was not in cutting cattle out of the trail herds, for whatever else she was, she was not stupid. It is not amiss to say that she was shrewd, calculating and usually knew what she wanted. No better evidence of it can be found than her unexplained arrival at old Tom Starr's place in Indian Territory in 1880.

Certainly she was not there by chance, nor was she in need of a hide-out. Judging by what eventuated, I believe she came up from Dallas with the definite intention of marrying handsome Sam Starr and allying herself with the Starr clan. Very likely she was running out of money. As a member of the rich and powerful Starr family she would have security for herself and her children. Two other considerations must be taken into account: on the occasion of her first visit to the wild, beautiful country along the South Canadian, she had fallen in love with it; she was now thirty-two, and it can be taken for granted that she wanted a man to share her bed.

It did not take Sam Starr long to decide that he wanted her for his woman. Sam Starr became her third "husband," and to quote a typical Croyism, "this time she got it in writing." On the fifth of June, 1880, they appeared before Abe Woodall, District Judge for the Canadian District, Cherokee Nation, and were married. It is so recorded in Volume 1 B, of the Canadian District records, and so attested by Henry J. Vann, clerk of the court.

With one exception, this marriage has been regarded very lightly by all writers, many of whom give it no more validity than Belle's "marriage" to Jim Reed. This is wrong. It was a legal marriage by Cherokee law, and since the United States recognized the authority of the tribal courts, it was per se an authentic marriage. By Indian law and white man's law, Belle Shirley became Belle Starr. It was important to her, for it involved Sam Starr's head-right of sixty acres of land in a bend of the South Canadian. In the event of his death, the headright would now go to her. A few words of explanation are called for.

Cherokee lands were held communally, not in severalty. A member of the Cherokee Nation could settle where he pleased, provided the land he wanted had not previously been granted to another member of the tribe. When his claim was approved, he had possession of the land in question; he owned such improvements as he might make, and he could transfer title to them and settle elsewhere, but the land itself did not belong to him; ownership rested with the Cherokee Nation.

There was a one-room cabin on the property, occupied by one of Sam Starr's numerous cousins. He moved out and Sam and Belle took possession. It was to be her home for the rest of her life. She named it Younger's Bend. The surrounding country was so wild and sparsely populated that game abounded; the river was filled with bass, crappies and enormous catfish. As a refuge for men on the scout, Younger's Bend had natural advantages that old Tom Starr's headquarters did not possess. It could be reached only through a winding narrow canyon. In the wooded hills that ringed it were caves in which men could hide and stolen livestock be held indefinitely. Some say that from the very beginning Belle planned to turn Younger's Bend into an outlaw stronghold and set herself up as the brains and director of their criminal activities. Though this is speculation based on hindsight, it is to be doubted. The number of her outlaw acquaintances was limited when she settled down at Younger's Bend. Two to three years passed before men on the scout began to find their way to her place on the South Canadian.

The first thing she did was to add several rooms to the cabin. Later, she had two additional cabins put up to accommodate her guests. She and Sam Starr soon became accomplished horse thieves. They worked at it so hard that it was not long before they were widely suspected. Tyner Hughes and other deputy marshals attached to the U.S. District Court at Fort Smith tried in vain to get evidence enough to warrant taking them into custody.

At this time, Pearl and little Eddie were living with their mother at Younger's Bend, but as more and more men began to drop in out of nowhere, the children were in the way. Eddie was sent back to his Grandmother Reed, in Missouri, and Pearl packed off to an aunt in Kansas.

Rascoe says: "Belle and Sam had scarcely got themselves organized in the marital state when an old friend of Belle's, but a stranger to Sam, dropped in on them and made himself at home for several weeks. Belle introduced the visitor as 'Mr. Williams from Texas.' " In the chronology he gives, he says: "1880. Belle visited by Jesse James and Younger boys at Younger's Bend after her marriage same year to Sam Starr."

This is an error. The year was 1882. Belle and Sam were married in 1880. As for the Youngers, they were tucked away behind the walls of Stillwater prison in Minnesota. It was from this visit that Jesse was to return to Missouri to be slain by Bob Ford. Jesse was not Belle's "old friend," she having met him only in the days he spent in Sycene, back in 1866. I even question that she introduced him as "Mr. Williams." There was no reason why she should.

The prosperity of Sam and Belle became too pronounced to go unnoticed. Not only the deputy marshals of the Fort Smith court but the Indian police as well were watching them now. Though the immediate neighbors of Sam and Belle were members of the Starr clan, by either blood or marriage, several miles to the east, the West clan had settled. Being John Ross adherents, they hated the Starrs and the Starrs hated them. The bitterness between the two families came to a head following the theft of two blooded horses belonging to a man named Crane. Frank West and his brother John, who was a member of the Indian police, appeared before the U.S. marshal in Fort Smith. In a sworn statement Frank

West charged that he had seen Sam Starr and his wife crossing his headright with the stolen horses in their possession. This was nine months after the animals disappeared. Warrants for the arrest of Belle and her husband were issued, and Deputy Marshal L. W. Marks and another man were sent out to serve them.

Belle and Sam had disposed of the horses and were back at Younger's Bend when a Starr runner brought them news that the marshals were on their way there. Belle and Sam left at once and spent the night in the cabin of a Negro family in the Osage Hills. The marshals picked up their trail and followed them. Concealing themselves until morning, they took Sam by surprise when he came out to feed and water the horses. When he failed to return to the cabin, Belle ran out to see what was wrong and found herself in the arms of the officers. They were taken to Fort Smith, where they were arraigned and trial date set. They made bond and were released. In addition to the charge of larceny, Belle was described in the indictment as "the leader of a band of horse thieves."

They came to trial on February 15, 1883. Belle had engaged J. Warren Reed, Judge Parker's nemesis, to defend them. He endeavored to prove that Frank West himself was the thief and that for self-protection and out of hatred for the Starrs he had filed the information against the defendants. Reed, no relation of Jim Reed, made much of the fact that West had waited so long before coming forward.

The trial lasted four days, and it created a sensation—a woman being charged with stealing horses and being the queen of a gang of horse thieves made spicy reading. Newspapers the country over played it up. Almost overnight fame of a dubious nature had come to Belle. The headlines referred to her as "The Bandit Queen" and "Queen of the Outlaws."

It took the jury only an hour to find Sam and her guilty. She was to face the famous "Hanging Judge" five times in her life, but never again was she to hear herself found guilty.

Parker reserved sentence until March 8. Belle had been convicted on two counts. He sentenced her to serve six months on each count in the Federal House of Correction, at Detroit, Michigan, a model prison for its day. Sam, guilty on the one count, got a year in the same institution. With time off for good behavior, it amounted to nine months.

Beyond any doubt, Belle and her husband were guilty as found. It is equally certain that if John West allowed nine months to pass before speaking out it was because he feared the Starr clan and the price he might have to pay for informing on Sam and Belle.

Before being taken off to prison, Belle is alleged to have written the following letter:

Pandemonium, Feb.—1883

Baby Pearl;

My dear little one: It is useless to attempt to conceal my trouble from you and though you are nothing but a child I have confidence that my darling will bear with fortitude what I now write.

I shall be away from you for months, baby, and have only this consolation to offer you, that never again will I be placed in such humiliating circumstances and that in the future your tender little heart shall never more ache, or a blush called to your cheek on your mother's account. Sam and I were tried here, John West the main witness against us. We were found guilty and sentenced to nine months at the house of correction, Detroit, Michigan, for which place we start in the morning.

Now Pearl there is a vast difference in that place and a penitentiary; you must bear that in mind, and not think of mama being shut up in a gloomy prison. It is said to be one of the finest institutions in the United States, surrounded by beautiful grounds, with fountains and everything nice. There I can have my education renewed, and I stand sadly in need of it. Sam will have to attend school and I think it is the best thing ever happened to him, and now you must not be unhappy and brood over our absence. It won't take the time long to glide by and as we come home we will get you and then we shall have such a nice time.

We will get your horse up and I will break him and you can ride John while I am gentling Loco. We will have Eddie with us and we will be as gay and happy as the birds we claim at home. Now baby you can either stay with grandma or your Mama Mc, just as you like and do the best you can until I come back, which won't be long. Tell Eddie that he can go down home with us and have a good time hunting and though I wish not to deprive Marion and

ma of him for any length of time yet I must keep him a while.
Love to ma and Marion.

Uncle Tom has stood by me nobly in our trouble, done everything that one *could* do. Now, baby, I will write to you often.
You must write to your grandma but don't tell her of this; and to
your Aunt Ellen, Mama Mc, but to no one else. Remember, I don't
care who writes to you, you must not answer. I say this because I
do not want you to correspond with anyone in the Indian Territory, my baby, my sweet little one, and you must mind me. Except
auntie; if you wish to hear from me auntie will let you know. If
you should write me, ma would find out where I am and, Pearl,
you must never let her know. Her head is overburdened with care
now and therefor you must keep this carefully guarded from her.

Destroy this letter as soon as read. As I told you before, if you
wish to stay with Mama Mc, I am willing. But you must devote
your time to your studies. Bye bye, sweet baby mine.

(signed)
Belle Starr

The foregoing is regarded as one of the important documents
on Belle Starr. It first appeared in *Hell on the Border,* and has
since been presented in almost every book dealing with Belle
Starr, Judge Parker and the outlaws of Indian Territory. Harman
says he copied it from the original written by Belle on the eve of
her departure for the Detroit penal institution.

It is impossible to write anything about the Fort Smith court
without leaning on *Hell on the Border.* It is a dull, trashy book,
but undeniably accurate when it confines itself to the day-to-day
history of the court. It becomes inaccurate, even probably fraudu-
lent, when it turns to the characters who appeared before Judge
Parker. Long passages have been lifted bodily from the *National
Police Gazette.*

You will find Samuel W. Harman credited with being "a newspaperman," a "Texas editor." House-to-house, doorbell-ringing
research in Fort Smith disclosed that his newspaper experience, if
any, was very limited; that he had run a hotel, either in Van Buren
or Fayetteville, Arkansas, and, in one or the other of those towns,
conducted a livery business; that he was what was known as a
"professional juror" in Judge Parker's court, which meant that his
name appeared on one venire after another. As nearly as possible,

Parker's juries were hand-picked by him. He made no bones about it. If a man would not see things his way, his name disappeared from the panel. Harman must have been to his liking. With one term of court merging into the next with hardly a break in between, a regularly employed juror had a good job.

Hell on the Border did not originate with Harman; it was J. Warren Reed's idea. In fact, he began the actual writing before the shrewd, dapper lawyer, who had cheated the Fort Smith gallows of many vicitims, called Harman in. With Reed looking over his shoulder, Harman went to work. When the book was finished, Reed put up the money for the first edition of one thousand copies, which were run off on the press of the *Fort Smith Elevator*. The first edition sold like hot-cakes, but the second printing found few buyers. When hard times caught up with Harman and Reed, they hawked the book at street corners and from house to house.

I have examined Belle's letter off and on for twenty years, and my early conviction that it was a colossal fake has mellowed to a watered-down skepticism that accepts certain passages as the genuine heartbreak and shame of a befuddled woman trying to retain her daughter's good opinion. The rest I still believe to be fakery.

Harman is the only person who ever saw the letter. If it was written on Belle's last night in Fort Smith, she had to write it in her cell. It may be that outgoing mail had to be examined by some prison official, who might have copied down a paragraph or two and passed it on to Harman. That was in 1883. He did not make use of it, if such was the case, until 1898, fifteen years later—a long time to hold on to notes and memorandums. But he may have been gathering material on the Fort Smith court without knowing how he was to use it. If so, he would have kept anything relating to Belle.

He produced other material that is just as shadowy as the letter—excerpts from Belle's diary (which no one else ever saw) and passages from an interview he alleges she had with J. W. Weaver, of the Fort Smith *Independent*. That he edited the letter, doctoring it to his purpose and lengthening it, is obvious. Place-dating it Pandemonium—a word that certainly was not in Belle's vocabulary—is a Harman touch. Signing it Belle Starr, rather than Mother, is another false note. For added verisimilitude, he tosses in the names of Aunt Ellen, Marion and Mama Mc. They have never been identified.

My conclusion is that the letter, almost in its entirety, is a hoax, largely written by Harman, possibly with a few lines by Belle.

12

Judge Parker Takes Over

❧

Because of the close association of Samuel Harman and J. Warren Reed, with the U.S. District Court for western Arkansas and the Indian Territory, it has been popularly believed, especially among writers, that anything one needs to know about Judge Isaac C. Parker and his war on the stream of killers, outlaws, rapists, horse thieves and lesser criminals on whom he sat in judgment for twenty-one years can be found in their book, *Hell on the Border; He Hanged Eighty-eight Men.*

That is true only when it concerns the court itself, but it gives no better than a hazy picture of Parker, the man, and is often unreliable in its coverage of the lawless and depraved who faced him. The title of the book contains an inaccuracy; Parker did sentence eighty-eight men to be hanged, but only seventy-nine came to their death on the gallows; one was killed while trying to escape; one died while awaiting sentence; seven won reversals (after that became possible in 1891) and received lesser sentences on being retried.

In previous books (*Wild, Woolly and Wicked* and *Red River Valley*) I have dwelt at some length on the "Hanging Judge" and

114

his Fort Smith court. Since then, what little new information I have discovered further justifies the opinions and conclusions I expressed. I can not do better than to restate them.

Under Judge William Storey, the U.S. District Court for the eighteen counties of western Arkansas and the Indian Territory had fallen into such disrepute, with charges of graft and bribery being made so openly, that Storey was about to be impeached when he wisely resigned. For three months the court was left without a presiding judge.

An examination of court records in Storey's time on the bench reveals that seventy-five per cent of the cases he tried were for minor violations of the law, largely having to do with the illegal manufacture and sale of whisky. Few were convicted, and the same was true of men brought before him to answer charges of having stolen their neighbors' timber, horses or other livestock. The cynical belief in Fort Smith was that if you could come up with some cash, you would go free and be able to continue in business. As for crimes of violence—murder, felonious assault and rape—you could count them on your fingers. And they were crimes committed in Arkansas; Indian Territory appears to have been a blank with Judge Storey, or perhaps he had convinced himself that any attempt to bring the law to that red earth wilderness of outlawry, stretching from Fort Smith on the east to the borders of Colorado far to the west, an area larger than Missouri and Connecticut combined, would be profitless as well as futile.

Let us catch up with Isaac Parker. He was from Ohio, born near Barnesville, in Belmont County, about thirty miles west of Wheeling, West Virginia, on October 15, 1838. What formal education he received was limited to the public schools of Barnesville and the Barnesville Classical Institute. The urge to "go west," to which so many Ohio boys were succumbing, took hold of him. Without having any destination, he went down the Ohio River by packet to St. Louis and then by shallow-draft steamboat to St. Joseph, Missouri.

St. Joe once had been an important way station for explorers and fur traders bound up the Missouri for the Far Northwest, men like Lewis and Clark, Peter Roubideaux, the Sublettes and Manuel Lisa. Later, it was to be the jumping-off place for the

Pony Express. Parker found it a thriving, bustling town, proud of its historic past. The year was 1859, and on slavery, the burning question of the day, it favored the cause of the South, but not predominantly so. Northerners, who had migrated to Missouri from Illinois and Iowa, were strong for the new antislavery Republican party, and they had the support of those Democrats who opposed slavery.

Why Parker decided to cast his lot in St. Joe is not clear, unless he foresaw that in the muddled state of local politics an astute young man—he was twenty-one—could advance himself. Though personally strongly Northern in his sentiments and rabidly antislavery, he was careful to straddle the fence at first, for he was an opportunist who knew what he wanted. After a year of supporting himself by odd jobs, studying law meanwhile, he passed the bar examinations and set himself up as an aggressive young lawyer.

To make himself look older he cultivated a brown mustache and imperial. He was tall, long-legged, his blue eyes penetrating and reflecting a temper which he could not always control. Wellman describes him as "plump, even rotund . . . his snow-white hair and white beard, with his bulbous nose and pink round cheeks, gave him more the look of a jovial Santa Claus than one of the most fearsome judges since the notorious Justice George Jeffreys, of the 'Bloody Assizes' in England in 1685."

It is an accurate description of Judge Parker as he was in his last days on the bench. The description is from the photograph widely used. Few people have seen any other pictured likeness of the man. Perhaps he looks more like a prosperous, well-fed butcher than Santa Claus. But that is a matter of opinion. Certainly it bears no resemblance to the Isaac Parker who arrived in Fort Smith in 1875.

Parker was keeping his ear to the ground and in 1862 got himself elected city attorney of St. Joseph, on the Democratic ticket. The following year, he was re-elected without opposition. His star was rising, and though he joined a Missouri Home Guard regiment, a Union outfit, it did not prevent him from being named a presidential elector. He cast his ballot for the re-election of Abraham Lincoln, and in the 1864 election he won the post of prosecuting attorney for the Ninth Judicial District. He had switched party labels and was roundly denounced by the Democratic press as a bolter and a turncoat.

It did not stop him from climbing the ladder. He seems to have liked the sound of his own voice. He was always available when a speech was needed. His political foes called him a "spellbinder," "a braying jackass with the American eagle in one hand and the Bible in the other." Reading one of his speeches is a chore. He had an unbearable prolixity and a fund of tedious homespun humor. It must have been what the voters wanted to hear, for in 1868 he was elected circuit judge of the Ninth District, to serve six years. He resigned after serving two years so that he might run for Congress. He won, not only in 1870 but again in 1872. He was on the way to becoming the wheel horse for the Republican party in Missouri, where Republican victories at the polls were becoming rare.

Parker overstepped himself in the election of 1874. He accepted the Republican nomination for United States senator and registered a thumping defeat. But the party was in power in Washington and in position to take care of the faithful. President Grant offered to name him chief justice of Utah Territory. It sounded good, but when Utah became a state, the job would vanish. He wanted something that promised to be more permanent. Parker was not unacquainted with the Fort Smith court, having served in the House on the Committee for Indian Affairs, where he introduced some legislation designed to better the economic condition of the Five Civilized Tribes. He used this limited knowledge of Indians to persuade Grant of his fitness for the Fort Smith post. He got the appointment, and though the court was designated a U.S. District Court, as its presiding officer, Parker had the status of a circuit court judge, which was for life tenure.

Before leaving Washington, Parker succeeded in having William Henry Harrison Clayton, a fellow Missourian, appointed federal prosecutor of the Fort Smith court. He could not have made a better choice. Clayton was a tireless, relentless prosecutor. Whatever success Parker achieved was due in large measure to Will Clayton.

Judge Parker's feeling that Utah would soon achieve statehood was very wide of the mark. It was not until January 4, 1896, that it entered the Union as the forty-fifth state. With the irony in which history so often indulges, it was in that same year that the Fort Smith court was abolished.

The Parkers—the Judge, his wife (the former Mary O'Toole of St. Joe) and their son Charlie, a lad of four or five—came from St. Louis by steamboat to Little Rock, where they changed to a shallow-draft boat to continue their journey up the Arkansas River to Fort Smith. Jimmy Parker, the baby of the family, was born seven months later. The new judge was expected, but there was no reception committee on hand to greet him when he stepped ashore. This was not so much a bit of personal insolence as an expression of the indifference and disrespect in which the court itself was held by the town's reputable citizens. They knew how it had functioned in the past—venal, impotent. They did not expect Isaac Parker to be any improvement on his predecessors.

Fort Smith was not, nor ever was, a cow town, bursting at the seams with hundreds of thirsty, hell-roarin' cowboys bound up the trail or stopping over on their way home to Texas (but you will find it described as such by the uninformed). It was tough and violent in the days when Fort Smith was an important army post, and it had become tougher after the military abandoned it. When Judge Parker saw it for the first time, it had more than a score of saloons, a floating population of gamblers, whisky peddlers, rivermen, Indian traders, blacklegs and prostitutes running into the hundreds.

The two-story brick and stone headquarters building of army days was now the courthouse. The courtroom, judge's chambers and jury room occupied the first floor, with the prosecutor, lesser court officials and the U.S. marshal quartered above; in the basement was the prison, two large rooms, thirty by fifty-five feet, where often in the years of the Parker regime as many as a hundred and fifty prisoners were held, some awaiting trial, others serving out short sentences that the court had imposed. In that rat and vermin infested hell-hole, no attempt was made to separate youthful first offenders from habitual criminals.

Sanitary conditions were unspeakable. Tubs of water for drinking and a urine barrel were wheeled in once a day. The air was poisonous and disease-ridden and poluted with the stench of human sweat and excrement. Four small barred windows did not let in light enough to dispel the depressing gloom. In the rainy season, the dank, rotting masonry that formed the walls dripped so much water that mattresses spread on the floor were wet for weeks at a time. Men who spoke from experience said Libby Prison and Andersonville were no worse.

"The food, supplied by a contractor, which cost the Government twenty-five cents a day per man, and should have been palatable at that price, was so bad that even men who were rough feeders couldn't eat it." I am quoting myself in *Wild, Woolly and Wicked*. "Even Parker, who never wasted any sympathy on the human fodder that came before him, was moved to complain to Washington. It resulted in some improvement in the food, after ten months of waiting, but nothing was done for years about the physical features of the crawling hell in which boys and men were caged."

Out in what had been the barracks yard, a small square building, constructed of concrete blocks, was built to house female prisoners. Previously they had been lodged in what had once been the garrison's brick ammunition dump. It was a Parker improvement, dictated by necessity. Over the years it was often occupied.

It was some time after Judge Parker's arrival in Fort Smith before the wheels of his treadmill of vengeance and justice began turning, with a veritable army of the accused—most of them guilty as charged—passing in review before him. Some matters had to be attended to first. In his official family there were two holdovers from the Storey regime—U.S. Marshal James F. Fagan and the court's hangman, George Maledon. It did not take him long to decide that Fagan was not the man to do the job he wanted done. He appealed to Washington, and the Department of Justice sent him D. P. Upham. Now he had a man who saw eye to eye with him. Before his race was run, he had other marshals, but none of them ever won the praise from him that he bestowed on Upham.

It was Upham who conceived the idea of hiring several hundred deputy marshals and sending them out with John Doe warrants, which could be served on anyone whom they might have reason to suspect of being engaged in a criminal activity. They were to be paid on a fee basis, which meant in effect that they were to be paid only when actually working, and in addition to their base pay were to be rewarded according to what they accomplished. He and Parker submitted a schedule of the moneys the deputies were to receive, and the Department of Justice gave its approval. It called for the following: mileage was to be allowed at the rate of six cents a mile when an officer was on official business. If he came back with a prisoner, he was to be paid ten cents a mile for himself and an equal amount on his prisoner. If he failed to bring in his man, he got nothing, and could not claim the nominal allowance of a dollar a day for expenses. Twenty-five per cent of his emoluments were to go to the chief marshal.

In practice, it left him little enough, seldom averaging out at more than two dollars a day; but though the work was dangerous —sixty-four deputy marshals were killed and three times that number wounded—men took the job for what money they could squeeze out of it, not for adventure or to serve the cause of justice. Because the pay was poor, there was a constant turnover of personnel. They were of three colors—black, red and white. The vast majority were uneducated and of only average intelligence. There were exceptions of course, men like Tyner Hughes, Bud Ledbetter and Heck Thomas. Years later Thomas was to win undying fame as one of the Three Guardsmen, working with Bill Tilghman and Chris Madsen. Ledbetter, of course, went on to carve a niche for himself in Oklahoma history.

A deputy marshal was not permitted to go out alone. If not accompanied by other marshals, he was to take a "posseman" with him. A posseman in this instance was a civilian whose services were engaged and paid for out of the deputy's own pocket.

Obviously it was more economical and expeditious to bring four, five or more wanted men in at a time than one. To make that possible, the prison van, or "tumbleweed wagon," came into existence. Horan describes it as "a large caboose-type building set on huge iron-rimmed wheels." It was nothing of the sort. It was a flat-bed wagon, equipped with bows and a canvas top that could be rolled back at will, and it was drawn by a team of horses. At a distance, it looked very much like a modified version of the well-known covered wagon. The vans were made in Fort Smith and rented to the U.S. marshal. Behind the driver's seat ran two benches extending to the tailgate. They were for prisoners, with leg irons bolted to the floor. The driver went unarmed to prevent a man from snatching his pistol.

The wagons went everywhere. If there was no road to where they were going, they took to the trails or cut across country, blazing a new trail. When they returned to Fort Smith after an absence of two or three weeks, there was seldom an empty seat in the wagons.

"When we drove through town, folks crowded to the edge of the sidewalks to see who we was bringin' in, some of 'em figgerin' that we might have latched on to friends of theirs," Eli Rector, the last surviving member of "Parker's deputies," recalled in an interview given just before his death in 1952.

When one goes over the long list of men who, at one time or another, served as officers of the Fort Smith court, some names, in addition to the few who were to become famous peace officers, leap out. There was Frank Dalton, no outlaw he, who was killed in the line of duty. His brothers, Bob, Grat and Emmett, who were to win greater fame outside the law than in it, also appear. And there is Bill Doolin, who miraculously escaped the disaster at Coffeyville and at the head of his own gang was to write his name large in the annals of outlawry.

"It takes brave men to enforce the law in Indian Territory," Parker once told a newspaper feature writer. He might better have said, "brave and reckless," for all too often the hunters and the hunted were tarred with the same brush, the line of demarcation between the lawless and the law-abiding being paper thin.

If Judge Parker had not been satisfied with Marshal Fagan, the reverse was true with the other holdover, George Maledon, the court's hangman, a quiet little man with a soft, foot-long beard and deep-set somber eyes that peered out from under a craggy façade and bushy brows. In addition to his job of hangman, he was charged with the responsibility of conducting prisoners on trial from the basement prison to the courtroom. In the past, he had had little to do on either count.

Prior to 1875, no one had paid any attention to the little Bavarian. Parker was to pluck him out of obscurity to make him notorious as "The Prince of Hangmen." On coming from Germany, his parents had settled in Detroit, Michigan. Sometime before the beginning of the War between the States, George Maledon had drifted into the Southwest. With the beginning of hostilities, he enlisted in the First Federal Arkansas Battery. When peace was declared, he returned to Fort Smith and, after several years on the police force, was appointed a deputy sheriff of Sebastian County. His next employment was as a guard and hangman for the U.S. District Court.

Wellman says: "Maledon oversaw the building of the famous scaffold at Fort Smith. It had a hinged platform thirty inches wide and twenty feet long, giving room for twelve men to stand upon it side by side. The master hangman, however, never was able to plunge that many to their death at once. On two occasions he did execute six men with one springing of his trap, three times five men, three times four men, and triple and double executions too numerous to excite comment."

He is in error in saying that on two occasions six men were hanged with one springing of the trap. It occurred but once. The only reason it did not happen a second time was because one of the condemned men received a presidential stay of execution several hours before he was to be hanged. As for Maledon overseeing the building of the gallows, which stood in a corner of the old barracks yard, he may well have done so. If he did, it was several years before Judge Parker became the presiding officer of the Fort Smith court, because it was built in 1873 and was waiting and unused when he arrived in 1875.

A few details should be given about the features of the grim death-machine. It reared up in the air for twelve feet and a sturdy six by six inch white pine beam, to which the hangman attached his ropes, ran from one end of the structure to the other. Charitably, a slanting roof had been built over the gallows so that the wretches who stood on the hinged platform, waiting to be plunged into eternity, should be protected from rain and the elements. Beneath the planks, mercifully concealed from view, there was a heavy iron trigger which controlled the hinged platform. A tug on a lever opened it, and the condemned plunged through the opening to fetch up at the end of the rope with their necks broken.

It was a matter of pride with Maledon that the men he dispatched never strangled to death—a broken neck, and it was all over in a matter of seconds. He stretched and softened his ropes with linseed oil before using them. He was often asked where he had learned to tie the hangman's knot he used. If he ever said, there is no record of it, but when he placed a noose about a prisoner's neck, it never failed to function. Many years later, when he and Harman were traveling from town to town, he with an assortment of the ropes and leg irons he had used, and Harman giving a free lecture on the Fort Smith court and the punishment of crime as a preliminary to selling his book, his proudest boast was that he never bungled a hanging. The mass execution of the six killers at one time was, to him, his greatest achievement. "Not one of them even twitched."

Though seventy-nine men were hanged on the Fort Smith gibbet, it was not always George Maledon who sprang the trap. On at least four occasions, due to illness or (believe it or not) because he was acquainted with the condemned, his assistant officiated.

For months after the court was abolished, the grisly contraption stood whitening in the Arkansas sun, visited by sight-seers and souvenir hunters, who made off with parts of it; and then the Fort Smith town council ordered it torn down and burned. If you were to visit the old barracks yard today, looking for reminders of the past, you would be disappointed. Everything is gone, and so are the old-timers and their memories. Only their tales remain.

13

Border Law

THERE IS LITTLE DOUBT that knowing he had the power of life and death over a realm vaster than most principalities unduly impressed Isaac Parker with his own importance. It was a trait that became more pronounced as the years passed.

It has been said, without proof being offered, that before leaving Washington, when he got his instructions on how he was to conduct his court, he was told by the Attorney General to forget about Arkansas and concentrate his attention on cleaning up Indian Territory. Whether he did get these orders or not, it was what he proceeded to do, and when he settled down to work it was with something of the efficiency of the modern-day assembly line. Between May 10, 1875, and September 1, 1896, he tried 13,-490 cases and won better than 8,500 convictions. Approximately one in every hundred of those found guilty was sentenced to death; for the others it was terms of imprisonment from one to forty-five years in one of the state penitentiaries that accepted federal prisoners by arrangement with the government. His court was in session six days a week, from seven thirty in the morning to noon and from one o'clock to six. In the fanatical war he waged on crime there was no time for letting up, one term of court running into the next, year after year.

Of the cases he heard, more than eighty-five per cent were for offenses committed in Indian Territory. It was his theory, often expressed, that certainty of punishment rather than punishment itself was the only way to combat crime. He put his theory into practice, and with the boundless vigor of a dedicated zealot, he inaugurated the greatest outlaw hunt in history. When the Territory's hardiest criminals heard his name, they shuddered, for it was synonymous with the gallows.

Never before in American jurisprudence was there such a court as his. From 1875 until 1889 there was no appeal from his decisions; his word was final, except on those very rare occasions when the President intervened.

In his war on crime his avowed purpose was to make honest men safe in the possession of their lives and their goods, and he never wavered. Progressively he became more and more an autocrat, far exceeding his authority. Repeatedly he tried cases that were properly the business of the Indian tribal courts. Though he proclaimed himself to be the great friend and protector of the Indians, he allowed no malefactor to slip through his fingers. When his deputies brought a man in, he presumed him to be guilty.

Parker was not bound by the customs of legal procedure established in other courts covering the conduct of the judge, prosecutor, the admission of evidence, and the rights of the defendant. They meant nothing to him; he did as he pleased. Defense counsel repeatedly protested his habit of biased harangues to the jury in favor of the prosecution at the outset of a trial, often brazenly demanding that they bring in a verdict of guilty.

As explained in the case of Sam Harman, jurors who would do his bidding were indispensable to him. Though he knew a jury was stacked in his favor, he would address it with religious fervor, quoting long passages from the Bible that was always on his cherry-wood desk. If he thundered emotionally in his harangues to a jury, it was as nothing compared with his frienzied excoriations of the guilty as they stood before him waiting to be sentenced. They were as lengthy as they were bitter, sometimes running thirty to forty minutes.

It has been said that they served no purpose other than to afford Parker an opportunity to gloat over the condemned with which I must disagree. Undoubtedly they must have given Judge Parker a measure of satisfaction, perhaps pleasure, for he was far more interested in convictions than the fine points of justice. But they had a purpose too; nothing was said in his courtroom that did not travel by word of mouth to the depths of the Territory where, he had reason to believe, they would act as a deterrent on crime.

Only once did a prisoner at the bar awaiting sentence find the spunk to face up to him. He was Henry Starr, the bandit. He had been tried and found guilty of murder. Knowing he was to be sentenced to die on the gallows and that he had nothing to lose may have given him the courage to speak up, though there seems never to have been much question about Henry Starr's courage. Parker began one of his usual tirades, when Starr cried:

"Don't try to stare me down, old Nero. I've looked many a better man than you in the eye. Cut out the rot and save your wind for your next victim. If I am a monster, you are a fiend, for I have put only one man to death, while almost as many men have been slaughtered by your jawbone as Samson slew with the jawbone of that other historic ass."

Parker was dumbfounded as he stared down from his desk, which stood on a raised platform. But he did not continue with his tirade. In clipped words he sentenced Starr to be hanged by the neck until he was dead. The date was February 20, 1895. Many years were to come and go, however, before Henry Starr reached the end of his life of outlawry. The judge was old, fat, white-haired (Wellman's description of him) and a hopeless diabetic. He and his court did not have far to go now. In another year, both would be gone.

Half a century and more after his death, with so much known about him—his life has been fairly well spelled out in at least a dozen books—there is a wide difference of opinion among historians regarding his merits and accomplishments. His admirers hold him up as a brave, noble, courageous Christian, the best frontier judge the country ever had, who punished the lawless and the vicious. Others just as vehemently label him a cruel, sadistic killer, a merciless tyrant immersed in the fatuous belief that he was the anointed of God sitting in judgment on his fellow men. Probably he was something of both.

You will read how the malaise that settles on all prisons on the day a man is to be hanged affected him. Court would not be sitting on those days, but he would be at his desk at his usual time and would spend the morning hours reading his Bible; that as the time of execution drew near, he would cross the deserted courtroom to a window from which he could see the gallows, in the corner of the barracks yard, and stand there with tears running down his cheeks until it was all over. When it was, he would return to his desk and sit there praying with bowed head.

That he may have pitied the men whom he condemned seems reasonable, but a brooding, penitent Parker is, to me, completely out of character. Believably he could have found solace in prayer and the Bible. But the Bible was also his sword. Whenever he was asked by interviewers if the men he had hanged troubled his conscience, he always replied: "I've never hanged a man. It is the law that has done it."

That was the real Parker—a man who believed so completely in the righteousness of what he was doing that remorse could not touch him. He was a fanatic, of course, but not a religious fanatic; his fanaticism was concerned with the punishment of crime. "Protect the innocent; let no guilty man escape." It was his life. Perhaps no instance reveals the depth of his feeling as clearly as the torrent of words with which he lashed the notorious Cherokee Bill when that savage slayer stood before him, convicted for the second time of murder. Cherokee Bill had just killed Larry Keating, a guard, in an attempted prison break. Here is part of it, taken from the court reporter's stenographic record. Reading it one almost can hear the words rushing from Parker's lips as he was carried away by his own eloquence:

"Cherokee Bill, you revel in the destruction of human life. The many murders you have committed, and their reckless and wanton character, show you to be a human monster. You most wantonly and wickedly stole the life of a brave and true man. You most wickedly slew him in your mad attempt to evade the punishment justly due for your many murders.

"Keating was a minister of peace; you were and are a minister of wickedness, of disorder, of crime, of murder. You have had a fair trial. . . . There is no doubt of your guilt of a most wicked, foul and unprovoked murder, shocking to every good man and woman in the land.

"I once before sentenced you to death for a horrible and wicked murder. I then appealed to your conscience by reminding you of your duty to your God, and to your own soul. The appeal reached not to your conscience, for you answered it by committing another most foul and dastardly murder. . . . Behind you lies a long red wake of human gore. Your hands are steeped in it and your heart reeks with infamy. With hideous mien you stood and fired shot after shot at the brave officers who gathered to control you, and now you ask mercy from this court . . . you, a creature whose very existence is a disgrace upon nature, a grievous burden to the atmosphere from which you draw breath. Away with you, you most fiendish of all monsters. . . . Better that you should have been strangled at birth than that you should ever have arrived at the age we call manhood.

"You will now listen to the sentence of the law, which is that you . . . be hanged by the neck until you are dead—dead—dead. May God whose laws you have broken have mercy on your soul."

This is Judge Isaac Parker, the crusader, under full steam, self-righteous, intemperate in his utterances. His critics, who denounced his methods, say that he accomplished very little, for all of his trying; that when he stepped down from the bench he had barely scratched the surface of crime in his jurisdiction; that conditions in Indian Territory were no better than when he took over. The wonder is that they were no worse. To acknowledge that he checked the rising tide of violence in the 70,000 square miles of wild, lawless country that was his bailiwick is to pay him his finest compliment. It is worth remembering that it was only a few years after his court was abolished and his former jurisdiction cut up that no less than seventy-two state and federal courts were established to replace it. But they were unable to stamp out lawlessness. In fact, even after Oklahoma achieved statehood in 1907, outlawry and banditry continued.

Before we go back to May 10, 1875, and Parker's first trial, the difficulties that beset him and ended his career call for comment. They began with his unfortunate correspondence with the Department of Justice and his indiscreet criticism of the Supreme Court. As a result of the extensive newspaper coverage that Eastern newspapers were giving Judge Parker and his court, most of it unfavorable, in which they were variously described as "the Fort Smith Death Factory," the "Slaughter House" and the "Butcher Parker," congressmen were being deluged with mail from their constituents demanding that he be removed and that the men he found guilty should have the right to appeal their convictions to the Supreme Court.

It was not only the press that was attacking Isaac Parker; from Fort Smith his implacable courtroom foe J. Warren Reed was bombarding the Department of Justice with complaints about the judge's illegal procedures, jury packing, biased charges to a jury, refusal to give defense counsel time to prepare his case. It had an accumulative effect. To Reed must go the distinction of being the man who pulled Parker down, and incidentally, though he does not appear to have given it any thought at the time, destroyed himself.

J. Warren Reed was an unknown lawyer when he and his wife arrived from California in 1879. He had practiced law in several states. When he saw the amount of legal work to be had in Parker's court, the busiest one in the country, he hastened to become a member of the Arkansas bar. He was shrewd, unscrupulous and a master of legal trickery. His fees were modest at first, but with success, they climbed sky high. Suddenly prosperous, he became the best-dressed man in Fort Smith, which put him in sharp contrast to Parker, who was a slovenly dresser.

His dandified appearance in court wearing a gray topper, fawn-colored gloves and carrying a silver-headed cane, seems to have annoyed the judge, or perhaps it was that from the first he recognized an enemy in Reed. Of the two, Reed was the better lawyer. He often bested Parker and was always a thorn in the Judge's side. When the court came under attack, relations between the two became bitter and acrimonious. Parker was aware of the prominent role Reed was playing in the battle to undermine him.

The showdown came on February 6, 1889, when Congress passed an act granting the right of appeal to the Supreme Court of the United States in all cases of conviction where the punishment was death. It was a staggering blow, but Reed was soon to show him how really serious it was. He had his opportunity now, and he began bombarding Washington with appeals to have verdicts set aside and new trials granted. Other lawyers followed his lead. Of forty-six appeals, the Supreme Court ruled in thirty cases that the prisoner had not had a fair trial. The judge was finished, his power broken. From the guilty awaiting sentence, the cry went up: "Get me Reed. He'll save me."

Other blows were to be received in that year of 1889. A new federal court was established at Paris, Texas, and it took away from the Fort Smith court jurisdiction over the Choctaw and Chickasaw Nations and the western half of the Territory. A federal court was established in Muskogee, with jurisdiction over the Creek Nation. On April 22, the first great opening of the Territory to white settlement occurred. It resulted in the formation of six counties in what came to be known as Old Oklahoma, and Beaver County in the Oklahoma Panhandle. Guthrie was named the capital, and a federal court established there. Parker's domain was disappearing like sand along a beach being washed away by the tide.

Congress was not finished with the Fort Smith court. On March 3, 1891, direct review of all cases involving murder and other major crimes was granted. No longer could Parker pack a jury or lead it as he had done for years. Will Clayton, his able prosecutor, who had stood by him loyally and fought Reed and the enemies of the court, must have realized that the end was near even though the judge went on doggedly. Parker had won a notable victory in the second trial of Cherokee Bill. Despite all of J. Warren Reed's maneuvering, he had not been able to save the Indian from going to the gallows. On July 30, 1896, he hanged his last man. Again Reed was the attorney for the defense, and again he appealed to the Supreme Court for a reversal, but the high court sustained Parker. It was a victory that had no savor; he was a weary, sick man, old beyond his years.

On September 1, the court crier arose and announced the decision of the Department of Justice: the District Court for western Arkansas and Indian Territory stood adjourned sine die.

The judge was home in bed on the day his court was abolished. He never left it. The end came on the morning of November 17, 1896.

In the end, tragedy touched the lives of all the principals in the history of the Fort Smith court. Parker's son Charlie, after getting out of one scrape after another, died under mysterious circumstances. Jimmy, the younger son, committed suicide. There can be little question but that the demise of the Fort Smith court hastened Parker's death. Annie Maledon, the hangman's only child, said to have been the prettiest girl in Fort Smith, ran off with a handsome, worthless scamp named Frank Carver, who, unknown to her, had a prison record. After living with Annie for a year or more in Colorado, he deserted her, only to come back some time later to find her living in Muskogee with another man. There was a street gunfight and she was mortally wounded. She was removed to the hospital in Fort Smith and died there some weeks later. Captain J. H. Mershon, who had succeeded Upham as chief marshal and served Parker for twelve years, went insane.

Will Clayton fared better than the others, but his life was darkened by the unhappiness of his daughter Anne, who married Charlie Parker. It was an unhappy marriage from the beginning. Charlie and his mother, who was drinking heavily, made things so miserable for the girl—she was only eighteen—that she packed up and left Fort Smith without saying where she was going. When what is now eastern Oklahoma was opened to white settlement, Clayton was named judge of the federal court at McAlister. That leaves only the fate of J. Warren Reed to be considered.

It seems incredible that it never occurred to Reed that in destroying Parker he was destroying the court itself and that he would be caught in the ruins, his livelihood swept away. For years he had had more legal work than he could attend to. Suddenly there was none, at least not the kind that had made him famous, with big retainers. Fort Smith was filled with lawyers, and they were now scrambling over one another to grab what little work there was. He hurried off to Muskogee and opened an office there, with a branch office in Tahlequah, the Cherokee capital. He did well enough at first, but too many new people were moving into the Territory who had never heard of him, and too many young lawyers who were as able as he. His practice dwindled away. He had defended one hundred and thirty-four men charged with capital crimes. Thanks to him, only two had suffered the ignominy of death on the gallows. By inventing alibis, using perjured witnesses, stopping at nothing, no matter how unscrupulous it might be, he had achieved fame. He could not understand why more people needing a good lawyer were not knocking on his door. To save money, he closed the Tahlequah office.

He began writing the book that was to be called *Hell on the Border; He Hanged Eighty-eight Men*. He had plenty of time for it, for there were fewer and fewer interruptions. But he found writing hard work. He sent for Sam Harman. Originally the purpose of the book had been to tell the story of the Fort Smith court; now it was the publicity it would give him, enabling him to regain his lost prestige and mend his fortunes, that became uppermost in his mind.

Reed had always been a hard drinker. Now he went to the bottle oftener and stayed longer, as the saying had it. By the time the book was published, he was broke. It failed to live up to his expectations. He ended up hawking it from house to house. He had become a bothersome, forgotten old man. He died in 1912 and was buried in Fort Smith. Very few people attended his funeral.

It is time to say something about the men and women whom they tried, defended, punished and often hanged. They are as unknown today as though they never existed. There are one or two exceptions: Belle Starr is remembered, possibly the Cherokee Kid and Henry Starr; Rufus Buck, Bill Cook, Texas Jack, the Verdigris Kid and a hundred others are blanks except on the pages of history. Anyone who ever heard of Judge Isaac Parker and his court knows vaguely that he hanged six men one morning; that they were vicious killers, every one of them, and richly deserved hanging. But who were they? Suppose we take a look at them.

William Clarke Quantrill, the notorious guerrilla leader

Fletch Taylor, one of Quantrill's ablest lieutenants; Frank and Jesse James

Mercaldo Archives

Cole Younger as he appeared when released from the Stillwater penitentiary, where he had served twenty-five years

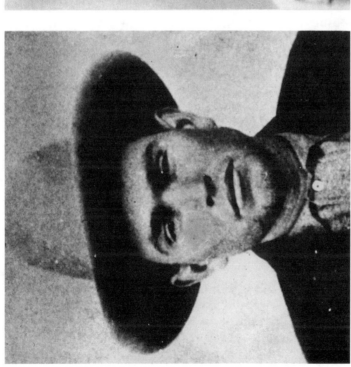

Kansas State Historical Society, Topeka

Bill Cook, leader of the Bill Cook Gang, who was finally run to earth near Fort Sumner, in the old Billy the Kid country

Isaac C. Parker, aged thirty-seven, when he began his reign as presiding officer of the Fort Smith U. S. District Court

Judge Parker, diabetic and old beyond his years, twelve months before his court was abolished in 1896

Belle Starr, outlaw queen of legend, as she really was, and her Cherokee paramour of the moment, Blue Duck. A photograph made in Fort Smith, Arkansas, after his release from the Southern Illinois Penitentiary.

Oklahoma Historical Society Archives

Cherokee Bill, who killed for the pleasure of killing, and his captors, on his arrival in Fort Smith, Arkansas, to face the "Hanging Judge." Reading left to right: Zeke Crittenden and Dick Crittenden, deputy marshals; Cherokee Bill; Clint Scales; Ike Rogers and deputy marshal Bill Smith.

Bob Dalton and his sweetheart Daisy Bryant, who was either the sister of Black Faced Charley Bryant, or his former mistress. The legend that after the killing of Bob Dalton she adopted the alias of Tom King and in male garb headed her own gang of horse thieves has never received much acceptance.

Mercaldo Archives

Kansas State Historical Society, Topeka

Aftermath of Coffeyville, which spelled the end of the Dalton Gang. Note the boy peering through a hole in the fence.

Henry Starr, who was among the first and certainly the last of the horseback outlaws of Oklahoma and Indian Territory. This picture was taken outside the jail at Chandler, Oklahoma, where he was being held following the double bank robbery at nearby Stroud.

14

Fort Smith and Hell

Parker's first case brought Dan Evans before him, charged with the murder of a Texas youth named Seabolt, out in the Creek Nation. This was the same Dan Evans who, with W. D. Wilder and Jim Reed, Belle Starr's late "husband," had tortured and robbed old Watt Grayson and his wife of $30,000. Evans was down on his luck, his share of the Grayson robbery long since frittered away on women and whisky. The circumstances in the case were these:

A deputy marshal was out in Eufala, doing some sleuthing, when word was brought to him that the body of a man had been found in a patch of timber on the North Canadian. He hurried to have a look at it. The young man had been shot in the head, the bullet entering from the back, which rather definitely made it a case of murder. His pockets had been turned inside out, which indicated robbery as the motive for the killing. The only identification the marshal found was the name Seabolt, printed on the cover of a notebook. What he could not understand was why young Seabolt was in his stocking feet.

With the help of several Creeks, who had accompanied him, he began searching for the missing footgear. A few hundred yards away, one of the Indians found an old, badly worn pair of shoes that had been tossed into the underbrush. It had rained the previous day, but the shoes were dry, proof enough that they had not been there long. In the soft earth were the sharp imprints of boot heels. It was now rather obvious that the killer had exchanged his worn-out shoes for young Seabolt's boots.

Downstream a quarter of a mile, in a shallow ravine, they found his horse. It had been shot. The saddle was gone. They concluded that it had been hidden or thrown into the river. Picking up the trail of a horseman heading toward Eufala, they followed it and overtook the man a mile west of town. He was wearing a pair of expensive new boots. When the marshal questioned him, he talked freely, denying, of course, that he knew anything about young Seabolt; but the deputy was so sure he had the killer that he took him into custody and bore him off to Fort Smith.

What little evidence could be produced against Evans was so circumstantial that the jury could not agree on a verdict. He was returned to the prison in the basement of the courthouse and was there awaiting a new trial when Judge Parker took over. Both he and prosecutor Clayton were convinced that Evans was guilty, but there was grave doubt in their minds that he could be convicted. And then something happened that put an entirely new light on the case. Clayton had a visitor.

The stranger was a Texan, from McKinney, down in Collin County. His name was Seabolt. He identified himself as the father of the boy who had been killed. He had known nothing about it until he read an account of Dan Evan's trial in the Dallas *News*. He informed Clayton that Evans and his son had left Texas together on a trip up through the Territory. Just before leaving home, he had bought his boy a pair of new boots.

"I liked 'em so well, Mr. Clayton, I bought a matching pair for myself."

He shoved out his legs and had Clayton examine his boots. They were exact duplicates of the boots Dan Evans was wearing.

"My boy had a little trouble with one of his boots—the one for his left foot. Somehow, he knocked the heel loose. Not having any cobbler's nails on the ranch, he hammered it back in place with horseshoe nails."

"How many nails did he use, Mr. Seabolt?"

"Three—I know because I watched him drive 'em in."

Now Clayton had all the ammunition he needed. When the new trial began, he had Evans remove his left boot. The heads of three horseshoe nails were visible in the heel, just as Seabolt had stated.

The boot was put in evidence as an exhibit for the prosecution. The father took the stand. That was enough for the jury. Twenty minutes after it left the box, it was back with a verdict of murder in the first degree.

It was a particularly heinous crime, and before passing sentence Parker delivered the first of the blistering excoriations that were to echo through the Fort Smith courtroom for twenty-one years. He sentenced Dan Evans to die on the gallows, but he did not set the day when the will of the court should be carried out. That was his prerogative. In view of what happened in the following weeks, one must wonder if even then he had in mind the mass execution that was to shock the nation.

Parker's deputies were beginning to swarm over the Cherokee and Creek Nations. Among the men in whom they were interested was Jim Moore, a professional horse thief. They chased him out of the hills west of the Verdigris River, only to lose him. Then two of them learned that he had been seen around Catoosa. They went after him. In Catoosa, they were told that Moore and another man had just stolen several horses from a rancher named Everetts. Accompanied by a posse, the two deputy marshals picked up the trail of Moore and his accomplice. It led them to Moore's stronghold on Pole Cat Creek, just across the Arkansas River. There was a battle, in the course of which William Spivey, a posseman, was killed by Moore. Night was at hand. The marshals decided to wait until daylight to rush the camp. In the morning, they found that the two men had disappeared.

Moore and his companion separated. Moore confessed later that he had caught a Katy train and rode it all the way to Eufala and then turned west up the North Canadian. He was getting out of the country now, knowing he was wanted for a murder that could be proved against him this time. (He boasted at the very last that he had killed six men.) Meeting a man driving a small herd of cattle to the Sac and Fox Agency, he went along with him, being helpful but planning to kill him and make the cattle his own. But things went awry. The two deputy marshals who had almost trapped him on Pole Cat Creek had driven sixty miles across country in their prison wagon, not expecting to see Moore again, when he walked right into their hands. They turned back down the North Fork and had their prisoner behind bars in Fort Smith four days later.

The evidence against Moore was of a nature to make it unnecessary for the court to waste much time on him. "You will be hanged by the neck until you are dead, dead, dead, and may God have mercy on your soul." The words were to become a popular refrain in the drab courtroom. But again no date of execution was set. In the deep freeze of the basement prison, the judge now had two specimens he could use in a monstrous demonstration to the outlaw world that crime does not pay. And more were coming. The crawling hell below stairs was beginning to bulge with men awaiting trial. Chief Marshal Upham and his deputies were bringing them in every day. Two deputies were shot to death in the Osage Hills. They were replaced, and the prison wagons continued to roll.

Although the first edition of *Hell on the Border* runs to 720 pages, the authors find room for only the briefest treatment of a man named John Whittington. That little, however, appears to be all we have about him. According to Reed-Harman, Whittington, a white man, lived down in the Chickasaw Nation, near Red River. The selling of whisky was forbidden in Indian Territory, but on the Texas side of the river a man could slake his thirst seven days a week and do it legally. Whittington was in the habit of crossing the Red at Colbert's Ferry and spending an hour or two at John Maupin's combination store and saloon. One Sunday, he crossed the river with his neighbor John Turner. They did considerable drinking. When Turner opened his purse to pay their score, Whittington saw that it contained a large sum of money.

After they had recrossed the river and were walking along a

wooded trail for home, Whittington, who was in back, picked up a club and felled Turner. Drawing a knife, he killed the unconscious man and robbed him.

It was his misfortune to have Turner's son come riding up the trail in time to witness the deed. The crime was reported to the Fort Smith marshals. Whittington confessed and threw himself on the mercy of the court, swearing that he was so drunk when he killed Turner that he didn't know what he was doing. Leniency might have been shown him, but prosecutor Clayton dredged up two other murders of which Whittington was suspected. That settled his fate with Parker. But since alcohol had been the cause of the prisoner's downfall, the judge could not forego delivering a tirade on the curse of whisky. Whittington became Number 3 in his collection of Terrible Examples.

Samuel W. Fooey, of Webbers Falls, a half-breed, born of a Cherokee mother and a white father, obligingly made himself available as Number 4. It happened this way. John Emmett Neff, a schoolteacher at one of the Indian schools in the Going Snake District, walked all the way to Tahlequah to collect his salary, which he had left untouched until it amounted to three hundred dollars. With the money in his purse, he decided on leaving Tahlequah to continue south and visit his parents, who lived on the Illinois River.

When night overtook him, he still had some distance to go. He stopped at a farmhouse, as was the custom of the country, and arranged to pay for his supper, lodging and breakfast. The charge was fifty cents, but in the morning when he wanted to pay his bill, the woman of the house could not change the five-dollar note he offered. Neff said he would leave the fifty cents at a store he knew he would be passing. This was satisfactory to the woman. Her brother, Sam Fooey, chanced to be visiting her. He got a glimpse of the money Neff was carrying. When Neff left, Fooey accompanied him, saying that he, too, was going home.

They stopped at the store Neff had mentioned and left the fifty cents. Neff was not seen again. About a year later an Indian boy found a skeleton in some weeds at the bank of the Illinois River. The news was communicated to the marshals. They made an investigation and found a book with Neff's name in it at the base of a nearby bluff. Since Sam Fooey was the last person known to have seen the schoolteacher, they questioned him. He told a decidedly lame story, and worse still for him, he had been spending more money than he could account for. He was brought to Fort Smith, tried and convicted. The sentence was death. But once again Parker refrained from stating the day of execution. He offered no explanation to court attendants and reporters. If anyone surmised the nature of the bombshell he was preparing there is no written record of it.

The forced removal of the Cherokee people from their homeland in the Carolinas and Georgia to Indian Territory, and the manner in which it was accomplished, might explain their being imbued with an undying hatred of the white man. That was true, however, of only a very few. That trifling minority made trouble for the Cherokee police and the Tribal Council as well as for whites. They were surly and refused to learn (or speak) the white man's language. A young full-blood living in the Flint District was typical. He was Smoker Mankiller, and he was as mean as his name.

One noon, he encountered a neighbor, William Short, a white man, eating his lunch under the trees on Sallisaw Creek. Short had been out hunting. His rifle was standing against the trunk of an elm. He was well-acquainted with Smoker Mankiller. He could speak some Cherokee. The Indian accepted his invitation to sit down and share his lunch. As he ate, young Smoker's attention focused sharply on the rifle. When he asked Short if he could examine it, the latter, remarkably unsuspicious, it would seem, said yes. The noontime peacefulness was shattered the moment the Indian got the rifle in his hands. He turned it on Short and shot him dead.

The thing that lifted this killing out of the ordinary was that Smoker Mankiller, having accomplished his purpose, threw the rifle on the ground, leisurely walked home and said nothing. That he did not take the rifle or prepare a story to cover himself can be explained only as a gesture of his contempt and hatred of white men.

When Short failed to return home that evening, a party of his friends set out to look for him. Shortly after daylight, a flock of circling buzzards led them to the body. Smoker Mankiller had been seen walking up the creek about noon of the preceding day. The remains of Short's unfinished lunch established the time of his death.

The Cherokee police were on hand when two U.S. marshals arrived. The dead man being white made it a matter for the federal officers. They questioned Smoker Mankiller, one of the police acting as interpreter. His truculent manner, rather than what he said, led to his being placed under arrest. They took him down Sallisaw Creek until they intercepted a prison wagon returning to Fort Smith from Tahlequah.

On the witness stand Smoker Mankiller made some damaging admissions. The jury returned a verdict of guilty. Judge Parker was the "red man's friend." Never before had he sentenced an Indian to death. It was now his duty to do so: murder was murder. Smoker Mankiller became object lesson Number 5.

The month of August was half gone when Edmund Campbell, a Negro farmer down in the Choctaw Nation who had been put upon in various ways by a neighboring farmer named Lawson Ross, also a Negro, decided that he had endured enough. Seizing his shotgun, he went to Ross' place and blew the latter's head off when he came to the door. Campbell admitted the killing and was soon facing Judge Parker. He was told that he must die for the crime he had committed. Parker departed from his custom and expressed his pity for the Negro, but in his war on crime, a man's color could not save him. Before Campbell was led away, the court announced that he and the five previously condemned men would be executed at ten o'clock on the morning of September 3. The public was invited to witness the multiple hanging.

Six men to be hanged with one springing of the trap! It created a sensation, as Parker intended it should. Up and down and across Indian Territory let men who were ready to kill for a pair of boots, a few hundred dollars or to satisfy a grudge take notice that the law, inexorable and inflexible, had arrived.

News of the sextuple hanging spread rapidly. Fort Smith began to fill up with strangers. Newspapermen from St. Louis and other distant cities began arriving. On the outskirts of town, farmers camped with their families. Many of them had driven forty to fifty miles to witness the hanging. When the morning of September 3 arrived it was estimated that two thousand people were crowded into the old barracks yard.

Promptly at ten o'clock the guards led the manacled prisoners across the yard to the gallows. Two by two they mounted the stairs that they were never to use again. Hangman Maledon showed them where they were to stand. When he was ready, they were asked if they had anything to say before the sentence of the court was carried out. Most of them did. Several ministers were on hand to help them to pray.

It was time to adjust a noose about the neck of each of the condemned men. That done, Maledon drew the long black hood over the head of each. The crowd was silent as he stepped to the end of the platform and jerked the lever. The hinged platform parted under the feet of the six killers, and they shot through the opening to oblivion.

Reaction the country over to the multiple hangings was largely unfavorable to Judge Parker. In some newspapers he was described as an "avenging tyrant," "a monster, drunk with power." He fared much better locally. Both the *Fort Smith Independent* and the *Fort Smith Elevator* hailed him as a fearless, dynamic leader who was determined to put down lawlessness in the Territory. There was no way of knowing the reaction of the culprits whom Parker was trying to impress with the terrible consequences of their wrongdoing. That it must have had some effect seems logical. But there was no lessening in the incidence of robbery and murder; the tumbleweed wagons continued to bring in their loads of human freight, and the court calendar remained jammed with cases waiting to be tried.

Far from admitting defeat, Parker hired more deputy marshals, guaranteed the safety of prosecution witnesses and speeded up payment of their fees. If the first mass hanging had not had the hoped-for results, perhaps a second experiment would. He began collecting condemned men as assiduously as some men collect rare coins. In seven months and two weeks, he was ready. On April 21, 1876, for the second time in little more than half a year, six men were to hang. Again, the public was free to witness the mass execution.

Any idea that only a few would attend, because people had been so revolted by what they had witnessed once, had to be abandoned, for it soon became apparent that another great crowd would be on hand. The first one had been orderly, even subdued, but this one came as to a picnic. The saloons had been open for hours, and that they had done a rushing business was evident from the number of drunks among the spectators.

Because of the last-minute stay that Osee Sanders received from President Grant, only five men went to their death that April morning. Sanders, a Cherokee fullblood, had committed a foul murder. He had an accomplice whom he refused to name. He deserved hanging more than most of the five men he should have joined on the gallows. Maledon got him eventually. Perhaps the reason for the presidental stay was that during the Civil War Sanders, as a member of the Third Cherokee Rifles, had fought on the Northern side.

The second mass hanging brought further condemnation on Judge Parker. That it proved to be any more of a deterrent on crime than the first is to be doubted. Never again were as many as five men to be executed at one time. The number dropped to four, then to three and up again to four. As has been stated, triple and double hangings continued with monotonous frequency.

It would be a mistake to conclude that Parker was gradually putting down lawlessness because there were fewer hangings in the eighties than in the first five years of his regime. There were other reasons; he was being hedged in in various ways and was being successfully challenged by J. Warren Reed. It is safe to say that some of the men who went to their death on the Fort Smith gallows in the middle and late seventies would have suffered no worse than long prison terms if they had come to trial ten years later.

Among the thousands on whom Isaac Parker sat in judgment, fewer than ten could properly be called outlaws—outlaws in the grand manner of the James-Younger Gang. Instead they were whisky peddlers, horse thieves, rapists and murderers, but they did not rob banks or hold up trains. If the printed pages of many who have preceded me are to be believed, outlawry, as such, centered and swirled about Belle Starr. She is said to have consorted with outlaws, sheltered them and taken at least four, each in his time, as her lovers. If so, except for Jesse James, who hid out at Younger's Bend for several weeks but had no dalliance with Belle, they were small fry. To give substance to the legend that she was the "Outlaw Queen," men like Henry Starr and Bill Cook, who were first-rate bandits, have been associated with her. It is surprising to read in Wellman's *A Dynasty of Western Outlaws:* "Two who had felt the influence of Belle Starr helped, almost as if by an inevitability, in the organization and growth of Cook's band [the Bill Cook Gang]. They were Henry Starr, Belle's nephew by her marriage with her Indian husband, Sam Starr; and Jim French, next to the last of Belle's lovers, who at times called himself Jim Starr at her behest."

To set the record straight: Henry Starr never had any contact with Belle; he was only sixteen when she was killed; the Bill Cook Gang did not come into existence until 1893, four years after her demise. And, of course, it was Jim July who, at times, went by the name of Jim Starr, not Jim French. Whatever his other qualifications may have been, and it would seem that they did not rate very high with Belle, for he did not last long at Younger's Bend, French, a Creek fullblood, never amounted to shucks as an outlaw.

Just who were the "notorious outlaws" who forgathered with her on the South Canadian? No one has named them. That they bootlegged corn whisky, stole horses, robbed lonely country stores and killed when they thought that necessary can be taken for granted. Among the men who shared her bed and board at Younger's Bend was a character named Blue Duck. Both Rascoe and Wellman call him "a white man known only by his fantastic alias, Blue Duck." They are mistaken. Blue Duck was a Cherokee. He was one of a large family living on Rogers Creek, a tributary of the Little Verdigris River, west of Oologah. His name in Cherokee was *Sha-con-gah Kaw-wan-nu.* It comes out Blue Duck in English.

The bedrock on which the Belle Starr, the "Bandit Queen," legend rests is that for the five years from 1884 to the time of her death in 1889, she conducted at Younger's Bend a gathering place for the most notorious horse thieves and bandits in the country. If so, one wonders why Judge Parker, only fifty miles away, and his several hundred deputy marshals permitted it to exist. Belle loved notoriety. Perhaps she had something to do with spreading the wild tales that were told about her. There is some reason to believe that Robert L. Owen, the part-Cherokee Indian agent at Muskogee, thought so. Owen was to have a distinguished career as a United States senator for Oklahoma, perhaps best remembered for his authorship of the Federal Reserve Act. He caused to be published in the Territorial newspapers the following, which was a copy of a letter he had written Belle:

July 6, 1887

Mrs. Belle Starr, Oklahoma, I. T.

Madam:—The complaint against you for harboring bad characters, has not, in my opinion, been established, and is now dismissed. I hope sincerely that you will faithfully carry out your promise to this office not to let such parties make your place a rendezvous.

Robert L. Owen,
United States Indian Agent.

15

The Mystery of Younger's Bend

W HEN Sam and Belle Starr returned to Younger's Bend after
serving out their sentences in the Federal House of Correction, at
Detroit, Michigan, they had been away a few days more than nine
months. Imprisonment had taught them nothing, and they were
no sooner back in their old surroundings than they resumed their
lawless lives.

In their absence, old Tom Starr, Sam's father, had kept a man
on the place and had developed it into a farm of sorts, with several
acres of corn and a truck patch, and stocked it with hogs, some of
which were ready for butchering. The horses had been well cared
for. A "yard" had been fenced off for them at the entrance to the
cave just west of the cabin. Christmas was still a few weeks away.
Belle sent for her daughter Pearl, now seventeen, and for her son
Eddie. The boy, who had been living with his Grandmother Reed,
in Missouri, was almost fifteen. It was at this time that Belle had
two new cabins built at Younger's Bend. They are referred to

facetiously by some as her "guest houses." Old photographs show
the three buildings, the original one and the two smaller, one-room
cabins. When full, they could not have housed many men, unless
her guests slept on the floor.

If there were any festivities at Younger's Bend during the holi-
day season of 1884/1885, they have not been recorded. All we
know for certain is that Belle was reunited with her children. Undoubtedly there were visitors, for both she and Sam had reputations by now that gave them a wide acquaintance among men who
were on the scout. As spring came along and horses were reported
stolen, Belle and her husband immediately came under suspicion.

This business of stealing horses merits some attention. Granted
that making off with a man's horse was properly considered a more
serious offense than is stealing a man's automobile today, when
considered from the standpoint of economics—that is, the financial
return to the thief—there is no comparison. A good horse was
worth no more than forty dollars, and a first-rate animal could be
had for fifty. In the patchwork history of border outlawry, blank
pages appear in the life of every character under discussion. To
bridge over those blank spots, it has become the custom for the
writer to beguile the reader with the fiction that his man was stealing horses—just to keep busy, it may be supposed, for a free-spend-
ing outlaw would have to steal a considerable number of horses to
make ends meet.

The foregoing is particularly true of the treatment given Belle
Starr. When nothing else is at hand, she is put down as stealing
horses, or what is better, as the brains of a horse thief ring—a big
operation which, it is inferred, was responsible for the theft of
scores of horses. Measure this against the known facts. In the nine
years she lived at Younger's Bend, she was arrested five times. On
four of those occasions she was accused of horse thievery. She was
found guilty but once, and it was for the larceny of only two
horses.

That Belle, her husband, her lovers and the unsavory characters
who were welcome at Younger's Bend were horse thieves can
hardly be denied, but it can not possibly account for the sums of
money with which she apparently was always supplied. She was
often in Fort Smith for a week at a time, shopping, gambling, and

enjoying its pleasures. She was there so frequently that, mounted on her blooded mare Venus, she became a familiar and dashing figure, simply but expensively dressed. If one of her friends got into trouble with the law, she was always on hand to go bond for him and arrange his defense. When a lawyer was needed, she went to the best and most expensive, J. Warren Reed. Over the years, she was his most lucrative client. Take the case of Blue Duck. He was the man of the hour with her when he shot and killed a boy in a drunken rage. He was convicted and sentenced to death. At her behest, in an all-out effort, Reed got his sentence commuted to life imprisonment. He was sent away to the Southern Illinois Penitentiary at Menard. Within a year, and how it was accomplished remains a mystery, she succeeded in having him pardoned.

It is beside the point that he was scarcely back in her arms when he was killed. The record says "by some party or parties unknown." Wellman offers the conjecture that the slayer was Belle's jealous husband, Sam Starr. There is little reason to doubt it. But how was Blue Duck's pardon arranged? The Department of Justice must have recommended it. That meant Washington. Money spoke as loudly then as it does today. If there was a payoff somewhere, Judge Parker had no part in it; he was untouchable. However it was brought about, it must have been costly, and Belle Starr was the only one to foot the bill.

Profits dervied from selling stolen horses could not have supplied her with the funds she required. Necessarily, she had to have another source of income. If it could be established what that other source was, the riddle of Younger's Bend would be no riddle at all. Unfortunately, no evidence exists by which that can be done. But contributing factors point the way to the only logical conclusion possible.

With one exception, the men with whom her name is associated in her days at Younger's Bend were Indians. They were a vicious, ignorant, illiterate lot. Unquestionably they regarded her as a wide cut above themselves, she who could read and write and who had demonstrated that she possessed what they lacked, namely brains. Why else would they have sought her advice and done her bidding? Rascoe says she was a "fix," using the term as it is used in the criminal world of today. One must completely agree with him.

On their own, when they got into trouble with the law, they were helpless. It was then that Belle became indispensable to them, arranging their defense with Reed, supplying perjured witnesses, manufacturing alibis. They were willing to pay for it.

When a robbery was contemplated, she very likely advised how it should be carried out, and she doubtless suggested "jobs" to them. It seems a certainty that she shared in the profits, in much the same way that her father-in-law Tom Starr had done for years. He took no part in the robbery of Watt Grayson, but it was generally believed that he got part of the loot. Only once was she charged with participating in a robbery. Allegedly dressed as a man, she and three others had robbed an old Choctaw named Ferrell and his three sons, down at Cache. For the second time she faced Judge Parker, but the indictment was dismissed for lack of evidence.

Following Sam Starr's return from his imprisonment in Detroit, not more than three months passed before he was accused of a post office robbery and implicated in the looting of the Creek National Treasury. The post office job brought the U.S. marshals looking for him, and the Creek, Cherokee and Choctaw Indian police were after him for the other offense. Sam wasted no time about going on the scout. When Marshals Hughes and Thomas reached Younger's Bend they found only Belle and the children there. But as the hunt for Sam moved away from the South Canadian, men began to come out of the brush to transact business with Belle.

Among others came a white man named John Middleton, a cousin of Jim Reed, Eddie's father, who was on the scout. He was a horse thief, small-time bandit, jailbreaker and the murderer of the sheriff of Lamar County, Texas, J. H. Black. Texas officers, posing as private citizens, were in the Territory looking for him. He found a safe and pleasant haven at Younger's Bend, for Belle became enamored of him as her affection for Sam cooled. The latter had an annoying habit of popping up, at long intervals and when least expected. To escape from these interruptions Belle agreed to go with Middleton to his mother's home in Logan County, Arkansas, each to take separate ways of getting there when they neared Fort Smith. Pearl was to accompany her mother; Eddie was sent back to Missouri.

Belle rented her farm and hired a boy to drive the covered wagon in which she and Pearl were to ride. Middleton was to tag along on horseback. They were ready to pull out when Sam Starr made another of his unexpected appearances. To their dismay, he insisted on going with them. Not being a complete fool, it may be presumed that he knew he was being cuckolded, but with Indian inscrutability, he said nothing. When the party reached a point on the Poteau River where Middleton was to turn off in order to avoid Fort Smith, Sam said he would go with him, Fort Smith being as unsafe for him as for Middleton.

Belle reached her destination without mishap, but Middleton was not there. Days passed without bringing him; then word reached her that a horse had been found tangled up in the brush on the Poteau River, which was in flood. What made it peculiarly interesting to her was that the sorrel horse was blind in the right eye. The description fitted the horse Middleton was riding. Downstream a few hundred yards, the badly decomposed body of a man, supposedly the animal's rider, was found. Belle left at once for Pocola, in the Choctaw Nation. The dead man proved to be John Middleton. He had been shot. Had the Texas officers caught up with him and killed him to avenge the slaying of Sheriff Black— or had Sam Starr taken advantage of the opportunity to appease his jealousy?

Though no one was ever charged with the crime, Belle must have been sure in her own mind that it was Sam who had squeezed the trigger. When she returned to Younger's Bend with Pearl, Sam Starr was there, looking as inscrutable as ever. He knew nothing about Middleton. They had found the Poteau running so high that he had refused to cross; Middelton had gone ahead. That was the last he had seen of him.

The horse Middleton was riding chanced to have been stolen. A man named A. G. McCarthy easily identified it as belonging to him. He swore out a complaint against Belle, accusing her of having been a party to the theft. When she was taken to Fort Smith to answer the charge, she produced a witness who swore that, whether the horse was stolen or not, he was present when Middleton paid a stranger fifty dollars in gold for the animal. It absolved Belle, and the charge was dropped.

For one reason or another, she was seeing a great deal of Judge Parker. From the consideration with which he treated her, it is possible that she had won his grudging respect as a worthy opponent. It may have given rise to the fantastic story that he asked her to participate in the mock holdup of a stagecoach which was to be the highlight of the entertainment that the Sebastian County Fair Association, of which he was president, was to present during Fair Week. As it is usually told, Belle was to lead the attack on the stage, in which Parker was to be a passenger. Presumably, she was to slip a live bullet in with the blanks, by accident, of course, and kill him. The holdup occurred as the association planned, but Belle took no part in it. She may have been present as a spectator, which is doubtful, for in their coverage of the affair the Fort Smith newspapers do not mention her name.

The Cherokee Indian police and Parker's deputies showed no sign of relaxing their hunt for Sam Starr. Time after time they came riding down Belle Starr Canyon to Younger's Bend. If they found no one there, and consequently made no arrests, it was because Belle was always warned in time that they were in the neighborhood. Her guests scattered like quail at their approach. To have the law always sniffing at his heels became too much for Sam, and he went on the scout, disappearing for months at a time. But though he was rarely seen at Younger's Bend, his numerous brothers, cousins and friends kept him informed about what went on there.

It was at this time that Belle took up with Blue Duck. She had been acquainted with him for a long time. He has been described as a handsome, burly giant, at the peak of his vigor. In a photograph of Belle and him, taken in Fort Smith on his return from Menard, he looks fat and flabby, moon-faced and slightly popeyed. Belle appears thin-lipped, bony and flat-chested, any trace of the beauty she may have one possessed completely gone. She was thirty-eight.

Blue Duck must have possessed the manly vigor with which he has been credited, for Belle went all out for him. She has been called a nymphomaniac. Perhaps she was. At least sexually she appears to have found no inconvenience in endless variety.

The most frequently encountered story dealing with Belle and

Blue Duck concerns an alleged trip to Dodge City to sell a herd of cattle. He is supposed to have lost the proceeds of the sale in a gambling room, and she to have held up the place at gunpoint, not only recovering the money he had lost but snatching up everything in sight and making her getaway with him. This tale traces back to Zoe Tilghman, the famous marshal's widow. It may be dismissed in its entirety. Belle Starr was never in Dodge City.

As previously stated, her romance with Blue Duck ended temporarily when he was put away for life for the killing of a youth named Wyrick. She got him back, no one knows how, but it was to be a brief reunion, for he was killed a few months later by some unknown party. Was the unknown assassin Sam Starr? Very likely.

This was in July, 1886. Sam had been on the scout almost continually for two years. Time was running out on him. Late in September Chief Bill Vann, of the Cherokee police, his younger brother R. F. Vann, Frank West (his testimony had convicted Sam and Belle and put them away for nine months) and a white deputy named Robinson caught him as he was riding through a cornfield.

Chief Vann called on him to surrender. When Sam raked his horse with the spurs (it was Belle's prize mare Venus) in a desperate attempt to escape, Vann emptied his pistol at him. Two of the slugs unseated Starr and another killed the mare. Sam was disarmed and taken to a farmhouse to have his wounds treated.

They were more serious than Chief Vann at first thought. He decided to keep Starr there overnight and move him in the morning. Leaving Frank West and Robinson to guard the prisoner, he and his brother went to a neighboring farmhouse to get accommodations for the night.

News of Sam's capture and where he was being held went winging along the Starr clan's grapevine, coupled with word that Frank West had aided the Vanns in making the arrest. No time was lost in doing something about it. Shortly before midnight, a score of Sam's brothers and relatives broke into the farmhouse, overpowered West and Robinson and carried Sam away to his father's stronghold. Two weeks later he was sufficiently recovered to visit Belle. She jarred him out of his complacency by informing him that Chief Vann was organizing a large posse of Cherokees to recapture him.

Belle demonstrated her sagacity by urging him to surrender himself to the District Court at Fort Smith, where with good counsel (J. Warren Reed) he would have a much better chance of defending himself than in one of the tribal courts. The Choctaw and Creek chiefs hated Tom Starr and his sons, holding them responsible for numerous thefts and robberies. With the Ross faction in command of the Cherokee Tribal Council, his chances of escaping the death penalty in a Cherokee court would be slim. It was excellent advice. Once he was in the custody of the federal government, the Indian police could not touch him.

Sam was persuaded. Belle notified Marshal Tyner Hughes that Sam wished to give himself up and for the marshal to meet her across the river from Younger's Bend as soon as he could get there.

Belle accompanied Hughes and Sam to Fort Smith. Sam was indicted and promptly released on bond, which she posted. Trial date was set originally for early January, but Reed was busy with other matters and had it set back to mid-February. His advice to Sam was to go home to Younger's Bend and keep out of trouble. Sam followed it until the evening of December 21, when the neighborhood was invited to a "stomp" dance at "Auntie" Lucy Surratt's place at Whitefield, a few miles away. Sam attended with Belle and Pearl. He went armed, "just in case." The dance was in progress when they arrived. The night was cold and a bonfire was blazing in the yard.

An Indian "stomp" dance was just what the names implies. It was always held outdoors. The dancers formed a circle and with short stomping steps moved clockwise until the caller gave a signal, then they started moving the other way, clasping hands as they danced and keeping time to the beating of an Indian drum.

They were stomping with a will that night to keep themselves warm. In the corner of the yard a group was gathered about the fire, hands extended to the blaze. When the Starrs had put their horses away, they walked over to the fire, Belle and Pearl in front and Sam a step behind. Belle was surprised to see Frank West squatting on the ground on the opposite side of the bonfire. Sam saw West and pushed her aside. He was half-drunk and in an ugly mood. He accused West of wounding him and killing Venus.

Frank got to his feet, protesting his innocence, but Sam refused

MONTANA
WYOMING
SOUTH DAKOTA
Missouri R.
James R.
RAPID CITY
PIERRE
CASPER
SCOTTSBLUFF
NEBRASKA
CHEYENNE
North Platte R.
South Platte R.
OMAHA
LINCOLN
Colorado R.
DENVER
COLORADO
KANSAS
COLORADO SPRINGS
Kansas R.
PUEBLO
Arkansas R.
Atchison Topeka & Santa
WICHITA
A.T. & S.F.
Cimarron R.
Cherokees
N. Canadian R.
Canadian R.
SANTA FE
Rock Island R.R.
INGALLS
CUSHING
GUTHRIE
Seminoles
Rio Grande
ALBUQUERQUE
OKLAHOMA CITY
OKLAH
Chickasaws
NEW MEXICO
Red R.
ROSWELL
TEXAS
FORT WORTH
DALLAS

Longrider Country

to listen. Whipping out his pistol, he shot him through the neck. As West went down, he managed to get a revolver out of his overcoat pocket and send a bullet crashing through Sam's side. Both men were mortally wounded. Sam staggered to a cottonwood and wrapped his arms around it to keep from falling. Life was running out of him, however, and he slid to the ground.

Both men were dead in a few minutes. The same wagon that bore Frank West to his home carried Sam's body to his father's place for burial in the Starr family graveyard.

Belle did not mourn him for long. His headright was now hers, and she was really independent for the first time in years. A strapping big Choctaw named Jack Spaniard came her way. He was even younger than Blue Duck. She took him to her bed, but not for long. He had killed a farmer named William Irwin. Parker's deputies came for him. He was tried, convicted and sentenced to death. Belle did her best for him. Reed got one stay after another, but he was fighting a losing battle. Belle had been in her grave for six months when Spaniard was executed.

A more serious problem than losing her lovers with monotonous regularity was hanging over Belle's head. She had always held Pearl on a tight rein, or thought she had. But Pearl was her mother's daughter, and considering the example she had set the girl, what happened would seem to have been inevitable. Belle had scotched several budding romances, but Pearl had outwitted her and in February 1887 could no longer conceal the fact that she was pregnant.

Strangely, the discovery outraged something in Belle, who had made the same mistake. Regardless of the life she had led, the kind of people with whom she had associated, in spite of everything, she had kept inviolate the dream that Pearl should be a lady. It could have been the one illusion of decency that sustained her. It was gone now. Though she raged and wept bitter tears, Pearl would not tell her who was responsible for her condition. Beside herself, Belle ordered her to leave Younger's Bend, swearing that she never wanted to see the baby—which she never did. She offered the girl money, but Pearl had spunk enough to refuse. She went to Siloam Springs, Arkansas, and there in April her child was born, a girl, whom she named Flossie.

Twenty years later Flossie put her name on a series of sensational articles about her mother and grandmother, in which she said she had been "abandoned" to relatives in Kansas when she was only a year old. That she was "abandoned" is undoubtedly an exaggeration, as she grew up in Oswego, Kansas, and seems to have had a normal childhood.

Belle attempted to relieve her loneliness by taking up with Jim French, a dreamy-eyed young Creek, a rustler, horse thief and all-around desperado, who had been run out of the Catoosa district by Judge Parker's deputies. By her standards, physical and mental, he proved to be worthless, and she soon sent him packing. (Jim French next appears in this narrative as a member of the Bill Cook Gang.) He had been gone only a few weeks when she brought her son Eddie down from Missouri again. He was no longer a boy. It was evident that the environment in which he had matured had turned him toward the path his father had followed. Belle recognized the signs. She was furious. They quarreled so violently that she is said to have used a whip on him more than once.

Things took a turn for the better when Pearl appeared at Younger's Bend and made her peace with her mother. Before summer was gone, the children had a new "papa"—Jim July, a Cherokee fullblood, a powerful man, fourteen years younger than she, not the handsomest of her many men, but a big improvement on the departed Jim French. From his record, he appears to have been an inveterate horse thief. The law had no other grudge against him. Belle made him change his name to Jim Starr. He was an educated Indian and spoke most of the tribal languages. As Jim Starr, he announced that he was "married" to Belle. Under tribal law just living with her would have constituted a "marriage," had she been a Cherokee. Since she was white, he was not her "husband," but it was an illusion he clung to until he was killed near Ardmore by Marshal Heck Thomas on January 26, 1890, while resisting arrest on a horse-stealing charge and for jumping bail.

The trouble for which Belle feared Eddie was headed caught up with him on July 12, 1888, when Judge Parker sentenced him to seven years in the Ohio State Penitentiary for horse stealing. Again Belle came to the rescue. Remarkable woman that she was, she succeeded in having Eddie released after serving three months.

On returning to Fort Smith, he secured an appointment as a deputy U.S. marshal, in which capacity he served for three years. On October 24, 1895, he shot and killed Dick and Zeke Crittenden, brothers and former deputy marshals, at Wagoner, Indian Territory, who were drunk and hurrahing the town. One of the brothers had seriously wounded a restaurant owner named Burns. Eddie was promptly exonerated, but a year later he was back in Wagoner, and in a drunken rage tried to run the owners of a saloon out of their own establishment. They killed him, and it was agreed that they had done the town a favor.

When Jim (July) Starr came to Younger's Bend he was under indictment for the theft of a horse. The marshals were not bothering him particularly, but as his connection with Belle began to give him prominence, the old indictment was dusted off and they were ordered to bring him in. With her usual acumen Belle realized that he was in trouble. She thought the charge against Jim could be beaten. She therefore urged him to surrender himself in Fort Smith as she had persuaded Sam Starr to do. When a man wanted voluntarily gave himself up it always tended to prejudice the court in his favor.

Jim took her advice, and on Saturday, February 2, he and Belle started for Fort Smith. They stopped at the store and post office on King Creek, about fifteen miles from Younger's Bend, on the south side of the South Canadian, where she paid their account of seventy-five dollars. They went on then and were twenty miles east of Whitefield when they parted, Jim to go on to Fort Smith and Belle to return home. But she was never to see Younger's Bend again. She spent the night with her friend Mrs. Richard Nail on San Bois Creek. She was back at the store on King Creek by noon. During the afternoon, she stopped at the cabin of Mrs. Hyram Barnes to get some sour cornbread, for which Mrs. Barnes was locally famous. When Belle rode in, her disgruntled neighbor Edgar Watson was in the yard talking to Barnes. Watson had a shotgun with him. Seeing Belle, he made an excuse and left at once. Barnes and his wife testified later that the time was half-past three.

At four o'clock Milo (Frog) Hoyt rode off the ferry and started east. A few moments later he heard a running horse approaching.

The animal was riderless. It dashed into the river, swam across and disappeared in the direction of Younger's Bend.

Hoyt rode rapidly in the direction from which the horse had come. He did not have to go far to learn what had happened. A blast of buckshot had tumbled Belle out of the saddle, and she lay beside the road, dead, blood covering her face and oozing through her jacket.

16

Beyond Reasonable Doubt

T HE STRANGE DEATH of Belle Starr is not as strange as some of the conjectures with which all but one of her leading commentators have surrounded it. They accept the Reed-Harman account in *Hell on the Border,* and several then add some fantastic trimmings of their own manufacture. Burton Rascoe in *Belle Starr* was the first to do it. The surmises and suspicions he raised have been echoed down to the present by other writers.

In brief, the accepted version of the killing of Belle Starr and the circumstances that led to it is this:

Edgar J. Watson, a newcomer to the neighborhood, had made an arrangement with Belle to farm her land, in addition to his own. Subsequently, a disagreement sprang up over the division of the money received from the crop. Bad feeling developed between them, and it became bitter when Belle was handed an opened letter at the Whitefield post office, which had been given to Watson by mistake, and which he had read. What was in the letter is not known, but Belle was so infuriated that she broke her arrangement with Watson and put another man on her land.

This quarrel is supposed to have supplied the motivation for what followed. When Belle came riding toward the ferry on Sunday afternoon, February 3, Watson was believed to have been hiding behind a tree and killed her as she passed, one barrel of his gun being loaded with buck and the other with turkey shot.

Pearl sent Jim (July) Starr a telegram from Eufala with the news. Free on bail, he came pounding home. He accused Watson of the crime. Watson protested his innocence. He was taken to Fort Smith, but there was so little evidence produced against him at the preliminary hearing before U.S. Commissioner Brizzolara that Jim Starr was given two weeks in which to find witnesses. This he was unable to do—Eddie Reed refused to testify against Watson, and the charge was dropped. The feeling along the South Canadian was such that Watson and his wife left the country. Later, he got into trouble at Van Buren, Arkansas, horse stealing, but he beat the case and disappeared. Wellman says, "He was convicted and sentenced to fifteen years. He escaped and was killed while resisting arrest." Watson was killed at Chokoloskee, Florida, on October 24, 1910. Both Wellman and Rascoe doubt that it was Edgar Watson who killed Belle. They suggest that the killer was young Eddie Reed. They give their reasons for coming to that conclusion; namely that he hated his mother because she tyrannized him, even whipping him with her quirt at times.

Rascoe said it first in 1941, and Wellman is only repeating him. Here is a direct quote from Rascoe, and it is far more sensational than anything that ever appeared in the *National Police Gazette*, which he denounces as trash:

> "Among the people in the Belle Starr country it is the commonly accepted belief that there were incestuous relations between Belle and her son and that she complicated this with extreme sadism."

This is unadulterated nonsense, invented, it would seem, to spike up a story that had a drab ending. No evidence to support it was ever produced. To fall back (after fifty years) on nothing better than that "in the Belle Starr country it is the commonly accepted belief" thoroughly damns it.

No writer has been as painstakingly careful in assembling the facts connected with the death of Belle Starr as has Homer Croy. In his *Last of the Great Outlaws* he devotes a chapter to his findings. He gives his sources, and they are not the usual ones. He went into the Belle Starr country for his information, found old tribal records and interviewed members of the Starr family (he gives names) and pursued the case of Edgar Watson to its gory end. It is a privilege to have his permission to quote him at some length.

He says that Belle and Mrs. Watson, an educated woman, had become good friends and that the latter confided to Belle that her husband had fled from Florida to escape a murder charge. Later, in a burst of temper, Belle let Watson know that she knew his secret. When Watson confronted his wife with her tattling, they had a violent quarrel. Neighbors noticed that she no longer had anything to do with Belle. Mrs. Watson said it was because Belle had broken her pledged word on the sharecrop arrangement, and she so testified at the hearing in Fort Smith.

Croy contends that with the bad feeling existing between Belle and Watson the man had every reason to fear what she might do with the information she had about him and that to prevent her from using it, he killed her. "If Belle had known a little more about Watson," he says, "she probably would have measured her words. That is, she would not have disclosed to him that she knew he was wanted in Florida for murder. He wasn't the quiet, inoffensive little man he appeared to be. Far from it. Here is the case history on Watson, supplied to me by Charleton W. Tebeau, of the University of Miami, which appears in *The Chokoloskee Bay Country, With Reminiscences by C. S. "Ted" Smallwood*, Copeland Studies in Florida History, 1955 edition. Smallwood was postmaster of Chokoloskee until 1941, when he retired in favor of his daughter Thelma.

"Ed Watson, of Chatham Bend, was always gettin' himself into trouble, him bein' that kind." This is Ted Smallwood speaking. "Durin' his lifetime he had three wives, all Columbia County women. He got into trouble here over a matter of shooting (his brother-in-law) and dusted out for Arkansas, then moved into Indian Territory, where he was a neighbor of Belle Starr. He promptly had trouble with her, which he ended by killing her. He got out of this and headed back for Florida.

"On the way, as he was comin' through Arcadia, he killed

Quinn Bass in a nasty shooting scrape. He got out of that, too, and for a while made a living cuttin' buttonwood and running it to Key West. Then he got into trouble with Adolphus Santini, one of our best citizens. It ended by him cutting Santini's throat, who had a scar the rest of his life. It cost Watson $200 to get out of that scrape, life bein' rather simple here in our Everglades section. Watson bought a claim on Lostman's Key from Winky Atwell. But before Watson could get on it, a man named Tucker got on it with his nephew and they wouldn't get off. It ended up by Watson killing Tucker and the nephew, and that cost him plenty.

"Then Watson killed a man named Tolens. This scrape cost him a lot of money. Watson came back to Chatham Bend and began makin' syrup, but was soon in trouble again. He killed Dutchy Melvin. In fact, one way or another, Watson was accused of killing or participatin' in the killing of seven men. One day he came to my place and said he was goin' to kill Leslie Cox, him becoming increasingly bold. He went to the mouth of the River and a few days later came back and Cox was dead.

"People had got aroused over Watson's wild ways. A crowd gathered at my landing and I knew trouble was in the offing. Watson's wife was with my wife, and we all felt apprehensive. I could hear his boat coming down the pass, and I didn't want any of it, the situation bein' what it was. Armed men were waiting. To make a long story short, I heard shooting and after a spell I went down to the landing and Watson was lyin' there, dead as you please. This was in October, 1910. They carried him to Rabbit Key and buried him. Some time later the body was dug up and taken to Fort Myers where it was reburied."

Other Florida sources confirm the foregoing. That the glib, plausible Watson, who killed so frequently and with so little compunction, was the man who murdered Belle Starr is hardly open to speculation.

Belle was buried in the yard of her place at Younger's Bend, with Cherokee rites. Pearl had a stone put up on her mother's grave. A few years later, it lay in pieces, knocked down by cattle. Few tourists ever got into that country to chip it away. Ghouls had opened the grave, however, and stolen the silver-handled pistol that had been buried with her. Legend has it that it was one of Cole Younger's pistols. This need not be taken seriously.

In a quite different category is the following deposition, which can be found in the Cherokee records, Volume 11.

> Personally appeared before me, M. Kraft and Charles Acton who state on oath that they heard Belle Starr say on several occasions, a short time before her death and while in sound mind, that if anything should happen or befall her, or that she should die, that the improvement on which she was living would be James L. Starr's. The improvement is situated on the Canadian River in the Cherokee Nation.
>
>

M. Kraft
Charles Acton

>
> Sworn and subscribed to before me this 25th day of February, 1889.
>
>

H. J. Vann, *Clerk*
Canadian District,
Cherokee Nation.

Unfortunately for Jim (July) Starr, he had less than a year to go before he was mortally wounded while resisting arrest, and in the meantime he was never in a position to establish his claim to Younger's Bend.

It is of passing interest to note that it was this same M. Kraft, an elderly man, whom Belle would have forced Pearl to acknowledge as the father of her unborn child.

Pearl lived a respectable life for some time after the death of her mother and married a man named Will Harrison, about whom little is known. She tired of the dull life she was leading, and the next Fort Smith heard of her she was an inmate of a "house" on the "Row," the town's red light district.

She claimed she had taken to that life in order to raise money to help her brother Eddie out of trouble. The record does not show that he was having any difficulty with the law at that time. She was soon the most popular prostitute in Fort Smith. She was pretty, and she also was Belle Starr's daughter, which undoubtedly had something to do with it. She divorced Harrison and opened an establishment of her own. Some said it was with money her mother had left her. There is no proof of it.

Two years later, she left Fort Smith, where she was no longer a celebrity, and went West to disappear from written history until her death is recorded in Douglas, Arizona, on July 8, 1925. She and Cole Younger share the dubious distinction of being the only ones among Belle Starr's intimates, through either blood or sex, to die of natural causes. The others—her brothers Preston and Bud, her son Eddie, her "husbands" and lovers (Jim Reed, Sam Starr, John Middleton, Blue Duck, Jack Spaniard, Jim French, Jim July)—all met violent deaths, a fate which she herself did not escape. Today, more than seventy years later, her name endures. Time has given it a patina of glamour and romance. Typical of the generosity with which Oklahoma regards the wild days of its beginnings is the life-size statue of Belle Starr by Joe Mora that stood for years at Ponca City, a gun-belt strapped around her waist and a rifle clasped in her hands, and now reposes in the beautiful Woolaroc Museum, midway between Bartlesville and Barnsdall, on State Highway 123.

Whatever else she may have been, she was, indeed, a remarkable woman.

17

Wiping Out the Cook Gang

❦

THOUGH IT IS LARGELY UNKNOWN, the Bill Cook Gang played an important role in the history of horseback outlawry in what is now eastern Oklahoma. If its life as an organized gang under the leadership of Bill Cook was brief, it was spectacular. In one week short of three months, they successfully committed ten assorted stagecoach, store, bank and railroad holdups. It is a record unmatched by the James-Younger Gang or any other. In the course of it, they killed only one man, which is another record.

The robbery of the John Schufeldt store and post office at Lenapah, in which a house painter by the name of Ernest Melton was killed, without cause, is often charged to the Bill Cook Gang. It was committed by former members of the gang, but the Cook Gang had previously disintegrated. Even when it was flourishing, it grabbed very few headlines, principally because it was running in competition with the Bill Doolin Gang, which was operating in the wetsern part of the Territory. Doolin, in his own right, and because of his connection with the Dalton brothers, was known to newspaper readers the country over; few people had ever heard of Bill Cook.

Ironically enough, two members of his gang were destined to become far better known in their time than he. One was Henry Starr, the gentleman bandit and bank robber, by marriage the nephew of Belle Starr. The other was Crawford Goldsby, alias Cherokee Bill, the bloodthirsty mad dog who killed for the love of killing and was accounted the most vicious of all Indian Territory–Oklahoma outlaws. Both organized gangs of their own when the U.S. deputy marshals and Indian police scattered and destroyed the Cook Gang. That was normal gang procedure. They were constantly being broken up and re-forming. That was as true of the Doolins as of the lesser gangs. As a consequence the work of the marshals was never finished.

The record on Bill Cook is fairly complete. He was the son of Jim Cook, a Southerner from Tennessee who had fought in the Union army. Like so many others, he drifted into Indian Territory after the war and married a quarter-blood Cherokee woman, which enabled him to acquire a headright near Fort Gibson. They had two sons, Bill, who was born in 1873, and James in 1877. The boys were orphaned when they were in their teens. They were placed in an Indian orphanage, from which Bill ran away in 1887. He was then barely fourteen. Though it was all the schooling he ever had, he was far above average in intelligence for his years. For four years he drifted from job to job on Cherokee farms and ranches. He began calling himself a cowboy. In a free use of the word, he was, but he was a farm hand, too.

Whisky got him into trouble. Among the men with whom he fraternized, there was a queer sort of glory in being able to take drink after drink with them. It called for more money than he could earn by honest labor. It was only a short step into bootlegging liquor to the Indians. He took it. It was not long before he was in jail. When he was put away a second time, he seemed to get hold of himself.

For a time he worked as posseman for Judge Parker's deputies. His brother Jim, then only seventeen, got into trouble in the Cherokee Nation, being charged with unlawful entry of a crossroads store. He fled to the Creek country, and Bill joined him. In short order, he gathered about him a choice gang of desperadoes, and on July 14, 1894, they held up and robbed the Fort Gibson–Muskogee stage.

Two days later, on July 16, in typical James-Younger style, they stopped a Frisco train at Red Forks, looted the express car and went through the coaches with the hungry grain sack. Two weeks later, on July 31, they stuck up the Lincoln County bank at Chandler. As they walked into the bank, J. M. Mitchell, the proprietor of the barbershop next door, ran out to arouse the town. Cherokee Bill, one of the gang, shot him dead.

Bank robbery had become so commonplace that no one, save the owners, got unduly excited about it. It was a different matter when an innocent citizen was killed. Heck Thomas and a group of fellow deputy marshals and Indian police descended on Chandler, swore in a posse and began an intensive hunt for the Cook Gang. The latter took the hint and lit out for the San Boise Mountains. Nothing more was heard of them until September 21, when they robbed the Parkinson general store at Okmulgee. Two weeks later they struck again. On October 5, they waylaid a wealthy Choctaw farmer returning home from Fort Gibson. The following day, October 6, they relieved another Indian of several hundred dollars almost within shooting distance of Fort Smith. They moved north then into country with which all were familiar.

They had given the marshals the slip this time, the hunt for them being centered below the South Canadian. They laid low until October 10, when they stopped a Missouri Pacific train at Claremore (the old Iron Mountain), forced the messenger to open the express safe and then went through the passengers. Cutting across country to the Missouri, Kansas and Texas Railroad at Chouteau, twenty miles away, they made it a full day by sticking up the agent and making off with the contents of his safe.

They were riding high. Money was rolling in. The Katy and the Missouri Pacific had posted rewards on them, dead or alive. Reward posters began to appear, tacked to tree trunks and fence corners. Instead of tearing them down, the gang scrawled derisive and insulting messages on them for the marshals to read. They were doing all the laughing now. In their exuberance, on October 20, they first wrecked and then robbed another Missouri Pacific train between Wagoner and Fort Gibson, piling ties on the tracks and derailing the locomotive. For the pure hell of it, they fired a flurry of shots at the passenger coaches after they were back in the saddle and dashing away. Up near Vinita on October 25, they waylaid three travelers in the course of the day, which could have netted them very little. The real purpose of the robberies was to throw dust in the marshals' eyes and lead them to believe that the Bill Cooks meant to spend the winter in the northeastern corner of the Territory, when, in fact, they were bound for the Choctaw country and Texas, it being Bill Cook's idea to give things a few months in which to cool off before the gang struck again.

With the exception of Cherokee Bill, the members of Cook's band have been put down by some commentators as cowboys. They were at best only part-time cowboys, working on and off for small outfits, and should not be confused with the traditional Texas cowboy, who lived his life on the open range. Henry Starr was a member of the Cook Gang only in its infancy and can not be connected with the rash of robberies and holdups they commited in 1894. Cherokee Bill broke away when Cook and his followers headed for Texas.

Among those whom the law tabbed as members of the Cook Gang were the Cook brothers, Sam McWilliams, alias the Verdigris Kid, Lon Gordon, Thurman Baldwin, alias Skeeter Baldwin, Elmer Lucas, alias Chicken Lucas, Curt Dayson, Hank Munson, Jim French (the same Jim French who had held Belle Starr's interest so briefly), George Sanders, Will Farris and Jess Snyder.

Eventually, Judge Parker got some of them. The Creek and Cherokee police and U.S. marshals snuffed out the rest.

In the exchange of shots that occurred when the gang robbed the Chandler bank, Chicken Lucas was struck in the hip by a slug from the rifle of a Creek policeman and was captured. A posse of police and deputy marshals located Henry Munson, Lon Gordon and Curt Dayson in a farmhouse west of Sapulpa. In the fierce gun battle that took place, Gordon and Munson were killed. Dayson threw out his rifle and surrendered. Subsequently, he and Lucas came up before Judge Parker. Lucas was sent away for ten years and Dayson for fifteen.

When Bill Cook lit out for Texas, Skeeter Baldwin, Jess Snyder and Will Farris went with him. Texas Rangers were waiting for them, and in a brief battle at Wichita Falls, Texas, Snyder and Farris were captured. Bill Cook and Skeeter Baldwin escaped and separated. The law was after Cook in earnest now, and he was trailed halfway across New Mexico before he was run to earth near old Fort Sumner, in Billy the Kid country.

Skeeter Baldwin was still running free. He was apparently quitting Texas and heading back into the Territory when he ran afoul of Texas Rangers in Clay County, on Red River.

Snyder and Farris had been returned to Fort Smith, promptly convicted and sentenced to long prison terms. It was now Bill Cook's and Skeeter Baldwin's turn. Parker sentenced Cook to forty-five years in a New York State penitentiary. Skeeter Baldwin received a sentence of thirty years in the same institution.

Of the original Cook Gang, only three remained at liberty: Jim French, the Verdigris Kid and George Sanders. Henry Starr and Cherokee Bill were at this time under sentence of death and languishing in the Fort Smith jail, though not for crimes committed while members of the Cook Gang.

French had been hiding out in the Cookson Hills, not far from Catoosa, which in the spring of 1895 was the terminus of the St. Louis and San Francisco Railroad and almost completely lawless. Early on the night of February 7, French, accompanied by a young Creek named Jess Cochran, slipped into Catoosa and at gunpoint forced two citizens to break open a window in the general store of Patton and Company, Catoosa's leading mercantile establishment, and enter the store. Using the two men as a shield, French and young Cochran followed them through the shattered window, according to the Reed-Harman account. What they call the "office" was in a small building in the back, detached from the store, and appears to have been a combination office and bedroom of Sam Irwin, the manager. A light burned within.

Through a window, French saw Irwin seated at his desk, his account books spread out before him, his back to the door. French started to raise his rifle, when he saw the muzzle of a double-barreled shotgun pointed at him. The gun was in the hands of the store's watchman, a man named Wilkins, who was seated in a rocking chair facing the door.

For some reason that must go unexplained, unless it was panic caused by seeing French pull back from the window, the young Indian sent a slug crashing through the door. Irwin leaped to his feet and flung the door open. The watchman's shotgun spurted flame and Jess Cochran went down with the top of his head blown off. With surprising coolness for him, French smashed the window with the butt of his rifle and sent a slug tearing through the manager's bowels. As he sank to the floor, mortally wounded, the watchman emptied the second barrel of his shotgun at French. He had aimed too high and the blast did no damage.

French was now momentarily in command. Charitably, he ordered Wilkins, the watchman, to help him lift Irwin off the floor and place him on his bed. It was a mistake. He then made Wilkins bring the young Indian's body into the office and place it on the floor. Why this was done, Reed-Harman fail to say. It could have had nothing to do with robbery, which French seems to have completely forgotten. And one wonders what the two "citizens" who had been forced to break into the store were doing all this time.

If we are to believe the Reed-Harman account, French now drew his pistol to kill the unarmed watchman, who fell to his knees, begging for his life. French took dead aim on him and was about to fire, when Sam Irwin, with a last effort, drew a revolver that was concealed under his pillow and fired twice, both bullets "tearing through French's neck just below the ears. After staggering about drunkenly for a moment, French bolted through the open door and with blood spurting from his wounds ran toward the Spunky River. He crawled into an abandoned Indian cabin, where his pursuers, led by Wilkins, found him. He was dying, but Wilkins finished him with a blast from his reloaded shotgun."

That left only the Verdigris Kid and George Sanders at large. On March 28, only a few weeks after Jim French came to the end of his tether, the Verdigris Kid, George Sanders and a young thug named Sam Butler ran out of luck as they were robbing a store at the little Arkansas River town of Braggs, eight miles down river from Fort Gibson. The Verdigris Kid and Sanders were shot to death. Sam Butler, the amateur badman, killed a store clerk named

Morris. It took the marshals six months to catch up with him. On August 1, Deputy John Davis surprised him as he was taking his ease under an apple tree at his mother's cabin on the Verdigris River. He was armed, and his first shot knocked Davis out of the saddle, fatally wounded. But Deputy Marshal Davis, one of Judge Parker's bravest men, lurched to his feet and put a bullet through Butler's heart.

The law could now write *finis* to the Cook Gang. Not one had escaped. The guns of the U.S. marshals and the Indian police had snuffed out the lives of Lon Gordon, Hank Munson, George Sanders, the Verdigris Kid and Sam Butler. Bill and Jim Cook, Jess Snyder, Will Farris, Chicken Lucas, Curt Dayson and Skeeter Baldwin were behind bars. Though it came late in Judge Parker's career, it was, in many ways, his greatest victory. His "certainty of punishment" had never been so potently expressed.

One thing remains to be said about the Cooks and that concerns the circumstances that put young Jim Cook into the Cherokee prison for eight years. So turn back to the spring of 1894, when after endless negotiations, the federal government purchased the so-called Cherokee Strip from the Cherokee Nation. When the Cherokees were forcibly removed to Indian Territory, in addition to their immense reservation, an expansion "outlet" was held in trust for them, a big slice of today's northern Oklahoma, running west from the original Cherokee reservation to the Oklahoma Panhandle. While title to it remained with the government, the Cherokee Nation had definite treaty rights to the "outlet," which, as usual where Indians were concerned, had been ignored when it was thrown open to white settlement on September 16 of the previous year, resulting in the sensational Cherokee Strip "run" that brought thousands of whites racing across the Kansas line to claim free land and make new homes in today's Oklahoma. It was to "quiet" all Cherokee claims to it that the purchase was made. Of the total amount paid, a third went into the Cherokee National Treasury. It left $6,640,000 to be divided individually among all who could make legitimate claim to being at least one-eighth Cherokee. After a lengthy checking of the tribal roles, the figure arrived at was $265.70 per person.

It is remarkable that in outlaw-infested Indian Territory six million dollars could be distributed without a major robbery taking place. This was accomplished, however. Thousands of Cherokee were begowked, robbed, cheated, but only after they had received their share of the "Strip" money. The distribution was the business of the Cherokee National Council, but the federal government could have exercised some supervision, which it completely failed to do. A blind man could have foreseen that putting such a huge sum of money in the hands of largely ignorant Indians was bound to result in their being ruthlessly exploited by white sharpers. Nothing was done to prevent it. The results were often tragic and often ludicrous.

In the weeks before the distribution was made, a horde of unscrupulous agents and racketeers crisscrossed the Cherokee country, selling the Indians things they did not need and did not know how to operate, all at extravagant prices, and on credit against their Strip money, taking notes in payment. A carload of cheap sewing machines and washing machines was unloaded at Gibson Station. On the "luxury" side came musical instruments, which the Cherokees could not play, and an endless variety of feminine finery.

When a distribution point was set up, the Cherokees flocked in by the hundreds to find a carnival atmosphere prevailing. Gamblers and bootleggers operated openly, along with thugs and pickpockets. At Tahlequah, the Cherokee capital, there were tent shows, a merry-go-round, every device for extracting money from the Indians. And the agents with their notes were there, too. They got their money before the man who had bought on credit got his.

Young Jim Cook had the necessary Cherokee blood in his veins to qualify for his $265.70, and he wanted it, as did his brother Bill and Cherokee Bill. Their names were on the Tahlequah roles, but since they were wanted by both the Indian police and the U.S. deputy marshals, they knew it would not be safe for them to appear in Tahlequah. To get their money, they hit upon the device of getting someone to go in and collect it for them. The person they chose was Effie Crittenden, Dick Crittenden's ex-wife. Dick Crittenden and his brother Zeke both held deputy marshal commissions at the time. They were the same Crittendens that Eddie Reed was to kill at Wagoner some time later.

Fifteen miles out of Tahlequah on the Fort Gibson road, Effie Crittenden conducted a place known as the Halfway House, where travelers could get lodgings and meals. What financial arrangement they made with her is not known, but she agreed to get their Strip money for them. She had no difficulty getting it, but when Ellis Rattling Gourd, chief of the Cherokee police, read the names on the letter she presented to the treasurer, he realized at once that the three men were in the neighborhood and very likely at the Halfway House. He was acquainted with all three. Spying on the place for several hours that afternoon, he saw Cherokee Bill come out and walk back to the privy. A little later, Bill Cook made the same journey, and finally young Jim Cook.

Ellis Rattling Gourd was back in the morning with a posse of seven men, including Sequoyah Houston, Dick and Zeke Crittenden, Bill Nickel and three others. Chief Rattling Gourd called on the outlaws to surrender, but their answer was a blast of gunfire. It was returned by the posse. Jim Cook, peering around a corner of the building, was seriously wounded by a slug from Dick Crittenden's rifle. He tossed away his Winchester as he went down and lying on the ground was struck several times more. A few moments later, Cherokee Bill stepped out boldly and killed Sequoyah Houston.

Though Rattling Gourd still had the odds heavily in his favor, he withdrew from the fight soon after Houston fell, taking all but the Crittendens with him. The latter had no choice about remaining, for they had found cover behind an old log smokehouse and were afraid to leave lest they be cut down before they reached the scrub timber seventy-five yards away. They kept up a desultory fight throughout the afternoon, but when darkness fell, they beat a retreat.

Jim Cook's condition was grave. Desperate as the chance was, his brother insisted on getting him to a doctor at Fort Gibson. The hazardous nature of the venture appealed to Cherokee Bill. Together, he and Bill Cook got Jim into the saddle, tied him down and went to Fort Gibson, leaving him there under the care of a physician and making good their escape. When Jim recovered from his wounds he was convicted of being a party to the killing of Sequoyah Houston and sentenced to eight years in the Cherokee prison. He escaped once, but was recaptured and served his full sentence. When he came out it was to find that life in the Territory had changed drastically; the Cook Gang was just a fading memory.

18

Cherokee Bill

BECAUSE OF THE ALIAS of Cherokee Bill, the only name by which he is known, Crawford Goldsby is widely and erroneously believed to have been a Cherokee Indian. Actually he was only an eighth Cherokee. The rest of him was a weird mixture of other bloods. George Goldsby, his father, saw honorable service as a trooper in the Tenth U.S. Cavalry, an all-Negro regiment, our first, which distinguished itself in the Apache campaigns in Arizona. On his enlistment papers he put himself down as a Negro, but in later years he claimed to be of mixed white, Mexican and Sioux Indian descent. The assorted blood strains from which Cherokee Bill sprang did not end there, for his father married Ellen Beck, who was half Negro, a fourth Cherokee and a fourth white. Perhaps the assorted origins of his parents clashed violently in Cherokee Bill and made him the cruel, psychopathic killer that he was. Certainly some of his murderous traits appeared in Clarence Goldsby, his younger brother.

Both boys were born at Fort Concho, Texas; Crawford on February 8, 1876, and Clarence two years later. The father was an industrious, upright man; the mother devoted to her small family.

174

To the very end she was fiercely loyal to her oldest boy. He was not much over thirteen when she packed him off to the Indian School at Cherokee, Kansas, and kept him there for three years. Being part Cherokee and having gone to school at Cherokee, Kansas, were enough to fasten the nickname of "Cherokee" on him. Where the "Bill" came from is not known.

His mother, as indomitable in her way as he was in his, insisted that he continue his education. With what must have entailed some sacrifice on her part, she sent him east to the Carlisle Industrial School for Indian youths, at Carlisle, Pennsylvania. Hundreds of Indian boys went to Carlisle. They came from many tribes. Apparently, Crawford Goldsby is the only one who returned home to become an outlaw.

He was at Carlisle for two years. But he had no aptitude for learning and no liking for the rigid discipline of the school. His father had passed away. His mother had remarried and was living in Fort Gibson with his brother Clarence and his stepfather William Lynch, a white man. His sister Maude had married and was living a few miles from Nowata. He moved in with his mother and was soon in trouble. Following a quarrel with a young Negro named Jake Lewis, he secured a pistol and shot him twice. Believing he had killed Lewis, he dusted off for the Cookson Hills to escape arrest. Lewis recovered, but by then Crawford Goldsby had met Bill and Jim Cook, young Henry Starr and others, and had taken part with them in several minor holdups and store robberies. At the time, the Cook Gang was just in the process of formation. New men were coming in—men like Sam McWilliams, alias the Verdigris Kid, and Skeeter Baldwin, with whom he was acquainted. The wild, free, dangerous life of the outlaw camp suited him. Crawford Goldsby was hardly a fitting name for an outlaw. He dropped it and became Cherokee Bill, by which he was to be known for the rest of his life. He was then barely eighteen.

Only the color of his skin revealed his Indian blood; his features were distinctly Negroid—round face, low forehead, thick pursed lips and kinky black hair. Though not quite six feet tall, he was a burly, broad-shouldered man possessing great physical strength. His eyes have been described by some as baleful, with a wild beast stare. Others describe them as impassive. In the few available photographs of him, they appear to me to be lighted with a mocking, contemptuous amusement.

When he and the Cooks had had their battle with the Cherokee police at the Halfway House, in June 1894, a year had passed since Henry Starr had broken with the Cooks and organized his own bandit crew. But adequate replacements were always at hand. On July 31, Cherokee Bill took part in his first bank robbery, the Lincoln County Bank at Chandler, and shot to death J. M. Mitchell, the barber. He was never tried for it, nor for the killing of Sequoyah Houston. That he killed others without being charged by the law with the crimes is not to be doubted. Though he is reputed to have killed thirteen—the Reed-Harman figure—I can pin only seven killings on him, including the slaying of Sam Collins, a Missouri-Pacific conductor who was shot to death when he insisted that Cherokee Bill pay his fare or get off his train.

That he participated in many of the Cook Gang robberies is well-known. But he did not have a hand in all of them. His ego being what it was, it followed that as his reputation grew, he had to be head man. Accordingly he broke away from the Cooks and with three men, their identity unknown, held up the Missouri Pacific–Iron Mountain depot at Nowata, in the course of which, without cause or reason, he killed station agent Dick Richards. It was this propensity for killing without cause that was making him the most feared outlaw in the Territory. He topped his other crimes by wantonly killing his sister Maude's husband, George Brown, because he felt he was entitled to some of the hogs that Brown's father had given his son. His first shot killed Brown, but in his frenzied rage he stood over the fallen man, squeezing the trigger of his pistol until it was empty.

On old maps of the Territory, Nowata, Claremore, Wagoner and Lenapah are bunched together in northeastern Oklahoma. On November 9, Cherokee Bill and two others, one of whom can be put down as Sam McWilliams, the Verdigris Kid, rode into Lenapah in broad daylight and entered the general store of Schufeldt and Son and at gunpoint compelled the younger Schufeldt to open the store's safe. It yielded several hundred dollars, which was as much as the bandits could reasonably have expected to get.

But when Cherokee Bill saw the clothing on display in the rear room of the store, as well as a rack of guns and a shelf of ammunition, he decided that this was an excellent opportunity to replenish his wardrobe and lay in a supply of cartridges. Rifle in hand, he forced young Schufeldt into the rear room and made him lay out the articles he wanted. Schufeldt was no fool. He knew with whom he was dealing, and he did as he was bidden.

There was a narrow vacant lot between the Schufeldt store and the restaurant next door, the interior of which was being re-painted. A man by the name of Ernest Melton was doing the painting. What drew him to the side door of the restaurant, the upper half of which was a glass panel, will never be known, but as he gazed idly across the open space between the buildings and through a window into Schufeldt's, he must have been startled to see John Schufeldt nervously waiting on a customer who kept him covered with a rifle.

Cherokee Bill flicked a glance at the window and saw Melton staring at him. Enraged at the painter's audacity in spying on him, he threw his rifle to his shoulder and slapped a shot at Melton that killed him instantly.

It was a brutal, senseless killing, but no more so than others he committed. The excuse could not be offered that in slaying Melton he was removing the only witness to the robbery, since there were others, notably Schufeldt. A few moments after the fatal shot was fired, he and his companions rode away.

If the killing of Ernest Melton was not quickly forgotten, as many others were, it was because at last the law had an air-tight case of murder against Cherokee Bill. Rewards for his capture, dead or alive, were stepped up until he was worth fifteen hundred dollars to anyone who could bring him in.

There was good reason to believe that he was hiding out in the rough, broken country and tangle of creeks west of the Verdigris River. Two of Parker's deputies, W. C. Smith and George Lawson, working out of Sapulpa, combed that country for two weeks without cutting his trail. However, they made an arrangement with a Cherokee half-blood, named Charles Patton, a Verdigris River native and personally acquainted with Cherokee Bill, that if he could locate him and get word to them in Sapulpa, they would split the reward money. Patton was agreeable to such an arrangement. He began drifting through the hills without arousing suspicion, since he was known to everyone and had had a little difficulty with the law himself. As luck would have it, he was watched as he was making camp on his second night out. When the watchers saw who it was, they hailed him and invited him to camp with them. It was Cherokee Bill and the Verdigris Kid.

Bill made light of Patton's news about the hornet's nest that had been stirred up by the affair at Lenapah. He did not bother to deny that he had killed the painter. He made statements that were afterward used against him. Patton got away the following morning and was soon back in Sapulpa. A posse was hurriedly organized and left for Cherokee Bill's hideout. He was still there, alone now. The posse exchanged a number of shots with him. His horse was hidden in the trees. They killed it before he could reach it. When they looked around for him, he was gone, and they were not foolhardy enough to pursue him into the junglelike willow brakes into which he had disappeared.

From Judge Parker came the order, "Get Cherokee Bill." The marshals tried, but weeks, and then months, passed without his being run down. He was reported as having been seen here and there in the Cherokee Nation or across the line in Creek country. But he had become a will-o'the-wisp and the marshals never caught sight of him.

The stream of settlers moving across the Territory from Arkansas, Kentucky and Missouri that followed the opening of the Cherokee Strip still continued. In some form of improvised covered wagon they drove across the Cherokee Reservation. The natives referred to them as "movers." Invariably, they had disposed of whatever property they owned and turned it into cash, which they had with them as they headed west. Though it was usually very little, many were held up and relieved of their hoard. At least two "movers" were killed in resisting the robbers. The attacks were made by two men, and the description the Cherokee police received fitted Cherokee Bill and the Verdigris Kid. Several country post offices were looted. The express office at Pryor Creek was entered during the night and an unsuccessful attempt made to blast open the safe. The crimes were charged to Cherokee Bill.

No evidence to substantiate it was forthcoming, but in the popular mind he had become such a menacing figure that it was taken for granted that he was guilty of every robbery and holdup that occurred.

Why it took the law so long to learn that Cherokee Bill had a sweetheart and to discover where he was meeting her at irregular intervals, despite the risk of capture, is a little difficult to understand. The love life of other outlaws had been their undoing. Winter was coming on, however, before Deputy W. C. Smith got around to doing something about it. Through a man named Clint Scales, a mixblood, who sometimes worked as a handyman, he learned that Cherokee Bill was in the habit of meeting his inamorata, named Maggie Glass, at the cabin of Ike Rogers, five miles east of Nowata. Scales got word to Rogers that Deputy Smith wanted to see him, and a meeting was arranged in Nowata.

Ike Rogers was a mixture of Indian, Negro and white blood, who sprang from a family of Negro freedmen. Croy says they had taken the name of Rogers from Will Rogers' father, Clement Vann Rogers. Ike had once held a deputy marshal's commission, but his reputation was bad and he lived without visible means of support.

Deputy Smith was reasonably sure that Ike would do anything for money. The proposition he made him was that he (Rogers) was to invite the girl to spend a few days with him and his wife and then get word to Cherokee Bill that she was there. Scales was to be watching the cabin, and when he saw Bill arrive, he was to drop in casually and spend the night there. They were to catch Cherokee Bill off guard and capture him, in return for which Ike Rogers and Scales were each to get a third of the reward money. Though fully aware of the dangerous nature of the part they were to play, they agreed to do it, and the trap was set. It was after the first of the year, before it was sprung. This brings us to Maggie Glass, the buxom, far from stupid Cherokee-Negro girl, who was the niece of Ike Rogers' wife.

When Cherokee Bill learned that Maggie was at Ike Rogers' place, waiting for him, he lost no time getting there. Several hours after he arrived, Clint Scales put in an appearance. Unquestionably the hours that followed were charged with dramatic dynamite

—Cherokee Bill unsuspecting, Maggie Glass suspicious of Rogers and Scales, and the latter, beneath their pretense of rough good-fellowship, playing their cat and mouse game, waiting for the moment to arrive that would enable them to get the drop on the outlaw. Though the situation was supercharged with drama that needed no embellishment, some writers, for thrill purposes, have added details that are strictly imaginary, saying among other things that Ike Rogers' wife was in on the plot and that she helped to subdue Cherokee Bill. There is nothing in statements made later by Rogers and Scales to indicate that she had anything to do with his capture.

According to Rogers' account, Bill and Maggie were alone for some time before supper. When all sat down to the table, Bill kept his rifle on his lap. Supper over, the three men played cards for small stakes. The game ran on for hours. Mrs. Rogers went to bed. Maggie begged Bill to quit playing, but he was winning, and he put her off. She went to bed with her aunt. The game continued until early morning.

For hours, Scales and Rogers had been watching Cherokee Bill like hawks, but hunted animal that he was, he watched them as warily as though he knew what was on their minds. When they were ready to turn in, Scales bedded down on the floor and Cherokee Bill got into bed with Rogers, his rifle on the blanket at his side.

Rogers said that he lay awake most of the time, that whenever he turned, his bedfellow turned, too. It must have been, as he claimed, a harrowing experience lying there alongside that human tiger who would kill him instantly if he were caught making a suspicious move.

Morning came. Breakfast over, Mrs. Rogers sent Maggie to a neighbor's a quarter of a mile away to buy a couple of chickens. The day was cold, it was January, but there was no snow on the ground. Certainly it imposed no hardship on the girl to send her on the errand. But some investigators contend that sending Maggie for the chickens was only an excuse to get her out of the house, and they use it to bolster their argument that Mrs. Rogers was a party to the plot to capture Cherokee Bill. From what followed, it would not appear that it made any difference whether Maggie was in the cabin or ten miles away; she had innocently served her purpose as bait and there was nothing further she could do.

The three men sat around before the fireplace, talking. Cherokee Bill began to "git fidgity," according to Rogers. "He said he'd have to be shovin' off. I told him to wait till Maggie got back. He rolled another cigarette and as he bent down to git a coal from the fire to light it, I picked up a chunk of firewood and hit him over the head hard enough to kill an ordinary man. It knocked him down. Scales and I jumped on him but before we could snap the handcuffs on his wrists, he let out a yell and leaped to his feet."

Rogers described the life and death struggle that followed, Cherokee Bill's desperate efforts to reach his rifle, half-stunned though he was, and how he (Rogers) and Scales finally got him on the floor and got his wrists manacled. He says the outlaw begged them to kill him then and there rather than to send him in to face Judge Parker.

Scales hitched Rogers' team to a wagon. With Cherokee Bill seated beside him, he started for Nowata, Rogers following on Scales' horse, his shotgun across his saddle bow. On the way to town, the outlaw in some manner managed to break the hand-cuffs (Rogers says by sheer strength) and made a desperate lunge for Scales' rifle. "Scales had to fall out of the wagon to keep from losing his Winchester," says Rogers, "while I kept Cherokee covered with my shotgun."

The outlaw went along quietly after that, obviously realizing that he was worth as much dead as alive to the two men who had betrayed him. On arriving in Nowata, he was turned over to Deputy Marshals Smith and George Lawson. News of Cherokee Bill's capture spread like wildfire, and a crowd gathered at the railroad station, where he was chained to the station safe. Word was telegraphed to Fort Smith, where another excited crowd gathered to await the train that was bringing him. Half a dozen deputy marshals, including the two Crittendens, were on hand to aid Deputies Smith and Lawson and frustrate any attempt at escape.

Obviously pleased and flattered by all the attention he was receiving, Cherokee Bill waved a pudgy hand at acquaintances in the crowd and readily consented to being photographed. One picture shows him lined up with his captors and the Crittenden

brothers, his right arm playfully draped over little Zeke Crittenden's shoulder as he reached for Zeke's pistol, which the latter
had had the good sense to remove. The ceremonies over, Bill was
bundled into a van and driven to the crowded Fort Smith prison,
where he received a riotous welcome from the inmates, who
crowded against the bars, hooting and hollering. He was pushed
in among them, but though the steel-barred doors clanged shut
on him, he was far from finished, and so was his younger brother
Clarence.

To digress briefly, the treacherous part Ike Rogers had played
in the capture of Cherokee Bill had made him no friends. As
weeks, then months, were consumed in the two trials of the notorious outlaw, finally resulting in his execution, the feeling
against Rogers grew. He was tough, and he pretended to ignore
the threats made against his life. But they were real enough. It
was generally believed that, sooner or later, young Clarence
Goldsby would avenge his brother. Relatives restrained the boy,
but he declared over and over that he meant to kill Rogers on
sight.

Time ran on, and nothing happened. Ike Rogers was living in
a hell of his own making. Finally, he could stand it no longer.
Clarence was working as a guard for the U.S. paymaster at Fort
Gibson. Ike sent word that he was coming to kill him. After some
drunken boasting in Nowata, he took the train for Fort Gibson.
Clarence was on the depot platform, waiting for him. Three and
a half years had passed since Rogers betrayed Cherokee Bill, but
it was as fresh in the boy's mind as though it had happened yesterday, and as Ike came down the car steps, he fired a single shot that
broke Ike's neck, killing him almost instantly.

Deputies W. C. Smith and the two Lawsons were on the station
platform, but the shooting had happened so suddenly that Clarence darted under the standing train and made good his escape
into the scrub timber, very likely with the blessing of the deputies.
Whatever became of him is not known, though some say he went
to Texas, where he was born.

Cherokee Bill came up for arraignment before Judge Parker,
charged with the murder of Ernest Melton, the Lenapah painter.
From the moment they first faced each other, the air was charged

with a personal enmity between judge and prisoner seldom recorded in any courtroom. Cherokee Bill had been a thorn in Parker's side for years, and he was prepared to show him no mercy. Though the evidence against the accused was overwhelming, he knew from the moment J. Warren Reed appeared as counsel for the defense that the case would be bitterly contested to the very end.

Bill's mother had retained Reed to represent her son. In some manner that has never adequately been explained, she raised the money to pay his usually exorbitant fee. Very likely the astute Reed, in his feud with Parker, was so anxious to take the case that money, for once, meant little or nothing to him. The trial was certain to attract tremendous attention, perhaps more than any other ever heard by the Fort Smith court. With the evidence against the notorious outlaw so strong, Reed undoubtedly expected Parker to run roughshod over the defendant's legal rights. Sufficiently goaded, he might overstep the rules of jurisprudence flagrantly enough to convince the U.S. Supreme Court that a fair trial could not be had in the Fort Smith court—which Reed had been contending for years.

The trial became an endless series of clashes between defense counsel and the bench. Bullied, exasperated beyond endurance, Parker laid down some rules of his own, limiting the cross-examination of witnesses by both the prosecution and the defense and refusing to grant Reed the delays he insisted he must have to call up additional witnesses. Those he put on the stand were "alibi" witnesses, who swore they had seen Cherokee Bill fifty miles south of Lenapah on the day Melton, the painter, was murdered. The prosecution produced seven, including John Schufeldt, who positively identified Cherokee Bill as Melton's slayer. The jury was out only a few minutes and returned with a verdict of guilty.

Parker delivered his famous excoriation of Cherokee Bill. As it ran on, minute after minute, the latter stood there unmoved, his mouth twisted in a sarcastic grin. The death sentence was pronounced and the day of execution named. His mother wept when she heard it. She had been in daily attendance. Bill spoke to her as he was being led away. "What's the matter with you, Ma, crying like that? I'm not a dead man yet by a long ways."

In truth, he was right, for Reed immediately took an appeal to the U.S. Supreme Court to have the verdict set aside, stipulating on five counts that Crawford Goldsby, alias Cherokee Bill, had not received a fair trial. It stayed the date of execution until the high court could review the case.

Months dragged by. Bill's mother had moved to Fort Smith to be near him. Every day she passed the prison, carrying a cane fishing pole and a lunch basket, as she went back and forth to the river to spend hours fishing. The guards let her stop outside the wall to speak to her son through the bars of his cell. The old vermin-infested basement hell-hole in which prisoners had been held during Parker's earlier years on the Fort Smith bench was no more. Conditions were still unspeakably bad, but cells had been installed and men were no longer herded together. When the temperature soared and the cells became unbearable, they were given the freedom of the corridors.

Among Cherokee Bill's fellow inmates was one with whom he was well acquainted from his days with the Cook Gang. He was Henry Starr, under sentence of death for the killing of Floyd Wilson, a deputy marshal (more about that later), the only homicide with which he was ever charged. His case had been appealed, and, like Cherokee Bill, he was waiting for the high court's decision. That the two men had some contact is likely, but Starr certainly had no part in the prison break the other was planning.

In some manner, two .41-caliber pistols were smuggled in to Cherokee Bill. During a routine check of the cells on July 10, one of them was found in his bucket. It has been said that he placed it there, where it was certain to be found, in order to quiet any possible suspicion that he might have a second pistol.

This seems to be specious reasoning, since he could have passed the weapon on to one of his fellow conspirators, or hidden it as he did the other by removing a brick in the wall and secreting it there.

Of course, he refused to say how the pistol came into his possession. It was agreed, however, that the revolver had been fastened to a pole and passed in through his barred cell window. His mother could have done it. She saw him twice a day, coming and going to the river. She could have carried the pistols in her lunch basket, fastened them to her fishing pole and put them in his hands.

But it was on Ben Howell, a two-bit thief who was serving ninety days for a minor theft and was considered harmless enough to have been made a trusty, that suspicion fell. He had disappeared just before the pistol was found in Cherokee Bill's bucket. He was recaptured and given an additional six months for breaking his parole. He stoutly denied having had anything to do with smuggling the weapons to Bill. The latter, before he was executed, "confessed" that he had got the six-guns from Howell. For all his faults, Cherokee Bill loved his mother, and he certainly would have lied rather than implicate her.

After supper on the evening of July 26, on what had been a hot, sultry day, not a breath of air stirring, the prisoners were allowed out in the corridors. At seven o'clock the signal was given for them to return to their cells. The men responded sullenly as a turnkey and guard came down each of the corridors, locking them up for the night. Turnkey Campbell Eoff and Lawrence Keating, a guard, started down the corridor in which the prisoners convicted of murder were held. Keating was armed with a pistol; Eoff, as was his habit, was unarmed.

Cherokee Bill had entered his cell, and there was no confusion until Eoff and Keating reached his cell door. He had removed his hidden revolver from its hiding place. Suddenly, Eoff and Keating found themselves covered. Keating was ordered to hand over his pistol, butt first. Instead of obeying, the guard backed away and started to draw. The outlaw fired instantly and Keating staggered back, mortally wounded, his face a bloody smear.

Eoff ran for the gate. Cherokee Bill, out into the corridor, blazed away at him. The shots went wide, however, and he escaped unharmed. Behind him came Keating, who dropped dead as he reached the cage and safety. Bedlam broke out all over the prison. Men who had not yet been locked up rushed from their cells, and a full-scale riot was ready to errupt. Guards and other prison officers drove them back at gunpoint.

Deputy Marshal Heck Brunner reached Eoff. He was armed with a sawed-off shotgun. He began firing down the corridor in which the trouble had begun. That he killed no one was only because Cherokee Bill and the other rioters had darted back into their cells. Bill had a supply of cartridges. Reloading his revolver, he traded shot for shot with the guards. Above the din of the shooting rose his shrill, nerve-wracking "gobbling." When an Indian "gobbled like a cock turkey" it was regarded by the superstitious Cherokees as the death cry.

With gunsmoke hanging heavily in the corridor, Henry Starr got Eoff's attention. With courage seldom, if ever, equaled by a man outside the law, he said quietly: "If you guards will stop shooting, I'll go into Bill's cell and get his gun."

His offer was accepted, and when he was released from his cell, he walked down the corridor. As the sounds of shooting died away, they heard him calling to Cherokee Bill. The latter had barricaded himself, but he permitted Starr to enter. What passed between them will never be known. Certainly it was more than Starr's laconic statement. "I just said, 'Bill, your mother wouldn't want you to do this. Give me your gun and call it quits.'"

Judge Parker was in St. Louis when Keating was killed. When he got the news, he started back to Fort Smith at once, but not before calling in reporters and denouncing the Supreme Court for interfering with the Fort Smith tribunal, recklessly granting appeals and setting aside the justly deserved convictions of known killers. It was ill-advised and hastened his downfall. Possibly, he no longer cared. His health was failing, but he came back to Fort Smith with a fresh burst of energy. At last he had such an iron-clad case against Cherokee Bill that even the learned judges in Washington would not dare to dispute it.

The second trial of Cherokee Bill was largely a repetition of the first. Again J. Warren Reed was counsel for the defense. He argued all one morning that the prisoner was already under sentence of death for killing Ernest Melton and could not be tried for his life a second time until the appeal taken in the Melton case had been acted upon by the Supreme Court. Parker was adamant. He told Reed to get ready to go to trial.

Of passing interest is the fact that the foreman of the jury was loquacious Sam Harman, subsequently co-author with Reed of *Hell on the Border*. The jury was out only thirteen minutes. For the second time Parker imposed the death penalty on Cherokee Bill. Then to the surprise of all, the Supreme Court sustained the verdict in the Melton Case, so when Cherokee Bill was marched to the gallows on March 17, 1896, it was for the killing of the Lenapah painter, not for the slaying of Lawrence Keating.

There was no one to share the spotlight with him; he had it all to himself. George Maledon was no longer the official hangman, having resigned some months previously. To turnkey Eoff fell the duty of springing the trap. Deputy Marshals George and Will Lawson adjusted the straps binding the doomed man's arms and legs. Father Pius, a Catholic priest, was on the platform with them, at the court's request.

Invitations to the hanging had been limited to one hundred, but hundreds of others, denied the privilege of the yard, witnessed it from the walls and adjoining rooftops. Before the black cap was adjusted, Cherokee Bill was asked if he had anything to say. His answer was a fitting epitaph to his ferocious career. "Hell, no," he snarled. "I came here to die, not to make a speech."

19

Three Who Went Wrong

THERE WERE THREE MEN who figured prominently enough in the outlaw history of the eastern section of Indian Territory, to which they were indigenous, to merit special attention. The first was Ned Christie. He had the distinction of giving Parker's deputies the longest and most determined battle they ever fought.

Ned Christie was born at Rabbit Trap, in the Cherokee Nation, in 1852. He was a fullblood, the son of Watt Christie a well-to-do, highly respected Indian. His father had taught him the trade of gunsmith and had seen to it that he was well-educated in the white man's ways and language.

Proof of the esteem in which Ned Christie was held in the community is found in the fact that when he was still in his early thirties he was elected to the Cherokee Tribal Council. Whisky tripped him—not that he "took to the bottle," it was just a friendly drinking bout with a companion. This ended in an altercation that became so heated that Deputy Marshal Dan Maples was called in to quell the disturbance. A gun went off and Maples was killed. It was never established who fired the shot. Other marshals rushed to the scene. Christie fled. His friend was captured. He swore that it was Ned Christie who killed Maples. The latter having fled, it was assumed that he was guilty. The law took after him, but he had friends who concealed him and relayed information to him. For four years Parker's deputies never caught sight of him.

If he was guilty of only half the robberies and thefts of horses which were charged to him, it was an imposing record. Though he was a dead shot with a rifle, he was not a killer. But he was an embarrassment to the deputy marshals and the Indian police. More than once he caught one riding alone and, from a safe distance, shot the horse out from under him and put him afoot. When the law chanced to come close to him in one place, he was next heard of a hundred miles away.

If Parker's deputies were nettled, so was the Judge. He called Heck Thomas into Fort Smith and ordered him to forget all else and bring Christie in, dead or alive. Thomas was the most dogged and courageous man he had.

For three months the man-hunter followed Christie's trail before he caught up with him. They exchanged shots. A bullet from Thomas' rifle struck Christie in the face, costing him an eye. But he escaped. An Indian doctor patched up his face, and he survived, though horribly disfigured. The once handsome man had always maintained that he was unjustly accused of the killing of Deputy Maples; now his disfigured face became a constant reminder of the treatment he had received, and it fed his hatred of white men.

October was almost gone when Heck Thomas was tipped off that Christie was deep in the hills, eighteen miles east of Tahlequah, and was "forting up" for the winter. "Forting up" was not just a figure of speech in this instance. He had four young Indians with him, and they built a log fort on an open meadow that could not be approached within a hundred yards without the attackers exposing themselves.

Heck Thomas made a careful reconnaissance of the fort and got away undetected. Parker was delighted with his report. At last, they had Ned Christie pinned down. To make sure that there would be no slip-up this time, he assigned seventeen deputies to the capture of Ned Christie, with Heck Thomas in charge. This was unprecedented; never in the history of the Fort Smith court had there been such a concentration of marshals as this.

Marshal Thomas talked it over with them. They were the best men Parker had, men like the two Lawsons, Paden Tolbert, Bill Smith, Bud Ledbetter. They knew that numbers alone was no guarantee of success; that many would be cut down if any attempt was made to rush the log fort. At this juncture Paden Tolbert startled them with a suggestion that they dismissed at first as ridiculous, but which after further consideration seemed to have some possibilities. A friend of his in Coffeyville, Kansas, had an old brass cannon, a sturdy three-pounder, which he was sure he could borrow. Loaded to the muzzle, it would make kindling of Ned Christie's crude fort.

In their inexperience—not one of them had ever fired a cannon —they had no reason to doubt that it would do all that Tolbert claimed. There was nothing comical to them about blasting Ned Christie to Kingdom Come, whatever the means employed. Coffeyville was a day's journey by train. The better part of a week would be lost before he got back and they could move.

But they sent him. In the meantime, Christie, not knowing what was afoot, had allowed two of his cohorts to return to their homes. On October 30, Heck Thomas and his brigade left Fort Smith by train for West Forks, Arkansas, where Paden Tolbert with his cannon was to meet them.

He arrived the following day. He not only had the cannon but had had the foresight to lay in a supply of dynamite, just in case the little three-pounder failed to accomplish its appointed task. Saddle horses, a flat-bed wagon and a span of mules were secured. The cannon was bolted to the floor, with its muzzle pointed out the rear, the plan being that when it came time to use it, the wagon would be guided into position by men manipulating the wagon-pole.

On the morning of November 2, the battle began, the marshals opening up a withering rifle fire on the fort. It drew a spirited answer from Christie and his two companions. By noon, it was apparent that no decision was to be reached in that manner. The wagon was brought up, and three men guided it toward the fort. Tolbert was in the wagon—in Coffeyville he had received some instructions on firing a cannon—and when he applied the match, there was a terrific explosion. The cannon vomited its supposedly lethal load. But nothing much happened. The bark flew from unpeeled logs and a few splinters went flying into the air.

A second try was had at much closer range. The result was equally discouraging. Tolbert decided it was time to use the dynamite. They pushed the wagon close to the wall. He planted the charge, lit the fuse and scampered back to safety.

This was different; the fort was demolished and only a twisted mass of logs remained. In the smoke and confusion, one of the Indians escaped. The other one was killed. Out of the ruins stepped Ned Christie, snapping his empty rifle. The marshals opened fire on him, and he toppled over and lay still.

The body was taken to Fort Smith, photographed and exhibited. Old Watt Christie came to claim it. He had it placed in a coffin and drove off with it to give it burial in the Rabbit Trap graveyard.

The marshals had rid themselves of Ned Christie, but with little honor. If it had taken them so long to catch up with him, it was undoubtedly because there was something of Robin Hood about Ned Christie. Most of his crimes were against white men. When he plundered an Indian it was usually a matter of robbing the rich to reward the poor.

There was nothing of Robin Hood in Rufus Buck, the young Yuchi (non-Muskhogean Creek) fullblood who, in his small way, was as vicious as Cherokee Bill and coupled with it a depravity rare even among Indian outlaws. He was born and raised near Okmulgee, in the Creek Nation. It was in that country that he committed his first robberies, minor crimes but so successfully carried out that three young Creeks, Sam Sampson, Meome July and Lewis Davis, were attracted to him. A fourth man, Lukey Davis, by name, a Creek Negro mixblood, accepted his leadership.

It was commonly believed that a mixture of Creek and Negro blood was a dangerous cross, and that the offspring of such a union was sure to be "mean." It was true enough in the case of Lukey Davis, but there would seem to be little reason to accept it as generally so. For several hundred years there had been a strong infiltration of Negro blood into the Creek tribe, more so than with the Cherokee, Choctaw and Chickasaw. Few Creeks were a hundred per cent Indian. Undoubtedly intermarriage had had some effect on Creek culture. That it worked any tribal character change or was responsible for the inflamed criminal instincts of some Creeks, such as those with whom Rufus Buck surrounded himself, must be dismissed as absurd.

If the life of the Buck Gang was brief—a year would cover it—it was deadly while it lasted. In midsummer of 1895, they killed four men, committed half a dozen robberies and raped a middle-aged widow by the name of Wilson, all five of them taking a turn at ravishing her, which set a record for criminality even in the sanguinary history of Indian Territory.

On Snake Creek, a trifling stream that heads near Sapulpa and flows into the Arkansas, they came to the cabin of Henry Hassan. It was lonely country, and Hassan and his wife knew nothing about the red trail their visitors had left behind them. They told him they would pay Mrs. Hassan if she would cook them a good dinner. She was happy to oblige. She was a comely woman. When they finished eating, instead of paying her and riding on, they forced her husband out into the yard and took turns guarding him while the others violated his wife.

Later in the day, they met a horseman, who was astride a good-looking animal. They surrounded him and said they wanted to trade horses. The stranger demurred, only to discover that he was going to trade whether he wanted to or not. The exchange was made and the man jogged away on the horse they had given him, glad to escape with his life.

East of Sapulpa, they encountered a traveler named Callahan. They robbed him of all he possessed, and then, to amuse themselves, they opened fire on him as he fled to safety. He raced into town with news of what had happened. The Creek Light Horse (Indian police) went after the Buck Gang but failed to find them. Posses of Indians and posses of whites took to the field. They had no better luck than the police.

Boldly, the Buck Gang rode into Okmulgee and robbed a store. Before the day was finished they robbed two more stores, some miles apart. When they saw a horse they fancied, they offered to trade for it. If the owner said no, they shot him and took the animal. Almost within sight of Eufala they met a Negro boy walking to town. Apparently for no better reason than to enjoy seeing him twitch as he died, they killed him.

They had the country terrorized by now. As the number of their crimes mounted, farm families feared for their lives. Then, suddenly, no more was heard of them for several months. With winter at hand, it was presumed they had holed up somewhere. The hunt for them continued, however.

With the opening of spring, U.S. Marshal S. Morton Rutherford came out from Fort Smith with a brigade of deputies, among them reliable Heck Thomas, Paden Tolbert and Bud Ledbetter. It took them weeks to track down the gang. The outlaws were camped in a mott of live oaks, three miles south of Muskogee, when Rutherford and his deputies surprised them. A furious battle, in which several hundred shots were fired, began at once. There was a hill behind the camp. Rufus Buck and his companions retreated to its highest point and held off the attackers for hours. When their ammunition was exhausted, they had no choice but to surrender.

Hands manacled and in leg irons, the prisoners were put in a wagon and taken into Muskogee. It was Marshal Rutherford's intention to hold them in the federal jail there overnight and take them by train to Fort Smith in the morning. But news of the capture of the Buck Gang preceded their arrival in town, and when the wagon bearing them turned up North Third Street, an angry mob of several hundred armed men made a rush for it and tried to drag the cowering wretches away from the officers and string them up at once. It was a Creek mob, ninety-five per cent so. As it surged about them, held off only by the pistols of Rutherford and his deputies, Rufus Buck, Lukey Davis and the others knew only too well that their crimes had outraged their own people and that they could expect less mercy from them than from white men.

The prisoners were hurried into the jail—a flimsy, wooden building, a story and a half high, surrounded by a stockade of pickets. Outside, an interruption took place. General Pleasant Porter, at that time the principal chief of the Creeks, climbed up on the empty wagon and appealed to the mob to disperse. He reminded them that Marshal Rutherford and his deputies would protect the prisoners with their lives.

"They are brave men," he told them. "Let them take these killers to Fort Smith in the morning, where Judge Parker will see that they pay for their crimes."

The mob refused to listen. Men were surging against the stockade as Rutherford stepped out, a rifle cradled in his arms. He could only say what other marshals and sheriffs have said in similar circumstances. It was largely an echo of what Pleasant Porter had told them. He added a warning.

"We captured those men. Though their hands are stained with blood, I intend to see that they are given a trial according to law. You may batter down the door and overpower us, but I warn you that the first man who comes through that gate will be shot."

As mobs will, it was slow to break up. Imperceptibly at first, men began to drift away. Half an hour later there was no one left in front of the jail. The night passed quietly, and in the morning —it was Sunday—there was no demonstration as Rufus Buck, Lewis Davis, Sam Sampson, Meome July and Lukey Davis were marched to the railroad station. Fort Smith was going to church when their captors led them down Garrison Avenue in chains to the Fort Smith prison. It was a spectacle that the town was never to see again—five murderers being escorted to their doom.

In due course, they came to trial. The verdict was guilty. Parker sentenced them to death—a sentence he was to pronounce only once more before his court was abolished.

Usually there are some expressions of sympathy for men who are about to die, especially when they are young. If there were any when the Rufus Buck band was led up the gallows' steps and placed on the hinged platform where so many others had stood, they were voiced silently by relatives. With a show of bravado, the five men called to acquaintances among the spectators before the black caps were pulled over their heads. A moment later the trap was sprung and they were sent plunging into eternity. It was, the local press agreed, a good day's work, well done.

In McAlester, Muskogee, Tulsa or Oklahoma City in the years between the two World Wars, an old man was often seen seated on a stool at a busy street corner, his long hair in braids, a battered Stetson on his head and wearing cowboy boots and a greasy-looking fringed buckskin jacket, literally covered with badges and souvenirs he had acquired in his travels. Always there was an open suitcase, much the worse for wear, on the sidewalk at his feet, containing stacks of a little twenty-eight-page booklet, purporting to be the true story of his life, which you could purchase for a dime each. He was Texas Jack, "the famous bandit"—and he was not the fake many people believed him to be. Few, however, had the temerity to question the authenticity of his published "True Adventures" to his face or to dispute his authorship. If he "wrote" the little paperback that sold thirty-five thousand copies or more, he had the help of some unknown newspaperman who knew how to put a sentence together. It is a collector's item today.

According to the record, Texas Jack was not a killer, but he was a first-class train and bank robber, and unlike other Indian Territory outlaws, he roamed far and wide. Working alone, he stuck up a Santa Fe express in Colorado, robbed a bank at Riverside, Texas, held up a stagecoach at Canyon Gap, Colorado, robbed another Texas bank in 1891 and followed it with holding up a San Antonio stage. Moving into Missouri, he knocked off the bank at Southwest City. In 1894, ten years after his first foray outside the law, he took part in his last robbery, a gang holdup of a Katy train at Blackstone Switch, eight miles north of Muskogee, a fiasco in which he was so seriously wounded that it brought his outlaw career to an end.

His honest name was Nathaniel Reed (no relation to the other Reeds who have appeared in this narrative), and he was born in Madison County, Arkansas, in 1862. It was not to escape from abject poverty that he turned to outlawry. Reading between the lines of his book, one gets the feeling that he accepted banditry as a profession in quite the same way in which he regarded medicine or the law.

The Blackstone Switch holdup, although bungled from first to last, due to ignorance, stupidity, cowardice and possibly treachery, is the high point of his career. When it was over, the courage and fortitude he exhibited, the incredible suffering he endured, make as moving a page as will be found in all outlaw history.

Five men took part in the planned holdup: Jim Dyer, the leader; Buss Luckey; Will Smith; Tom Root, a Cherokee fullblood; and Texas Jack. They had someone in Dallas keeping them informed about bullion shipments that were going through to St. Louis. They went to the switch, the spot selected for the robbery, and rehearsed what each man was to do. They were ready when word came on November 13. After dark, they rendezvoused at the switch as planned. Jim Dyer failed to put in an appearance. At first, they thought he was just late, but as train-time neared and he had not come, they figured something had happened to him. They decided to go ahead as they had planned. Texas Jack took charge. He cut the switchlock. When the train was in sight, he threw the switch.

The engineer saw the red light ahead. He tooted the whistle. What the bandits did not know was that it was a signal to the seven deputy marshals riding in the express car to be ready. The railroad company had been tipped off that a holdup was likely. The seven deputies, among them Bud Ledbetter and Paden Tolbert, had boarded the express car at Muskogee. The train took the siding and slowed to a stop.

Texas Jack says he ran to the express car with sticks of dynamite and told the two express messengers to throw out their hardware, or there would be trouble. Their answer was to begin shooting. The train was composed of a smoker, three coaches and a sleeper. Leaving the others to guard the express car, he went through the passengers with the familiar grain sack. He says he got quite a collection of money and jewelry. With Smith and Luckey, he ran back along the side of the train. When they reached the express car, they found the door standing open.

"At this moment I happened to raise my eyes upward and caught a shadow between the two cars. I saw a man with a six-shooter in his hand. He was so close I thought he was going to hit me on the head with it. I bent so as to stoop beneath the sill of the car. He fired, and there was a hot burning sensation in my body. The bullet struck the upper part of my left hip, ranged downward, cutting through the bladder and lower bowels and emerging on the right side of the back part of my thigh. I fired back, but in my upset state was not accurate. Then I discovered that my help had run off and left me. I whistled, which was the signal we had prearranged. Tom Root came to where I was. I informed him I had been hit and told him to guard the car till I got part way to my horse so they wouldn't capture me."

It was Ledbetter who shot him, which had a tinge of irony, since they had grown up a few miles from each other in Madison County.

They got Texas Jack in the saddle, but he had to stop every quarter of a mile to drain his bladder. He believed he was done for, and so did they. When they were two and a half miles from Blackstone Switch, he said he could go no further. They spread a blanket for him—the night was bitter cold—and he used the grain sack for a pillow. He asked them to come back and bury him when they could do so safely. All knew that with daylight the deputy marshals would be scouring the country for them.

They returned the next evening, expecting to find him dead, but he was still alive. They had brought no food. Water was what he needed more than anything else. They got it for him. This was on Wednesday. He lay where he was until Friday night. Will Smith and Tom Root, the Indian, came again and found him in extreme agony. They built a fire and thawed him out. Tom Root had brought him a jug of buttermilk and a pan of *sofkey* (Indian corn mush). They also brought discouraging news; during the afternoon they had seen two groups of deputy marshals combing the Verdigris River bottoms, and to the north, a posse of Indians was working the country.

The two men stayed with him all night, doing what they could to ease his pain. Before dawn, they prepared to leave. He told them not to come back; that it was too dangerous. They agreed. An hour after sunup, he saw deputy marshals and possemen searching along the river. They were getting close. At any time they might find him. There was nothing he could do about it. All that day, Saturday, he lay there, and all Saturday night and all day Sunday. That evening, with fortitude born of desperation, he pulled on his boots, and using his rifle as a crutch, he headed east, crawling and stumbling through the brush, dragging the heavy grain sack with him.

It took him all night to make two miles. In the morning, he was too exhausted to continue and was about to crawl into a briar patch and rest, when he heard a Negro catching up his mule. He hobbled up to him and asked if he could get breakfast. The answer was yes. The Negro's wife set him down to a good meal—the first he had had in five days. He tried to get them to take him in for a few days. They refused, surmising that he was the bandit for whom the deputy marshals were searching. They had burned the brakes along the river and had orders to burn the fields of anyone who harbored him.

He went on, hiding or sleeping in the brush by day and traveling by night. He was bleeding less by now, but never out of agony. Finally, he grew so weak that he had to bury the heavy bag containing the loot from the Blackstone robbery under a tree.

Somehow, he found the stamina to hobble on for another eight miles, never making more than a mile or two a day. That a man in his condition, starving, half-frozen, could go on at all was nothing less than incredible. When hope was all but gone, a woman befriended him, hid him in her cotton field and fed and cared for him. Through her he got word to Jim and Pete Dyer, warning them that unless they helped him to get out of the Territory, he was going to give himself up and do some talking that would implicate them in a half a dozen robberies. They had not taken part in the Blackstone job, but Jim Dyer had planned it, and that could be used against him. The threat bore fruit and they arranged with a man driving north in a covered wagon with his family to take him along. Eleven days later, more dead than alive, he crossed the line into Seneca, Missouri.

He was a bandit, a criminal. Perhaps he deserves no pity, but his iron will and tenacity must be admired.

Outside of Seneca, he hired a man named Lawrence to care for him. He desperately needed a doctor, but he dared not risk sending for one. Weeks passed. By February he was sufficiently mended to make his way to his brother's farm in Madison County, Arkansas.

"I did not know what to do," he says. "The fates seemed to be barking at me. I had also got a considerable dose of religion, so I wrote Judge Isaac C. Parker I was ready to surrender, let come what may. This was the eighteenth day of March, 1895."

He and Tom Root confessed their part in the Blackstone robbery and were promised that if their confessions led to the conviction of the other members of the gang they would be freed on parole.

For twenty months he languished in the Fort Smith prison, receiving medical attention the while. Jim Dyer, Buss Luckey and Will Smith were finally rounded up. All five went to trial and four were convicted. Jim Dyer's strange conduct in connection with the Blackstone Switch robbery was revealed for what it was when his attorney, ubiquitous J. Warren Reed, presented evidence that it was Dyer who had tipped off the Muskogee marshal's office that the train was to be stopped, and had been working with the law, rather than against it—which undoubtedly was true. He was acquitted. Texas Jack and Tom Root were sentenced to five years, but they were paroled and released, as Parker had promised.

On November 18, still on crutches, Texas Jack hobbled out of the Fort Smith prison, a free man, to be met with the news that the famous "Hanging Judge" had just breathed his last.

Like Cole Younger and Frank James, he began exhibiting himself with carnival companies and Wild West Shows as "Texas Jack, the famous bandit and train robber," giving a moral lecture on the folly of crime, and selling his books. He died in Tulsa in 1950, at age eighty-eight. He was the last of the thousands who had faced Isaac Parker—a "reformed" outlaw who outlived them all.

20

The Dalton Boys

F OR WELL OVER half a century, and with little justification, the Daltons have been bracketed with the James-Youngers as one of the two most formidable organized bands of horseback outlaws the country has ever known. Jesse James and his longriders were professionals, the elite of their trade, and the disaster that befell them at Northfield, Minnesota, did little to add to or detract from their reputation.

With the Daltons, it was the debacle at Coffeyville on the morning of October 5, 1892, that projected them into national prominence. Five-strong they rode into Coffeyville that morning. Half an hour later, four were dead and the fifth so riddled with bullets that he survived only by a miracle. Along with them, they took the town marshal and three others to death and wounded three more. It was a gory morning. It provided such publications as the *National Police Gazette* and newspapers looking for the sensational with a field day. It "made" the Daltons. If it had not occurred, they would have passed into history for what they really were— first-class amateurs, at best.

Both before and after Coffeyville robberies and holdups were attributed to them in which they had no part. It put muscle on the myth that the "ferocious Daltons" were "the most cold-blooded robbers in the history of the West." Who could doubt it when it was widely heralded that they were blood kin, cousins (really, second cousins) to the notorious Younger brothers?

That was the clincher. A stream of cheap books, each one claiming to be the true and authentic account of their (the Daltons) astonishing career of crime, began rolling off the presses, and the end is not yet.

But the daddy of them all is *The Dalton Brothers* by an "Eye-Witness." It is the "Bible" on the Dalton boys. The identity of the author has never been disclosed. That he was a newspaperman, employed either in Coffeyville or no farther away than Kansas City, seems likely. Obviously, Eye-Witness realized that time was of the essence, and he must have bent to his task shortly after the smoke of battle drifted away, for he produced a 50,000-word manuscript in time to have it printed and published with a 1892 copyright line. Its first appearance was as a yellow paperback at twenty-five cents, and its success was phenomenal. (It has recently been handsomely reprinted in boards.)

Though much of it is hastily written trash, it can not be faulted when it concerns itself with what happened when the Daltons rode into Coffeyville to do what Jesse James had never done—crack two banks at once. It is a detailed, factual account, the best we have. That Eye-Witness got some of his material from Deputy U.S. Marshal Ransom Payne can hardly be doubted. Payne was attached to the U.S. marshal's office in Guthrie, Oklahoma. According to Eye-Witness, Payne trailed the Daltons relentlessly, but he appears to have been like the horseman on the tavern sign, always riding but never getting anywhere. He never captured any of the Dalton Gang. But Eye-Witness tries valiantly to portray him as a heroic, relentless man-hunter. Rascoe speculates that this was the payoff Eye-Witness made with Payne in return for the information he received. It is the best explanation to be found. It must be doubted, however, that Ransom Payne was a tip-off man for the Daltons and other outlaw gangs, as has been alleged.

Before an attempt at separating fact from fiction in the outlaw depredations of the Dalton boys, some family history must be injected. At the beginning of the Civil War, Louis Dalton, the father, left Jackson County, Missouri, with his family, for an unimproved farm he had purchased, eight miles north of Coffeyville, Kansas. It was there that eight of his sons and three of his daughters grew to adulthood. They were lean years for the Daltons. To make both ends meet, Ben and the older boys went out to work by the day for other farmers.

Frank was the first to break away from home. He went to Fort Smith and was commissioned a Parker deputy marshal. It was dangerous work, but it paid better than tilling a neighbor's fields for seventy-five cents a day. As for personal danger, all of the Daltons seem to have paid it little heed. In 1884, Frank was killed by Indian horse thieves while making an arrest. Four years later, Grat (Grattan) was wounded while riding for the "Hanging Judge." Following him, Bob and Emmett, his younger brothers, served briefly as officers of the law. It has been said, and cannot be questioned, that journeying over the Territory as deputy marshals provided Grat, Bob and Emmett Dalton with an excellent knowledge of various hideouts, where stolen horses could be held until it was safe to run them across the line for sale in Kansas, as well as acquainting them with where the best animals were to be found. It was knowledge they were to put to use a short time later.

Bill Dalton, next in years to Frank, left Kansas to seek his fortune in the gold fields of Montana, possibly as early as 1885, with what luck it is not known. But he went on to California and established himself on a small ranch near the town of Livingston, in Merced County. He married the daughter of a prominent rancher in that neighborhood and became active in "politics"— which meant throwing himself into the fight the ranchers of the San Joaquin Valley were waging against "The Octopus," the Southern Pacific Railroad Corporation, and its avowed policy of creating and maintaining a monopoly of transportation in California, and of exacting "from that monopoly the utmost possible profit." [1]

When that part of the original Indian Territory known as Old Oklahoma was opened to white settlement on April 22, 1889, Louis Dalton and his sons joined the rush for free land, and he and four of his boys, Ben, Charles, Henry and Littleton, took up claims near the present town of Dover, ten miles north of King-fisher. Whether Bob, Grat and Emmett were with them at first can not be stated with certainty, but they were often there with their father, mother and sisters in the months that followed. It was at this time that the cleavage between the Dalton boys occurred; Bob, Grat and Emmett drifting into outlawry, and Ben, Charles, Henry and Littleton staying with their land and leading honorable lives.

In 1890 Louis Dalton returned to Coffeyville in failing health and died there soon after his return. His wife, daughters and three farmer sons continued to live on in Oklahoma. It is with Bob, Grat and Emmett that we are concerned.

Emmett was the handsomest of the three, Grat the oldest. It was Bob who was always the leader, a wild, reckless man, a stranger to fear, who could ride like the wind and had few equals in handling a rifle or six-gun. He had killed his first man, Charles Montgomery, when he was not yet twenty. At the time, Emmett and he were serving as deputy marshals. Montgomery had served time for selling whisky to Indians and had a bad reputation. Bob's story was that he had caught him stealing a horse. Being an officer of the law, his tale was accepted. It appears, however, that Minnie Johnson, the girl with whom he was in love, had flouted him for Montgomery.

No one can say with certainty when Bob, Grat and Emmett Dalton began stealing horses in Old Oklahoma and the Cherokee Strip and running them across the line into Kansas. Their prosperity at the time of their father's death in 1890 would indicate that they were already operating as successful horsethieves. The members of the Cherokee Strip Livestock Association were running thousands of cattle and horses in the Strip under lease from Cherokees. When they began to notice that many fine animals were disappearing from their ranges, they hired stock detectives in an effort to find out the identity of the thieves. It was not until 1891 was well along that suspicion fell on the Daltons.

Eye-Witness says that in the summer of 1891, Grat Dalton was arrested on the suspicion of stealing horses and was taken under heavy guard to Fort Smith to face Judge Parker, only to be released for lack of evidence. The story has been accepted and passed on by numerous writers. No evidence has ever been produced to substantiate it. It was likely concocted by Eye-Witness for the sole purpose of providing a steppingstone to the alleged participation of the Daltons in the robbery of a Southern Pacific train at Alila, California. He says: "Bob and Emmett thought [it] prudent to make themselves scarce for a while . . . and obeying some mysterious invitation—perhaps one from their brother William, settled at that time in California—disappeared suddenly this side of the Rocky mountains, and were seen and heard no more about their habitual haunts."

His subject was the "astonishing careers of the Daltons, the most cold-blooded robbers in the history of the West," and he must have realized that up to this time they had not done anything "astonishing." He remedied that by using the robbery of a Southern Pacific train in far-off California and putting them in the middle of it. It is as neat a blending of fact and wild-eyed fiction as one is likely to encounter. This is how he tells it:

On the night of February 6, 1891, the Southern Pacific's Atlantic Express was flagged down by four masked men at the way station of Alila (now Earlimart), south of the town of Tulare. When the express messenger refused to open his door, George Radliff, the fireman, was ordered to demolish it with his coal pick. This was done. In what was believed to be an attempt to break away, the fireman was shot to death. The express messenger had escaped by the other door, taking with him the keys to the safe. As a consequence, the robbers got very little for their trouble. Rewards were offered by the railroad and express companies. "By an unheard-of streak of luck," says Eye-Witness, "two of the probably guilty parties fell into the hands of the police before the week was ended.

"They proved to be a California gentleman of political prominence in those parts, by name William Dalton, and his brother, just fresh from the Indian Territory, and whose recent exploits were soon exposed—Grat Dalton himself. Thinking himself absolutely unsuspected, since this was the very first raid attempted by his gang that side of the Rockies, he had boldly taken refuge upon his brother's place. A chain of circumstantial evidence traced him from the Alila cañon to his present shelter, and the engineer and messenger both declared under oath that they heard his voice on that eventful night of the 6th of February, and that size and general outlines corresponded exactly with that of the robber left in charge of the engine.

"This fact, of course, saved Grat from the gallows, as the shots that had killed poor Radliff had been fired by the men that stood about the express car. . . . Will Dalton's political pull helped him, undoubtedly, to establish the alibi which made him apparently a total stranger to the Alila hold-up."

As Eye-Witness tells it, a Tulare County jury acquitted Bill but found Grat guilty, and the court sentenced him to twenty years in Folsom Penitentiary. He says: "Grat's brothers were with him in the Tulare County outrage." He produces no evidence to support it. In fact, we have only his word for it that any of the Daltons were involved in the Alila robbery. He is vague about Grat's trial and his accomplices, which would have been of the first importance, if it ever occurred, since it would have been the only time one of the Dalton boys was found guilty by a court of law.

The one thing we can be sure of is that Bill Dalton was not living near Alila at the time. Eye-Witness gives very few dates, and though he goes to great lengths in describing Grat's hair-raising "escape," he can do no better than say it occurred "on a fine morning in early April"—which may be interpreted as being between the first and the tenth of the month. In itself it is enough to make one doubt that Bob, Grat and Emmett Dalton were ever in California. Eye-Witness further arouses skepticism by having them return posthaste to their old haunts in Indian and Oklahoma territories—the one place where the law was certain to look for them —which is to be doubted.

It can be granted that if they returned to their familiar haunts from California, they would have been careful enough to do it in a roundabout way, which would have taken a week to ten days. April would have been more than half gone. Measure that against the indisputable fact that on May 9, at the head of an organized gang, they robbed a Santa Fe train at Wharton (now Perry), Oklahoma.

With them they had men like the redoubtable Bill Doolin, Black-Faced Charley Bryant, Bill Powers and Dick Broadwell—all cowboys who had been employed on Oscar Halsell's big H X Bar spread on the Cimarron River, north of Guthrie, the new capital of Oklahoma Territory—hard-headed men, and it can be presumed that they were not persuaded overnight to give up their cowboy trade and plunge into outlawry. The Wharton robbery was carried out successfully. Though the proceeds were small—less than two thousand dollars—it must have called for some preparation and reconnoitering.

To organize an outlaw gang from green material, plan a train holdup and carry it out, all within two weeks or so, stretches one's credulity beyond the breaking point. It is my belief that the Daltons never left Oklahoma that spring; that they were consorting with their friends on the H X Bar or waiting for the grass to come green again as they took their ease in one of their caves along the Cimarron. Certainly Bob Dalton had no desire to go roaming, for he had acquired a new love, Daisy Bryant, the comely and buxom sister of Black-Faced Charley Bryant, and established her in the little town of Hennessey, twenty miles north of Kingfisher.

Further, if Grat's alleged "escape" from the moving train that was taking him under guard to Folsom Penitentiary never happened but was invented, it discredits the whole episode of the Daltons being in California and participating in the Alila robbery. Here is the "escape" as Eye-Witness tells it:

"Two deputy sheriffs had been entrusted with the task of bringing Grat Dalton from the Tulare County jail to the state penitentiary. Knowing the man to be an athlete and a fearless desperado, they had decided to have his feet tied together with a leather thong, allowing their prisoner to take short steps only, while by turns each of the deputy sheriffs would link one of his wrists to one of the man's wrists by means of a double manacle. Thus it seemed that no possible escape could be effected. By using a day-train full of people there was no danger of an attempt at rescue by Grat's confederates.

"So the trio started on its trip on a fine morning in early April, 1891. The temperature was very hot, as it usually is at that time of the year over all southern California, and the window next to which sat the prisoner had been thrown open. While the train was running at full speed—forty-five miles an hour—between

Fresno and Berenda, the deputy sheriff who was tied up to the prisoner felt so drowsy that he let his head droop upon his breast, while he sunk in a delightful doze. His companion was having a chat and a smoke with a friend at the further end of the car.

"Suddenly Grat Dalton rose from his seat with a jerk that awoke his bewildered neighbor. By a magic that has never been explained to this day, the bracelet around the prisoner's wrist fell upon the seat, while the man himself pitched headforemost and with lightning rapidity through the open window. A great noise of water was heard outside, and the excited passengers, now all shouting and crowding to that side of the train, could just see the form of the escaped prisoner swallowed up by the blue waters of a running stream.

"The whole thing had not lasted five seconds, and the officers were gazing at each other with comic desolation, without even thinking of having the train stopped, when it slacked speed upon the conductor's spontaneously pulling the bell-rope.

"The deputy sheriffs started out in hot pursuit, but their search was fruitless.

"All they found on the river bank, close to the point where the incredible plunge had taken place, was the leather thong and the fresh hoofprints of a couple of horses that had evidently been kept waiting for the pre-arranged escape of Grat Dalton."

Dismiss the two deputy sheriffs by admitting that they could have been bought to play their parts in such an escape. Consider the car window. The windows of day coaches in those days were small. Could a man as big as Grat Dalton have "plunged" through one? And the unnamed river? Was it the San Joaquin? If so, the bridge was not an open trestle but an iron bridge. Could a man have "plunged" through the window of a train traveling forty-five miles an hour and not have had his brains dashed out by striking one of the bridge struts?

It would have been a feat to leap from a window of a standing train and reach the river, running high at that time of the year, uninjured. Of course, it never happened. The "escape" and everything connected with it reveal, even under casual examination, what it is—highly sensational fiction in the best *Police Gazette* style; and though it has been accepted without question by many

writers, honesty compels one to reject it. The usually caustic Rascoe, in his long introduction to the reprint edition of *The Dalton
Brothers,* by Eye-Witness, says with understandable mildness, being
indebted to the publisher:

"I don't accept, without more conclusive evidence than I have
been able to unearth, the account in this book or elsewhere, that
Emmett, or any of the Daltons, ever went to California or that
their bandit careers began with the Tulare County train robbery.
Nearly all fictionalized stories of outlaws, including those of the
Jim Reed gang, Sam Bass and the James boys, have the gimmick
about an apprenticeship in California. The actual holdups tried
or effected by the Daltons started, I am inclined to believe, with
the hold-up of the Santa Fe express train at Wharton on May 8th,
(9th), 1891." [2]

21

Prelude to Coffeyville

THE WHARTON ROBBERY was carried out successfully, the means employed closely following the pattern used for years by the James-Younger Gang.

The Guthrie-Wichita Express, northbound, was due to pass Wharton at 10:13 P.M. According to the published timetable of the Santa Fe, it would stop there only on signal. A few minutes before it was due, two armed men, the lower part of their faces masked with bandanas, took the agent-operator by surprise and ordered him to set the lights against the Guthrie-Wichita Express. After he had done as they asked, they tied his hands and bound him to a chair.

When the engineer saw the signals set against him, he acknowledged it with a toot of the whistle and cut the throttle. With brakes squealing, the locomotive clanked to a stop at the station. One of the bandits scurried up the iron steps of the locomotive to the cab and took charge of the engineer and fireman. The messenger ran back the door of the express car a foot or two and peered out to learn the reason for this unexpected stop. He found himself covered. He backed away, hands in the air. The conductor got down from a rear coach and ran toward the platform in time to see two masked men climbing into the express car. A warning shot out of the dark stopped him.

With the business end of a rifle boring into his back, the messenger obligingly opened the safe and stuffed its contents—not more than fifteen hundred dollars—into the waiting grain sack. Little as it was, it seems to have satisfied the bandits, for they did not go through the coaches. The two who were in the express car were about to leap out onto the platform when one of them saw that the station agent had freed himself from his bonds and was bending over the telegraph key, frantically calling for help. Whipping up his rifle, the bandit sent a slug crashing through the window that killed him where he sat. A few minutes later, the robbers were in the saddle and riding away with a whoop and a holler.

The Wharton robbery was to have some repercussions. According to the train crew of the Guthrie-Wichita Express, the masked bandits had numbered only three. They may have seen only three, but at least four others were in the offing. What is remarkable, and unbelievable, is the express messenger's tale that he recognized Bob Dalton and Black-Faced Charley Bryant as the two men who had compelled him to open the safe. That an express messenger, running on the Guthrie-Arkansas City Division, was sufficiently acquainted with Bob Dalton to identify him, though the lower half of his face was masked, is unlikely. He was correct in naming Bryant as the slayer of the Wharton agent, but his identification was probably based on the fact that the man who fired the fatal shot had a powder burn on his left cheek, below the eye. In a saloon brawl, a gun had been fired so close to Bryant's face that the powder was embedded beneath the skin, giving him his nickname of Black-Faced Charley.

But the story was believed and had a wide circulation. For the first time the phrase "the Dalton Gang" appeared in newspapers and gave Bob and his brothers a local celebrity.

Being thoroughly acquainted with the country, the gang had reached Wharton without being seen. Doubtless they could have retreated with equal ease if they had resisted the temptation to make off with a bunch of horses they encountered shortly after daybreak at the head of Beaver Creek, northwest of Orlando. Rounding up the animals and driving them along consumed time. When they reached Skeleton Creek, they believed themselves safe enough from pursuit to drive the horses into the heavy scrub and buckbrush and hold them there until evening. But the theft of the animals had been discovered, and a posse of cowboys and ranchmen had taken to the saddle at once.

The bandits were taking their ease in the live oak and black-jack scrub when the posse caught up with them. There was a brisk exchange of shots. The possemen knew nothing about what had occurred at Wharton the previous evening. If they had known, it might have made them more cautious; but believing they were tangling only with horse thieves, they charged into the timber, hoping to drive them out into the open. The maneuver failed, the gunfire becoming so vicious they were forced to retreat. As they dropped back to confer, they discovered that one of their number, W. T. Starmer, was missing. They correctly surmised that he had been killed. While they were deciding on what to do next, the outlaws quietly decamped, taking the stolen horses with them.

The slaying of Starmer was the second killing the law could charge to the newly organized Dalton Gang. Following that clash with private citizens—not the law—at what some writers call the "Twin Mounds" fight, there comes a hiatus in the criminal career of the Dalton brothers that remains inexplicable. As though the earth had opened and swallowed them, they disappeared for approximately thirteen months. Though many have tried, no chronicler of outlawry has been able to do better than nibble around the edges of that mystery, and it remains a blank, such as occurred for much shorter intervals in the life story of Belle Starr.

It is generally accepted that Bill Doolin, Dick Broadwell and Bill Powers, though under suspicion of having had a hand in the Wharton robbery, had returned to the H X Bar ranch and gone to work for Oscar Halsell. We know that Black-Faced Charley Bryant, never a man of any importance, was seen at long intervals in or around the little town of Hennessey, very likely visiting his sister, and always alone. If during that long period he was in any difficulty with the law, other than the Wharton affair, it does not appear in the record.

The Santa Fe had offered a reward of a thousand dollars for information leading to the arrest and conviction of the robbers and a special reward of a thousand dollars for the capture, dead or alive, of the man who had killed their Wharton agent. Descriptions of the wanted men given by the train crew were sent out. Since the express messenger had seen the fatal shot fired by a man with a black powder burn on his left cheek, several men so marked were picked up, but they had no difficulty proving their innocence.

And then Deputy Marshal Ed Short, headquartering in Hennessey, an experienced man with bulldog tenacity, perhaps the most dependable deputy attached to the U.S. marshal's office at Guthrie, began putting two and two together. It was well into August. He shook his head when he thought of it; he had had the answer almost in his hand for weeks. Perhaps it was because he was so close to it that it had not occurred to him before. He knew Charley Bryant by sight and was aware of Daisy Bryant's intimacy with Bob Dalton. It added up to the conviction that Black-Faced Charley Bryant was the wanted man. Without consulting Guthrie —there was the little matter of the thousand-dollar reward in his mind—he set out on his own to locate him.

The capture of Bryant is told several ways. Eye-Witness has him being taken at the love nest that Bob Dalton provided for Daisy Bryant, with his ubiquitous hero, Deputy Ransom Payne, leading the posse that surrounded the place and took Charley Bryant into custody. In this, as is usually the case when he steps beyond the town limits of Coffeyville, he is grossly mistaken. Ransom Payne had nothing to do with the taking of Black Faced Charley Bryant; Ed Short did it singlehandedly. And it occurred, not in Daisy's cottage, but in the Rhodes Hotel in the heart of Hennessey.

When Short began looking for his man, he went first to the 3 Circle Z ranch, west of town, where Bryant was last known to have been employed. He was not there. The marshal was told that Charley was sick and had left to seek a doctor's care. Whether or not he was tipped off that he would find his man in the Rhodes Hotel, a ramshackle clapboard building, two stories high, run by Ben Thorne, an ex-cowman, and his sister, we do not know. But

Bryant was there, in bed in an upper floor room. When Jean Thorne went up the stairs with the patient's noonday dinner, Short crept up behind her and was through the door before Black-Faced Charley could snatch up a gun from the chair at his bedside. He was ordered to get into his clothes and was then handcuffed.

It must have been Short's desire to get the prisoner to Guthrie as soon as possible, but undoubtedly he was even more anxious to get Bryant out of Hennessey before an attempt could be made to rescue him. Accordingly, he took the first Rock Island train north for Wichita, where he could lodge him overnight in the federal jail and then double back to Guthrie via the Santa Fe. Timing it so that he would arrive at the depot as the train for the north was pulling in, he marched Bryant out of the hotel and sat down with him in the baggage car.

It all had been so easily accomplished that Ed Short may have been lulled into carlessness as the local rattled along. Bryant sat bent over, the picture of dejection as he stared at his manacled wrists.

When the train stopped at Waukomis, a few miles south of Enid, Short told the baggageman he was going to step out onto the depot platform for a minute and stretch his legs. He gave the baggageman his revolver, and after warning him to keep an eye on the prisoner, opened the rear door of the car and stepped down.

The baggageman had work to do. After watching Bryant for a minute or two, he foolishly placed the six-gun on his desk. Bryant pounced on it with a tigerish leap, and though his wrists were shackled, this did not prevent him from seizing the pistol. It was the work of only a few seconds to make the baggageman run back the door on the side of the car opposite the depot platform and leap out. The next we know for certain is that men and women preparing to board the train were suddenly startled to see a man standing on the car steps, a pistol clutched in his manacled hands.

Bryant saw Short standing in front of the depot, ten feet away, and began firing at once as rapidly as he could squeeze the trigger. Either the first or second shot struck the marshal, inflicting a fatal wound. Stricken though he was, Short brought up his rifle and fired twice, both shots ripping into Bryant. The latter pitched forward and rolled down the steps. A human bulldog to the last, Ed

Short reached out as he sagged to the platform and clutched Bryant's legs. Black-Faced Charley was dead, and as Jim Collins, the Rock Island conductor, bent down over the dying marshal, Short breathed his last.

With the killing of Black-Faced Charley Bryant, any doubt of his connection with the Daltons disappeared, and likewise of their responsibility for the Wharton holdup. The hunt for the others was intensified. No trace of them could be found. Daisy Bryant was arrested as a material witness, but no evidence could be produced to warrant holding her. When she quietly disappeared from her home, the rumor spread that she had slipped away to meet Bob Dalton. Actually, she was in Guthrie, conducting herself circumspectly.[1]

But what of Bob, Grat and Emmett Dalton? It would be of the greatest interest to know where they were and what they were doing. Very likely it would puncture the myth that they were the foremost horseback outlaws of their day. Oklahoma Territory, as a political entity, was new; law enforcement was too weak to cope with a raw, new land; settlements that blossomed as tent cities overnight were just beginning their metamorphosis into lively, established communities. The Daltons were wanted, but they were not being hunted aggressively enough to make them take cover for thirteen months—not if they were the ferocious desperadoes, the "most cold-blooded robbers in the history of the West" that they were reputed to be.

It was the custom of outlaw bands to take time off from their criminal pursuits and enjoy the proceeds of their robberies. In this instance, it could not have been true of the Daltons, for the loot gathered at Wharton, divided seven ways, coupled with their horse-stealing activities, could not have given them money enough to sustain themselves for thirteen months. It has been suggested that they spent this long interval in reorganizing. This may be doubted, for when they struck again the personnel had not changed. In fact, with the exception of Charley Bryant, it remained intact up to the disaster at Coffeyville.

Of course, robberies were occurring with monotonous frequency. When they were committed by "parties unknown," the Daltons were suspected. But no evidence to that effect was ever produced. When their whereabouts continued to be a mystery, the rumor grew that they had quit the Territory and were somewhere in Texas. Perhaps the best surmise was that they were idling their time away down in Greer County, on Red River. This was wild, thinly populated country. The Texas Boundary Commission was still debating whether Greer County belonged to Texas or Oklahoma. As a result, law enforcement suffered, except when Texas Rangers crossed the river in search of wanted men. They were not interested in the Daltons.

On June 1, 1892, another Santa Fe train was held up at Red Rock, only twelve miles north of Wharton; this time it was the Dalton Gang, and there was no doubt about it. The southbound Texas Fast Express was due to pass Red Rock station at 9:40 in the evening, with Guthrie its next scheduled stop. It never got past Red Rock this night. A few minutes before it was due, two masked men walked into the boxlike depot and ordered the agent to set the signals against the express. Facing two armed men, and having a normal interest in self-preservation, he obliged. When the engineer saw the signal lights set against him, he closed the throttle and the train rolled up to the depot and stopped.

Some cattle were shipped from Red Rock, which accounted for its existence. Aside from the depot, shipping pens and two stores, the rest of the town could have been covered with a horse blanket. Knowing there would be no interference by the citizenry of the tiny hamlet, the bandits went to work with businesslike efficiency.

In addition to his brothers Grat and Emmett, Bob Dalton again had Bill Doolin, Dick Broadwell and Bill Powers with him. There was no confusion; this job had been rehearsed and each man knew what he was to do.

One of them, Wellman reports in his *A Dynasty of Western Outlaws,* was Black-Faced Charley Bryant, and he says it was at Red Rock that the slaying of the station agent occurred. He is mistaken; the killing of the agent took place at Wharton on May 9, 1891. It was on Sunday, August 23, 1891 that Bryant and Ed Short dueled to death on the station platform at Waukomis—nine months prior to the Red Rock robbery. There is a precedent for this error. It first got into print when Gordon Hines wrote *Okla-*

hombres for the great U.S. Marshal Evett Dumas Nix, in 1929.

If the Dalton brothers can not be regarded as range cowboys turned outlaw, the others can. They were the genuine article, men who had never known any other calling. Black-browed Bill Doolin, a rawboned six-footer, could barely read or write, but he was resolute, nerveless, shrewd, intelligent and a born leader of men, which he was to prove before he was finished. Bill Powers was an unsmiling cowboy roughneck, hard as nails; young Dick Broadwell just a laughing, inexperienced boy who had more iron than judgment in his makeup.

Bill Powers and young Broadwell climbed hurriedly into the cab of the panting locomotive and cowed the engineer and fireman with their rifles. Two of the Daltons, Bob and Emmett, ran up the steps of the first coach and went through the train, relieving the passengers of their money and valuables. In the meantime, Doolin and Grat had leaped into the express car and found the messenger and the shotgun guard, who was riding with him, playing checkers. Before the two men could jerk to their feet, the bandits had them covered.

The safe was opened. By report it yielded very little. The railroad company put the loss at only a few hundred dollars. It undoubtedly was a great deal more than that; minimizing its losses was railroad company policy, pursued in the hope of discouraging further holdups.

In light of the events that followed, one can be sure that Greer County had no place in the plans of the Daltons when they scattered after the Red Rock robbery. Before they parted, they had agreed on a rendezvous. The place chosen was an admirable hide-out for men on the scout. Bob, Grat and Emmett had discovered it when they were serving their hitches as deputy marshals for the Fort Smith court. It was a limestone cave, tucked away on the old Berryhill farm, just above where the Cimarron flows into the Arkansas River. Roughly speaking, it was about fifty miles southeast of Red Rock, just over the invisible line separating the Creek Nation and what was left of the original Indian Territory from Oklahoma Territory.

For half a century and more, in and around the little town of Mannford, named for Tom Mann who established the ferry there, the cave, with its overhanging shelf of rock, was known as the "Dalton Cave." There, according to local legend, Tom Bartee, a Creek half-blood, hid and fed the Daltons. The cave and other historical points of interest will soon be gone forever, along with Mannford and the neighboring village of Keystone, drowned out by the backed-up water that will be impounded by the Keystone Dam across the Arkansas.

The best reason for believing that Bob Dalton and his long-riders lay hidden in the retreat at Mannford in the weeks following the Red Rock robbery lies in the fact that when they struck again it was at the little town of Adair, in the Cherokee Nation, roughly only fifty miles east of Mannford. Presuming that they traveled by night, they could very easily have left the so-called Dalton Cave and been across the Verdigris River before daylight. On the second night, a matter of a few hours riding would have brought them to Pryor Creek (not the town of that name) where, later, it was reported they had been seen.

It often has been said in connection with various train robberies that the bandits were tipped off that a particular train was carrying a large sum of money. There may have been occasions when this happened, but they were rare. The James-Youngers, who stopped more trains than any other band of outlaws, never received that sort of information. It was a gamble with them; they either hit the jackpot or got very little. The Daltons had netted only several thousand dollars from the Wharton and Red Rock holdups. Luck smiled on them at Adair. It was their most profitable job, the proceeds amounting, it was claimed, to $17,000.

Adair lies about halfway between Muskogee and Parsons, Kansas, on the Cherokee Division of the Katy Railroad. Its population today is numbered only in the hundreds, and it was even smaller on the night of July 14, 1892, when six armed men rode into town from the direction of Pryor Creek, some three or four miles to the west, and went directly to the railroad station. It was sometime after nine o'clock. Most of the inhabitants had already retired for the night or were indoors. The railroad agent offered no resistance when the bandits barged in. He was bound, gagged and deposited in a corner of his tiny office.

With time to spare—the northbound train was not due until

9:45—the robbers looted the station till, which must have yielded very little. This observation seems justified, because in all of the many accounts of the Adair holdup, no mention is made of travelers waiting to board the train or of passengers alighting from it. It is only one of many mystifying aspects of what occurred that evening.

For some reason, not easily explained, Adair seems to have been a regularly scheduled stop for Number 2, the northbound express. With so little of interest happening in a town of that size, it seems that its arrival and departure would have drawn at least a few idlers to the station.

We are told that the bandits "backed a spring wagon up to the express car and in an almost leisurely manner loaded the loot into it." That they required a wagon in which to make off with $17,000 passes belief. That they would have burdened themselves with a vehicle of any description is equally incredible. There is wide disagreement as to whether the gang went through the coaches with the always handy grain sack. Some say no; others produce accounts of alleged passengers in the sleeping car at the rear of the train who were forced to contribute. They are obviously untrue, for if the bandits had "worked" the cars they would not have failed to go through the smoker, in which ten armed guards, led by Captain J. J. Kinney of the Indian police, were riding, which would have changed the complexion of things in a hurry.

Several explanations are offered for the presence of an armed guard of that strength on Number 2 this particular night. One commentator says the Missouri, Kansas and Texas had got word that it was to be attacked. It is easier to believe that it was because the $17,000 in the express car was an unusually valuable shipment for the financially impoverished Katy to be carrying that Captain Kinney and his men had been hired to see it through from Muskogee to Vinita. However that may be, what followed was a curious blending of comedy and tragedy.

When Number 2 came to a stop, two of the bandits swung up into the cab and took charge of the engineer and fireman. Conductor George Scales and a colored porter hurried up the platform, very likely to get orders from the agent. They were quickly taken in charge. George Williams, the express agent, at first refused to open up as ordered, but he changed his mind when he was told that if the door was not opened the car would be blown up.

The night was warm. The car windows were open. One of the guards, a Cherokee half-blood named LaFlore, thrust out his head to learn the meaning of the delay and the excited voices at the door of the express car. He pulled it in in a hurry as a spatter of rifle shots greeted him. It removed any doubt that this was a holdup. Instead of rushing out and making a fight of it, Captain Kinney ordered his men to crouch down at the windows and shoot from there, which they were disgracefully content to do.

Their cowardly conduct explains, perhaps, why they were not riding in the express car, close to the money they were hired to protect, instead of drinking and lolling in the smoker.

Several hundred shots were fired, the guards blazing away without effect and the bandits blasting back at them. Ricocheting slugs ripped into Kinney and two of his men, inflicting trifling wounds. Finally, several of the guards scrambled out on the opposite side of the train and began shooting between and from under the cars. It accomplished nothing. None of the bandits was struck, and when they were finished, they fired a farewell blast and galloped off.

Adair was thoroughly aroused by now. In the drugstore, one of several stores facing the back of the depot across an open space of a hundred yards or more, the town's two physicians, Dr. W. L. Goff and Dr. Youngblood, were standing, when a bullet crashed through the flimsy wall and mortally wounded Goff. A few moments later, Dr. Youngblood was struck. It was thought at first that he too would die. He recovered, however. That it was slugs from the high-powered rifles of the cowardly guards that felled the two doctors can hardly be disputed, since the bandits were firing in the opposite direction.

The Adair holdup was a major robbery. At last, Bob Dalton had what he had always craved—proven mastery over men and fame as the greatest bandit leader of his day. He was only twenty-two. No one knows when the Coffeyville exploit began yeasting in his mind. It could have been as he rode away from Adair at the head of his gang of longriders. The next time, he very likely told himself, it would be something spectacular.

22

Coffeyville

FOLLOWING the Adair holdup, the Dalton Gang again disappeared in mystifying fashion. A score of deputy marshals, the Cherokee police and the Creek Light Horse (the Creek police), spurred on by the rewards posted by the Katy, totaling $6,000, failed to turn them up. Rumors circulated that they had been seen in Denison, Texas, even in Fort Smith, "living it up," but when investigated, the tales proved to have no substance.

There is some reason for believing that they returned to Mannford and the Dalton Cave and buried their loot in that neighborhood. When he appeared to be dying from the wounds received in the Coffeyville battle, Emmett Dalton said, when questioned about their hiding place: "We had a rendezvous near Tulsey Town." Tulsey Town, the old Creek village which became Tulsa, was, at the time, of little importance. Mannford was only twenty miles away. His vagueness, even in extremity, is understandable, if the gang had buried money in or near the Dalton Cave. In later years, after he came out of prison, Emmett refused to be pinned down. Possibly, he dug up the money.

We have his word for it that in the weeks before the Coffeyville raid on October 5, 1892, Bob visited the town at least once. It is often asked why he chose Coffeyville as the target for the exploit that was to end in the destruction of the Dalton Gang. It would seem he had three or four reasons. It was the home town of the Daltons. They were acquainted with the roads leading into and out of it and familiar with the streets, alleys and buildings of the business section. An alley debouched into Walnut Street, on the eastern side of the plaza, almost at the southwest door of the C. M. Condon and Company Bank. The First National Bank was situated directly across Union Street on the far side of the square. There was a vacant lot between the Condon institution and the Opera House, on its north side. If the horses were left in the Walnut Street alley, the vacant lot provided a handy means of retreating to them when the looting of the First National had been accomplished.

Robbing the two banks was an enterprise fraught with danger, but the proximity of the institutions to each other and the ease with which they could be reached provided some reason for believing it could be carried out successfully. Viewed in that light, the Coffeyville raid of the Daltons was not, as has so often been said, the foolhardy attempt of a vainglorious man (Bob Dalton) to outdo Jesse James, and doomed to failure from the beginning. Another factor must have entered into his reasoning. He and his brothers had grown up with a boyish awe for the "rich" Condon and First National banks. Coffeyville had become a prosperous farming town. Undoubtedly they expected to find the coffers of the two institutions bulging with money.

Up to this time they had stolen horses and held up three trains —that is the provable extent of their crimes—but they had robbed no banks. To gain some experience, they might have been expected to go after smaller game on their first venture. Instead, they put caution aside and headed north from their hide-out to, as the cliché puts it, kill two birds with one stone.

The only information we have regarding how that decision was arrived at and how the gang reached Coffeyville is contained in the vague and somewhat contradictory statement made by Emmett Dalton a day or two after the raid. In his book *When the Daltons Rode,* published many years later, he enlarges on it. He says that when Bob first suggested that they "knock off" the two Coffeyville banks, only Dick Broadwell was in favor of it, which is believable, for Broadwell had made Bob Dalton his hero and would have followed him on any venture.

Grat Dalton and Bill Powers were then won over to the idea. Out of love for his brothers, as Emmett tells it, he had to go along with them. Hard-headed Bill Doolin was the last to agree.

Here is a passage, greatly condensed, covering the gang's fifty-mile ride from their hideout to the Kansas line.

"On the morning of October 3rd, we saddled up north of Tulsa in the Osage Nation and rode about twenty miles toward Coffeyville. . . . We camped in the timbered hills on the head of Hickory Creek, about twelve miles from Coffeyville, on the night of the 4th, and in the night we saddled up and rode to the Davis farm on the Onion Creek bottoms, and this morning (the 5th) we fed our horses some corn."

They were now only three or four miles, slightly to the southwest, from their destination. After they had breakfasted, they shaved, all but Bill Powers, who sported a heavy brown mustache and refused to part with it. The tonsorial attention they gave themselves was not prompted by a desire to appear at their best before the home-town folk. They had an excellent reason for shaving, and vanity had nothing to do with it. In his pocket, each man carried a black false beard which was to be his disguise—no bandana masks this time. Anyone who has had occasion to wear a false beard knows it will cling far more securely to a smooth cheek, dampened with gum arabic, than to a two- or three-day-old stubble of whiskers. Resorting to such amateur theatrics was a mistake that was to cost them dearly.

According to plan, they were in sight of Coffeyville a few minutes after nine o'clock on the sunlit morning of October 5. A short distance from town they encountered a man and his wife driving west. A bit later they passed two men who also were driving west. The sight of a group of armed men jogging toward town was unusual enough to attract the attention of the occupants of the two buggies. They counted them, and in testimony given later, all agreed that they passed six men. And yet a few minutes later, as the bandits jogged down Eighth Street and turned into Maple

Street, which brought them to the alley in which they hitched their horses, they were seen by a score of people who counted only five.

This mysterious discrepancy in figures has long since been explained. The sixth, or missing, man was Bill Doolin. His horse had suddenly gone lame. With the sense he usually displayed, he turned back to steal a good-looking sorrel he had seen grazing in a roadside field. He exchanged animals and set off at a driving gallop to overtake the others. He was too late. At the edge of town, he was met with the news that the Dalton Gang had been obliterated. He lost no time getting out of Kansas. One ludicrous account has him warning everyone he met that the Daltons had just robbed both Coffeyville banks and that he was riding to alert people that the bandits were believed to be heading that way. Doolin was made of sterner stuff than that.

Once the Daltons are in Coffeyville, Eye-Witness is on safe ground. In a minor tour de force, he records every step they took, every shot they fired and every shot that was fired at them. Unfortunately, he supplies so many details of what happened in the gory twelve to fifteen minutes following the arrival of the bandits in the alley, which they were to use in reaching the plaza, that his account tends to become confusing.

He says the gang did not adjust their false beards "and mustaches" until they had tethered their horses. He attaches no significance to it, but it is further proof of the contention that in the business of banditry the Daltons were amateurs rather than professionals. For them to have waited until they were in the alley to put on their disguises, which must have cost them several minutes, when time was of the very essence to them, reveals the caliber of their thinking and tabs them for the second-raters they were.

The robbers emerged from the alley, walking rapidly, Grat, Powers and Broadwell in front, abreast, and Bob and Emmett a step behind. Alex McKenna stood on the steps of his dry-goods and grocery store at the alley's mouth. The bandits passed within a few feet of him. He gave them a casual glance and then looked a second time. The blue-black beards looked suspiciously false to him. Behind one, he thought he recognized Bob Dalton.

As McKenna watched, he saw three of the five men walk into the Condon Bank; after a moment's hesitation the other two hurried across Union Street and disappeared through the doors of the First National. His suspicions definitely aroused by now, he moved to the edge of the store steps from where, through the plate glass windows, he could observe what went on in the Condon counting room. Any doubt that the bank was being robbed, and very likely the First National as well, disappeared the instant he saw Charles Ball, the cashier, and Charles Carpenter, one of the owners, standing at the counter with hands raised and a rifle pointed at their heads.

McKenna hurried inside his store and cried a warning to his customers and clerks. The alarm went winging around the plaza. Very few men had a weapon they could lay their hands on, but in the town's three hardware stores rifles and cartridges were passed out to whoever asked for them. It was Northfield all over again.

In the Condon Bank the robbery was not proceeding as planned. There was $18,000 in the safe, but cashier Ball informed Grat and his companions that the time lock on it was set for 9:45 and that it could not be opened before then. It meant waiting three minutes. That could not have seemed like much of a wait to Grat. But those lost three minutes sealed the fate of the Dalton Gang. Had Grat known it, the safe had been open since eight o'clock. If he had given the steel door a tug, it would have swung free in his hand.

As the bandits waited, a man named Levan, a moneylender and dealer in mortgages, stepped in. He was made prisoner, as was a clerk from one of the stores who had a draft to be cashed. They were not harmed, other than being forced to stretch out and hug the floor. They were no sooner down than a slug thudded into the door. It came from the south end of the square. A few moments later, bullets from a dozen rifles shattered the plate glass windows. Remarkably, the only casualty they inflicted was from a piece of flying glass that nicked Dick Broadwell's arm.

Across the street in the First National, Bob and Emmett were having better luck. When they came in, Thomas G. Ayers, the cashier, and W. H. Shepherd, the teller, were at the counter, and a customer named Brewster was transacting some business with Ayers. The bandits quickly covered the three men with their Winchesters. Emmett then hurried into the back room where the bookkeeping department was located, took Bert Ayers, the cashier's son, by surprise and herded him into the counting room.

Bob Dalton was acquainted with the cashier. Addressing him by name, he ordered him to turn over all the money in the bank. Ayers reluctantly tossed the currency and gold on the counter into the sack Bob handed him, and then brought out the money in the vault, the total amounting to $20,240.

With the well-filled grain sack securely knotted, Emmett tossed it over his shoulder and followed Bob to the door. Using the two Ayers, Brewster and Shepherd as a screen, the bandits emerged from the bank, intending to cross the street and pass by the Condon Bank by way of the vacant lot. But as they stepped out, a blast of shots from the south side swept the square. Realizing that crossing the street would be suicidal, they let their prisoners go and scurried back through the bank to the alley in the rear. Cashier Ayers and his companions darted into Isham Brothers, hardware dealers, next door, and armed themselves.

Just before they entered, young Lucius Baldwin, a clerk, had snatched up a pistol and run through the store to the alley, hoping to take the bandits from the rear. When the two Daltons came out of the bank and found Baldwin confronting them, one or the other, very likely Bob, killed him without a moment's hesitation. Running up the alley to Eighth Street, a matter of fifty yards, they turned west to cross the north side of the plaza. Once across, another twenty-five yards would bring them to a side alley by which they could reach their horses.

From in front of the Eldridge House, they had an open view of the plaza. From different directions, at least a dozen hastily armed men were pouring a stream of lead into the Condon Bank. Bob must have realized then that Grat, Powers and Broadwell were trapped inside and would be lucky to escape alive.

Several hundred feet away, on the sidewalk in front of Brown's shoe store, Charlie Brown, the elderly proprietor, and George Cubine, a shoemaker, were standing, their attention fixed on the entrance of the First National, several doors away. They evidently believed the robbers to be still inside. Cubine was armed with a heavy six-gun. He had it trained on the bank doors. Infuriated by the way things were going, Bob Dalton whipped up his Winchester and put a bullet through Cubine's heart. As Brown bent down to grasp the revolver from Cubine's stiffening fingers, a second shot from Bob Dalton's rifle snuffed out his life.

On the porch in front of Isham Brothers there was a display of farm tools, kitchen utensils and hardwood tubs. A movement there caught Bob's eye. Looking closer, he saw a rifle being aimed at him. Only the head and shoulders of the man holding it were visible, but that was target enough for him. Unerring shot that he was, he fired before the other could press his trigger. The man fell back out of sight, unconscious, blood streaming from the deep furrow that had been cut on the side of his head. He was Tom Ayers, the First National's cashier. In Isham's, he had seized a rifle and immediately stepped out to do his part in stopping the escape of the bandits.

Ayers was not aware that Bob and Emmett Dalton had left the bank until they started to run across the north side of the plaza. Before he recovered from his surprise, he saw Cubine and Charlie Brown shot down. It was but a moment later that he was struck. The shots fired at the north end of the plaza drew the attention of the three members of the gang penned down in the Condon Bank. They were as surprised as Ayers to see Bob and Emmett running up Eighth Street. It told Grat, Powers and Broadwell that they had to make a break, take the $3,000 that was in the sack and try to get across Walnut Street and into the alley.

Somehow they got across the bullet-racked street without being cut down. Charlie Gump, a laborer, tried to stop them. Powers shot the pistol out of the man's hand. The moment they entered the alley they were out of the line of gunfire from lower Walnut Street and the south end of the square, but across the way, the group of men who rushed out of Isham's had an unobstructed view of the alley. Into it they poured what would have been a withering fire if their aim had been better. Matt Reynolds, the coolest of the lot, stepped aside and slapped a bullet into Bill Powers that half-turned him around. Powers retaliated with a snap shot that shattered Reynold's right foot, and ran on. Though a shot fired from the second floor of the Condon Bank wounded Broadwell, it did not stop him.

Bob and Emmett Dalton, running north up the alley at the rear of buildings facing the square, met Grat and the others where the two alleys intersected. It put them not more than sixty feet from their horses which they had left hitched to the fence that was part of John Kloehr's livery barn and wagon yard. Up to that moment Bob and Emmett were unscathed, and although Powers, Broadwell and Grat were wounded and bleeding, all five were still dangerously alive.

Kloehr, regarded as the best shot in town, had been in the fight on the plaza. When he had seen the bandits rush out of the Condon Bank, he ran through Boswell's general store and reached the rear of his livery stable. Hurrying about his barn, he came up behind the board fence, on the other side of which, a few yards away, the bandits were securing the grain sacks to saddle horns and preparing to race out of Coffeyville. As he peered through the fence, Kloehr was dumbfounded to see City Marshal Connelly run out into the alley beyond the bandits.

According to the testimony Kloehr gave later, Connelly glanced up the alley to the westward, apparently thinking he had come out behind the Daltons, when they were behind him. Grat killed the marshal before he could turn around.

Connelly is regarded as one of the heroes of the Coffeyville battle. Doubtless he took part in the battle on the plaza, but I can not find that he did anything to distinguish himself other than to get himself killed—and foolishly.

Concealed behind the fence, Kloehr caught Bob Dalton as he was ejecting a shell from his Winchester and killed him with a shot through the bowels. Bob caught sight of him, and though mortally stricken, he snapped a shot at the liveryman. It sped harmlessly over Kloehr's head. The bandit leader took a step or two and was clutching the fence when a second shot by Kloehr tumbled him into the dust.

Gunfire from the group in front of Isham's swelled in violence as they saw that the marshal and Bob Dalton were down. A team of horses drawing an oil wagon blocked escape from the alley. Bill Powers killed the horses. He was swinging into the saddle when a bullet tore through his breast. With a convulsive gasp, he flung up his hands and fell to the ground dead. In that moment of desperation, Grat caught a glimpse of Kloehr. He whipped up his rifle but the liveryman was too quick for him. His Winchester cracked again and Grat was snuffed out with a gaping hole through his throat.

There was bedlam in the narrow alley by now. Two of the bandits' horses, rearing, frantic, went down, legs thrashing as they rolled over on their backs and died. In that hail of screaming lead, Emmett and Broadwell leaped into the saddle and sped up the alley toward Maple Street and probable escape, once they had turned the corner. Broadwell was struck. The first slug would have been fatal, but he was struck a second and a third time. With blood spurting from his mouth, and clutching his saddle horn with both hands, he turned the corner and disappeared from view. He got as far as the creamery on the Independence road, north of town. He had his bridle rein clutched in his hand holding on to his horse, when they found him dead in the tall grass at the road-side.

What of Emmett Dalton? John Kloehr and half a dozen others agreed that he had reached the Maple Street corner with Broadwell when he suddenly turned back, apparently realizing only then that Bob and Grat were not with him. Eye-Witness says:

"Emmett Dalton, boy as he was with the down of his twentieth year on his lip to mark his youth, did as incredible a thing as men ever looked upon. . . . In all that terrible, constant fire which fed the narrow crossway with leaden bullets, he deliberately rode back the whole distance to where his brother Bob lay dead, dismounted and tried to lift him upon the saddle of his horse that he might bear him away.

"A bullet from a Winchester shattered his right arm near the shoulder, making a mere mass of splinters of the bone.

"Bob's body dropped and Emmett, holding the rein as best he could, sought to use his left hand. A load of buckshot struck him in the back and side. Carey Seaman, a barber, fired the shot . . . and Emmett Dalton fell unconscious by the side of his brother, his arm shattered, his thigh broken, and a dozen buckshot in his back."

Rascoe sneers at this rescue attempt, denies that it happened, principally, it seems, because it so closely parallels Cole Younger's turning back under fire to rescue his brother at Northfield. Stripped of the elaborations it has received, one may accept the story as true. There is no reason for doubting the Emmett Dalton incident just because of its similarity to one that occurred sixteen years before.

Eye-Witness was either in Coffeyville at the time of the raid or shortly thereafter. To a certainty, he pieced his story together from the information he gathered from men who had participated in the fighting—the bloodiest fifteen minutes in the annals of Western outlawry. Four citizens killed; four wounded among the defenders. On the other side of the ledger, Bob and Grat Dalton, Dick Broadwell and Bill Powers were dead, Emmett lying helpless in the Farmers' Home, a small inn on Eighth Street, to which he had been removed after the battle by Sheriff Callahan and placed under guard.

Following the raid, Coffeyville seethed with excitement for several days. There was irresponsible talk about lynching Emmett. Sheriff Callahan squelched it, but it was not until October 11 that he considered it safe to remove the youngest of the Daltons to the Montgomery County jail at Independence. Emmett's mother and brother Ben had come up from their farm in Oklahoma and were joined by Bill Dalton. On the strength of Emmett's statement that Bob had nine hundred dollars on him when he rode into Coffeyville, Bill threatened to sue the town for its return. It was not taken seriously, but when a careful accounting of the sums taken from the two banks was made and the money returned to its rightful owners, it was found that there was a surplus of nine hundred dollars. Whether the Dalton family ever recovered it is not known.

Months passed before Emmett's condition was sufficiently improved for him to stand trial. He was promptly convicted and sentenced to twenty-five years in the state prison at Lansing for his part in the Coffeyville raid. It was there that he slowly fought his way back to health. After he had served fourteen years, President Theodore Roosevelt granted him a full pardon. He was a tall, lean man in his middle fifties, with a springy step and straight as an arrow, when I talked with him on several occasions in California, in 1928. He died in Los Angeles on July 13, 1937—sixty-five years old—the last of the Daltons.

Of the Coffeyville raid it can truly be said that Bob Dalton made good his alleged boast to outdo Jesse James. He did—but surely not in the way he intended.

23

The Doolin Gang

WHEN BILL DOOLIN returned to Oklahoma Territory, unchastened by the debacle at Coffeyville, he hid out at one of the remote line camps on Halsell's sprawling H X Bar range, where he was among friends, men who were, at least in spirit, every bit as lawless as he. He was all of thirty at the time. The son of Mack Doolin, a poor Arkansas farmer, he had been on his own since boyhood. Early poverty had sharpened his wits and filled him with a hard self-reliance that made him a natural leader.

It was on the H X Bar that he recruited the Doolin Gang, which was to rate second only to the James-Youngers among horseback outlaws. In three years, as Marshal Evett Nix figured it, they made off with $165,000 from their train and bank robberies.

Having selected the men he wanted, Doolin left the H X Bar and moved into the old Dalton Cave at Mannford. There they were to join him. An unexpected recruit, Bill Dalton, found his way there. Coffeyville had blasted Bill's career beyond repair. How he learned that Doolin was organizing his own gang is not known. But outlawry seemed to be all that he had left to him.

At first, say some commentators, Doolin was of two minds about

231

having Dalton riding with him, fearing that Bill might try to make himself leader of the gang. They fail to name the source of their information. Certainly Doolin never made any statement of the sort; neither did Dalton. All we know is that the two Bills robbed and plundered together until Dalton was killed.

Bitter Creek Newcomb (his honest name was George Newcomb) and Ol, or Oliver, Yountis, alias Crescent Sam, were the first of Doolin's carefully hand-picked longriders to reach the rendezvous at Mannford. They brought him word that the others would be along as soon as they had "settled up some things." In his impatience to make a strike and get back before an early storm left enough snow on the ground to make tracking easy, Doolin decided not to wait for the others. With Bill Dalton, Newcomb and Yountis, he led the way into Kansas. It was the middle of November, only five weeks after Coffeyville.

Spearville, a little town on the main line of the Santa Fe, a dozen miles east of Dodge City, was their destination. Very likely, cracking the Spearville bank was something that Doolin and Bob Dalton had talked over at some time and never got around to doing anything about.

The Spearville robbery was surprisingly easy, and very profitable, amounting to approximately $18,000, which the bandits divided equally among themselves. They got out of Kansas, and none too soon, for Chalk Beeson, the sheriff of Ford County, and a posse had cut their trail and were pounding hard after them. They separated as they crossed the Strip, Doolin and Newcomb heading for the Dalton Cave, Bill Dalton continuing directly south to the Dalton farm at Dover, and Ol Yountis making tracks for his sister's home near Orlando—a decision prompted by the fact that Chalk Beeson, the ex-buffalo hunter, part owner of the Long Branch Saloon and organizer of the famous Dodge City Cowboy Band, was right on their heels, he having the rather eccentric notion that his jurisdiction did not end until he caught the men he was chasing.

Doolin, Bitter Creek Newcomb and Bill Dalton got away safely, but the horse Yountis was riding went lame. In desperation, he drove the animal until it could go no further. He was still twelve to fifteen miles from his sister's place when he met a stranger.

Wasting no time, Yountis killed him, exchanged horses and got away.

The sheriff found the murdered man and the foundered horse. It had cast a shoe, which identified it as the fleeing bandit's horse. Refusing to give up, Beeson went on to Orlando and got in touch by wire with the U.S. marshal's office in Guthrie. Deputy marshals Madsen, Thomas and Houston joined him in Orlando as day was breaking. Yountis had been in trouble with the law on several previous occasions. Madsen reasoned that Ol Yountis was very likely the man they wanted.

They went to his sister's place and had the house surrounded before it was full day. They had not been waiting long, when Yountis stepped out and started for the barn, carrying a feed bag. Heck Thomas called on him to throw up his hands. Yountis reached into the bag and pulled out a six-gun. Thomas ducked behind the stone fence as orange flame spurted from the barrel. With Yountis' attention fixed on Thomas, Chris Madsen, the remarkable Dane, stepped out from the corner of the barn and staggered him with a bullet that would have killed had it not struck the thick sheaf of bills in the pocketbook Yountis was carrying in his breast pocket. Before he could right himself, Thomas and Houston blasted the life out of him with their Winchesters.

Sheriff Beeson counted the money Yountis had on him. It amounted to almost $4,500—his share of the Spearville robbery.

Undaunted by the slaying of Ol Yountis, the men Doolin had expected began dropping in until all were gathered in the Mannford retreat. They did not remain there long. Initiating a policy, which he was to follow throughout his career as a bandit leader, of never being where the law expected him to be, they left the Dalton Cave and established themselves in an equally secure and more commodious cave in the wild brakes of the Cimarron River, twenty miles to the west. Below the river, in the Sac and Fox country, a safe distance away, there was a wide place in the road with a few stores and houses that called itself Cushing—one day to explode into the brawling, boisterous oil capital of Oklahoma. In the other direction was the little town of Ingalls—a name to be forever associated with the Doolin Gang.

The roster of the Doolin Gang by the winter of 1892/1893

numbered ten. There was Doolin, himself; Bill Dalton; George Waightman, alias Red Buck, a homicidal brute; Jack Blake, alias Tulsa Jack; Charlie Pierce; William Grimes (or Clifton), known as Dynamite Dick because it was claimed that he "loaded" his cartridges with a few grains of dynamite; Little Dick West, the wild man who refused to sleep under a roof and was deadly with a six-gun; young Roy Daugherty, alias Arkansas Tom, who was devoted to Doolin as young Broadwell had been to Bob Dalton; Little Bill Raidler, a scowling, educated ugly duckling who liked to quote poetry around a campfire—and Bitter Creek Newcomb.

Almost every commentator or competent historian grows lyrical when he introduces George "Bitter Creek" Newcomb. He is always described as big, handsome, young, devil-may-care, with an eye for a pretty girl. This note is struck again and again until the reader is presented with a romantic (and spurious) image of Bitter Creek, which is used to lend credibility to the good old shopworn legend of the mythical Rose of the Cimarron's love for her outlaw sweetheart. But more of that later.

On May 26, 1893, the Doolin Gang crossed into Kansas for the second time and held up a Santa Fe express at Cimarron, the town that had grown up where the old Santa Fe Trail crossed the Arkansas River, known then as Cimarron Crossing. They did well again in money, taking south with them almost $13,000.

But they were not home free yet. By telegraph the U.S. marshal's office at Guthrie was apprised of the robbery. Deputy Madsen's advice was sought on how to intercept the bandits. In former years, Chris had served as an army scout at Camp Supply (now Supply, Oklahoma). Knowing that country, he reasoned that the Doolins would follow the old Jones and Plummer trail until they were within ten to fifteen miles of Supply, swing north to bypass it and then go down Buffalo Creek to the Cimarron. A wire to the commandant at supply requested him to dispatch a party of cavalrymen and Indian scouts to the head of Buffalo Creek to meet Madsen. Chris had correctly surmised the route the gang was taking, but he and the military were a few minutes too late to cut them off. They saw them, however, and in a running fight, a bullet struck Doolin in the right foot. The bandits had been careful to conserve their horses. The animals were still fresh, and the gang soon disappeared to the east.

Doolin had the bullet removed from his foot at a friendly cow camp in the Strip, with Arkansas Tom remaining at his side to take care of him. The others made it safely back to the gang's headquarters in the Cimarron brakes.

Some of the heat was taken off the hunt for the Doolins by the depredations of the Bill Cook Gang, which was running wild east of the invisible line that officially separated Oklahoma Territory from Indian Territory. Judge Parker was still in power at Fort Smith, but his deputies were too busy in their own bailiwick to be of much assistance to the peace officers working out of Guthrie.

Henry Starr, the noted "lone bandit," was temporarily behind bars. Several score of lesser lights in the outlaw firmament were very much on the loose. Their activities and the marauding of the big name bandits were responsible for only a fraction of the lawlessness that gripped Oklahoma Territory. Some idea of how completely law enforcement had broken down can be gained from Marshal Nix's statement that in the few years of its existence, the federal prison at Guthrie housed fifty thousand prisoners, the crimes with which they were charged ranging from murder, armed robbery, larceny, rape, arson to violations of the liquor laws.

Marshal Grimes, a better than average officer, had proven that he was unable to cope with it. In 1892, a presidential election year, in which Grover Cleveland was the successful candidate, a petition carrying the signatures of several hundred prominent Oklahomans, requesting the President to appoint a federal marshal who could restore law and order, was forwarded to the territorial delegate in Washington. Three men were anxious to win the appointment. Cattleman Oscar Halsell, owner of the big H X Bar ranch and a silent partner in the wholesale grocery firm of Nix and Company, began beating the drum for Evett Nix.

Nix was reluctant even to consider it, feeling that if the job were offered him he could not accept in fairness to the business and his partner. Halsell resolved that impasse by agreeing to come in as an active partner. So many of his cowboys had drifted into outlawry that he may have felt peculiarly responsible for the plight in which the Territory found itself. His confidence in Evett Nix was great, and it was not misplaced. Due to his efforts, Nix was summoned to Washington by the Department of Justice. Whatever he had to say to those who interviewed him must have impressed them, for shortly after the inauguration ceremonies were over, President Cleveland appointed him U.S. marshal of Oklahoma Territory. He could not have chosen a better man.

I have recently reread the Nix obituaries as printed in the Tulsa *Tribune* and the *Daily Oklahoman*. They follow the facts as I know them, but they err when they speak about the number of outlaws he killed. So far as I know, Evett Dumas Nix never killed anyone. He was not a gunfighter and never pretended to be. He was a businessman, an executive, and he brought order out of chaos by putting together the greatest organization of frontier field marshals this country has ever known.

From Parker, he weaned away the two best men the Hanging Judge had—Bud (Frank) Ledbetter and Heck Thomas—and coupled them with Chris Madsen and Bill Tilghman, the former marshal of Dodge City and under-sheriff of Ford County. That trio, Tilghman, Thomas and Madsen, were to win fame as "The Three Guardsmen"—honored names in Oklahoma today. "Uncle" Bud Ledbetter should be ranked with them. He was every bit their equal.

Charlie Colcord, John Hixon, Frank Canton, Jim Masterson, Bat's elder brother, Lafe Shadley, Tom Houston and Dick Speed constituted the dependable inner circle of the battalion of deputy marshals with which Nix surrounded himself. There were others, many others, for he had stipulated before accepting the marshalship that he should have the authority to enlist as many men as he felt the situation warranted. At times, the number soared to a hundred and fifty—not as large as the force Judge Parker had deputized, but far more efficient. The first order of business was to smash the Doolin Gang. Tilghman, Thomas, Madsen, Hixon and a few others of their caliber were assigned to do it.

The Doolins were flush, and all through the summer of 1893 they lay low. Unlike the Cooks and other lesser gangs, they did not jeopardize their safety by indulging in minor robberies and horse-stealing forays. They knew, via the outlaw grapevine, that Marshal Nix had assigned his best man-hunters to the job of hunting them down. Bill Doolin was personally acquainted with Nix. He respected the man. He knew the quiet, soft-spoken Nix was not the kind to give up until he accomplished what he had set out to do.

But Doolin knew, as everyone else did, that the Cherokee Strip was to be thrown open to settlement on September 16, 1893, in the greatest "run" for free land the country has ever known. Across the line in Kansas, thousands of people were gathering at Caldwell, Hunnewell and Arkansas City. In Oklahoma Territory, other thousands would be lined up to rush into the Strip from the south. Chaos would follow. Nix and his deputies would be swamped as they struggled to establish law and order, for, in one way or another, and as surely as there was a sun in the sky, the Strip would be settled by the six-gun.

Doolin must have been convinced that it would be a long time before Marshal Nix's man-hunters got around to making things tough for him. It was a miscalculation on his part that almost proved fatal. This brings us to the Battle of Ingalls—and here truth and fiction must go their separate ways.

With the right ingredients, a mixture of fact and fancy can be concocted that, when spiked with a strong dash of romance and shaken well, will give one an entertaining and readily acceptable draft of pseudo history. The ingredients were all present at Ingalls. The alleged story of what happened there, first brewed by Richard S. Graves, in 1915, has since been served up by a score of writers, so that almost half a century later we are quaffing the original recipe. Maybe it is too late to set the record straight, but it is at least worth trying.

Ingalls, we have been told, was the "joy" town for the Doolin Gang, whose stronghold was twenty miles to the south, in a bend of the Cimarron. There they came to drink and gamble and be entertained by the three or four girls the Widow Mary Pierce had installed in her two-story "hotel" for their pleasure ("hotel" is always used in quotes, the inference being that the girls were whores and Mrs. Pierce's establishment a backwoods bagnio). The barn where the bandits kept their horses was around the corner. There were two saloons, Ransom and Murray's Trilby being favored by the outlaws, and several stores, a few houses. That was the size and shape of Ingalls in legend.

This is hogwash. I have before me a plan of Ingalls as it was on September 1, 1893, the day of the fight. It was on a surveyed townsite, with a population of about one hundred and fifty men, women and children, and among its places of business, in addition to the saloons, were Bradley's general store, Perry's grocery, Nix's restaurant, two blacksmith shops, two livery barns, a shoe shop, a drugstore, a third grocery, Mary Pierce's hotel and around the corner on Second Street, George Ransom's O.K. hotel, where, according to Dr. Pickering's diary, the bandits "boarded" when they were in town. The latter establishment did not merit the name of hotel.

It is also worthy of note that Ingalls had a new schoolhouse, costing twelve hundred dollars; no trifling sum for so small a community in those days. On the same street with the schoolhouse was the Methodist Episcopal Church, North. (Frankly, I am helping myself to information gathered by the Reverend Leslie McRill who, on two occasions, in the early 1900's, was the pastor of that church.) And there was the post office—the first post office established in Oklahoma Territory.

Three doctors cared for the health of the town; Dr. J. H. Pickering, Dr. Selph and Dr. Call, the latter the stepfather of Rose Dunn, the fifteen-year-old girl who became the mythical "Cimarron Rose." The phrase "Rose of the Cimarron" was not coined until twenty-two years later, when it saw print for the first time in Richard S. Graves' paperback booklet *Oklahoma Outlaws—a Graphic History*.

It was not until mid-July that Bill Doolin and his men became frequent visitors in Ingalls. According to the old-time residents with whom Reverend McRill conversed on many occasions, "it was difficult for some to believe that the soft-spoken, quiet fellows they saw in and around town were outlaws. They sometimes gave the preacher money, and conducted themselves in a gentlemanly manner as any ordinary citizen might." The same note is struck in the Pickering diary, which McRill was fortunate enough to rescue from oblivion.

"It was a happening, not of the people's choice, that the notorious band of outlaws chose that community as a favorite hang-out. There were those in the community, doubtless, who did shel-ter and sympathize with the law-breakers, just as there were many who did not give aid or sympathy. . . . They drank in the saloons, played poker, furnished oysters for country dances and took as much part in community affairs as any of the early day settlers. In that day seldom was it asked where a man came from."

Though the Doolins were often in Ingalls during the latter part of July and throughout August, they apparently took turns at coming in, and never more than five or six were in town at one time. On the day of the battle, only six were trapped there.

This contrasts violently with the picture we have been given for years of a gang of "drunken, swashbuckling outlaws bellying up to the bar in the Trilby saloon, gambling their money away on dice, poker and faro, or tumbling into bed with one of Mary Pierce's harlots when the mood seized them."

I have mentioned Dr. Pickering's diary. His spelling is bad, but as McRill says, "Dr. Pickering's diary, not written to satisfy literary purposes, but to preserve what happened that day as he saw it, brings to us the account of an eye-witness. Many of the citizens, including Dr. Pickering's whole family, were in the caves (this was cyclone country) for safety all during the fight, and while there saw little of what was transpiring above ground. But the doctor stayed above ground, as did the other doctors, and all attended the wounded as soon as called."

The diary, carefully guarded over the years by Mollie Pickering, the doctor's eldest daughter, is the only really authentic docu-ment we have covering the Ingalls fight. We have had the Ingalls story from a score of writers, but it is always the same story, passed on from one to another.

It got off to a bad start with Richard Graves' long-since forgotten and grossly inaccurate travesty *Oklahoma Outlaws—A Graphic History*, in 1915. The line of succession is easily followed. In 1923, J. A. Newson published his *The Life and Practice of the Wild and Modern Indian*. What he has to say about peace officers and outlaws is borrowed from Graves. In 1926, Zoe Tilghman, widow of the famous marshal, followed the same pattern in *Out-law Days*. In 1927, Sutton and MacDonald repeated it once more in *Hands Up!* In 1929, Gordon Hines incorporated it in *Okla-hombres,* the Marshal Nix story. More recently, James D. Horan accepted it in his companion books *Desperate Men* and *Desperate Women.* So does Wellman in his *A Dynasty of Western Outlaws* —and, I confess, I did some years ago in a magazine piece.

The Pickering diary tears a number of gaping holes in the old, familiar Ingalls story. Despite its quaint spelling and crude grammer, reminiscent of William Clark's journal of the Lewis and Clark Expedition, it rings true. Perhaps most remarkable of all, he does not mention Rose Dunn, alias "Rose of the Cimarron," and the bedsheet business at Mary Pierce's "hotel."

Sometime in July, in addition to his other duties, Marshal Nix was informed that he was to recruit a force of a thousand men to patrol the southern line of the Cherokee Strip and assist the military in preventing "sooners" from rushing in to stake claims before the official bugle blew at twelve noon, on September 16. Temporarily unable to devote himself to his resolve to rid the Territory of outlaw bands, the Doolin Gang in particular, he welcomed Deputy Marshal Orrington (Red) Lucas' offer to take to the brush with a posseman for several weeks and locate the whereabouts of the Doolins.

It was an extremely dangerous undertaking. Lucas realized it, but he volunteered to go. Several days later, he left Guthrie with a companion and followed the Cimarron into Payne County. Toward the end of the month, they wandered into Ingalls. This is the way Dr. Pickering reports it:

"In July Wm. Doolan [Doolin], George Newcomb [alias Bitter Creek], Tom Jones [alias Arkansas Tom], Danimite [Dynamite Dick], Tulsa Jack and Bill Dalton began to come here frequently & in a short time they all staid here except Dalton. He was out at B. Dunn's [Bee Dunn's ranch two and a half miles southeast of Ingalls]. As a rule they were quite [sic] & peaceable. They all went heavily armed & constantly on their guard, generlly went 2 together. They boarded at the O.K. Hotel, staid at B. Dunn's when not in town.

"The last of this month [July] a man by the name of Dock Roberts and Red Lucas came to town looking up a proposed Rail Road rout. Both parties took in the haunts of the outlaws.

They were both jovial fellows & soon was drinking & playing cards with them. They left and came back in a week & said they were here to locate a booth, a place for intended settlers to register and get certificates to make a race for land or town lots [in the Strip]. They staid here until the last week in August then left."

Obviously, when they left the first time it was to get word to Marshal Nix that they had located the Doolins. When they left the second time it was to avoid being caught in the middle of the battle that was bound to occur when the contingent of marshals and possemen, whom they knew to be on the way, reached Ingalls.

They got away none too soon. Early on the morning of September 1, they found two wagonloads of marshals camped in a ravine three miles west of town. Four hours later gunfire was ripping the main street of Ingalls.

24

The Battle of Ingalls

WHEN MARSHAL NIX LEARNED from Red Lucas that the Doolins were frequenting Ingalls, he lost no time organizing a force of deputy marshals to capture them, dead or alive. Bud Ledbetter, Heck Thomas and Chris Madsen, busy on other important assignments, were not available, and Bill Tilghman, who would have been his first choice to lead it, was laid up with a broken ankle. He turned to John Hixon and put him in command and assigned Frank Canton, Charlie Colcord, Jim Masterson, Dick Speed, Tom Houston, Lafe Shadley and other reliable men—twelve in all—to accompany him.

To disguise the nature of the expedition, Nix hit on the idea of sending it out as a party of "movers" traveling in covered wagons who went here and there looking for land, visiting kinsfolks or just plain "seein' the country." Real movers always had a chicken coop on the back of the wagon, a plow lashed to the side, and camped out where night overtook them. Nix's "movers" lacked one convincing touch: they had no women or children with them. But for better or worse, they started across the Red Hills in two wagons (Dr. Pickering says there were three) for Ingalls.

Hixon led his posse down the Cimarron until they struck a small creek that came in from the northwest. Following the stream, they passed a mile to the east of the town and then swung back so that they came into Ingalls from the north. By this maneuver they had the main street (identified as Ash Street on the plat) open before them.

Shortly after ten o'clock, the first shot was fired. A man ran up the street from the shoe shop in the direction of Bradley's store. A member of the posse, never identified, believing the man had seen them and was carrying word to the outlaws, struck him down with a bullet from his rifle. I have five accounts of the Battle of Ingalls spread out on my desk. Only two of them mention this incident. One refers to the victim as a boy, and the other as a young man. Croy, in an unpublished manuscript, identifies him as a boy named Briggs. In the Pickering diary he is Walker. No mention is made of his being a boy or a young man. Since Pickering treated him after the fight, he hardly could have been mistaken. He speaks of a Frank Briggs being slightly wounded as the outlaws were leaving Ingalls.

The position of those members of the Doolin Gang who were in Ingalls that morning has been well established. Doolin, Dalton, Dynamite Dick, Tulsa Jack and Bitter Creek were in Ransom and Murray's saloon; Arkansas Tom, alias Tom Jones in Ingalls, was sick in bed in a room on the second floor of Mary Pierce's hotel. With the shot that felled Walker, the bandits surmised instantly that they were under attack. Arkansas Tom from the window of his room saw the marshals working their way up the street, taking advantage of what cover they could find. Their fire was concentrated on the saloon, the slugs from their rifles shattering the windows and boring through the flimsy wooden walls.

Doolin and his men cleared the jagged pieces of glass out of their way and, leaning out, began returning the fire of the posse. There was a lot of blind shooting, neither side being able to find a target. When it quieted momentarily, Jerry Simonds darted out of the blacksmith shop opposite Perry's grocery and started across the street. He was struck down, mortally wounded, but managed to crawl into the store.

It was then, or even before, that Bitter Creek got his horse, which could not have been stabled in the livery barn with the horses of the others, "and was riding up to a small building where Said Conly staid & the marshals thinking he was known [wise] to the move fired on him," says Pickering. He speaks of it being the first shot fired, and if so, it occured before Walker was cut down. Here is a quote from the diary: "Dick Speed marshal from Perkins fired the first shot. The magazine was knocked of [f] his, Bitter Creek's, gun & he was shot in the leg. He made his escape to the southwest."

This not only differs from his thrilling escape with his sweetheart, the "Cimarron Rose," as we have been told again and again, but ignores her completely. What the storytellers have been asking us to believe for years is that Bitter Creek ran out of Ransom and Murray's saloon and had almost reached the town pump at the intersection of Ash and Second streets, when his rifle was shattered and he received a wound that flattened him in the dust. Hearing the shot, the Rose is supposed to have rushed to a second-floor window of the Pierce Hotel and seen him lying helpless in the street. Wanting to get to him, but unable to use the front entrance because of the lead that was flying, she made a rope of bedsheets, lowered a rifle and cartridges to the ground and then slid down the rope herself. Picking up the rifle and ammunition, she reached Bitter Creek, got him to his feet and dragged him around the corner to the barn and his horse. With her help, he managed to get into the saddle. Mounting behind him they fled out the back door—but not for far. The injured Bitter Creek, we have been told, fell out of the saddle, and Rose could not lift him a second time. Red Buck, the merciless villain of the piece, gallops past and leaves them to their fate. But when he overtakes Doolin, the latter asks where Bitter Creek and the Rose are. "Hell!" snarls Red Buck. "We ain't got no time to fool with him and that girl! They're back there—"

He starts to ride on, but a bullet from Doolin's six-gun knocks his hat off. "Come back, you yellow dog!" shouts Doolin. "We're not running out on Bitter Creek and the girl."

I do not know how or by whom this dialogue was recorded for posterity. It would have been difficult, even with a modern tape recorder, seeing that Red Buck missed the Ingalls fight and was miles away. But suppose we leave the world of make-believe and get back to reality.

Kneeling at his window, Arkansas Tom was taking pot shots at the marshals. Jim Masterson was shooting from behind a tree at the side of Light's barn. Arkansas Tom no sooner spotted him than bark began flying from the tree. Looking for a way out, Masterson flung himself into a ditch and tumbled over Hixon who was lying there, firing over the lip of the ditch. The two of them directed their aim at the hotel window. By now, Doolin, Dalton, Dynamite Dick and Tulsa Jack were out of the saloon and shooting as they dodged in and out between the buildings, working toward the stable where their horses were quartered. A bullet cut across the back of Doolin's neck and dropped him for a moment, but he regained his feet and made the barn. So did the others.

They were now in a position to do some effective sniping. The shooting became so hot that Hixon ordered his men to drop back. As Deputy Tom Houston zigzagged across the street for a doorway, a bullet from Arkansas Tom's rifle struck him in the stomach and doubled him over. He was dragged out of the line of fire, but it was too late. Why Hixon, who certainly had been informed where the outlaws kept their horses, had not taken possession of the barn before a shot was fired passes understanding. His courage can not be questioned, but his leadership can. He and his deputies were on foot; once the gang were mounted, pursuing them would be impossible.

After Houston fell, Hixon moved his men. According to the standard tale on Ingalls, Arkansas Tom went up a ladder into the attic and punched holes in the shingles and continued his deadly sniping. This story originated in the Guthrie *Oklahoma State Capital* several days after the battle and has been ricocheting down the years ever since. Here it is in part:

"He [Arkansas Tom] finding himself alone upstairs when the firing began, punched a hole in two sides of the roof with his Winchester, and this with the two windows, one at each end, gave him command of the whole town, the building in which he was, being the only two-story structure.

"Some wonderful shooting and daring deeds were done on both sides but this man out of sight in the building did most of the shooting that killed and wounded. He picked his man whenever he wanted to, and for one hour from 10 to 11 o'clock, poured down shot on the besieging party, and on citizens who appeared."

Such nonsense always amused the old-timers in Ingalls, who pointed out that holes punched in the roof would have given Arkansas Tom a view of the heavens and nothing else.

Following the mortal wounding of Tom Houston, the marshals had scattered. Shadley, Frank Canton and one or two others had made their way around behind the buildings and came out on the main street to the south of the Trilby saloon, where the fighting had started. Others had swung around to the west, the obvious intention of all being to close in on the stable, pin down the gang and prevent their escape. From the stable door, the outlaws were shooting at anything that moved. Marshal Dick Speed made a courageous attempt to reach the town pump and watering trough, from where he could fire into the barn. Doolin, bleeding and half-crazed with pain, caught the movement. His first shot went wide, but bracing himself against the side of the open door, he fired again, and Speed pitched forward on his face, dead.

By now the four men in the barn were mounted. Doolin and Dynamite Dick dashed out through the back door; Dalton and Tulsa Jack came out the wide front door. A bullet, believed to have been fired by Marshal Lafe Shadley, struck Dalton's horse in the jaw. Dalton managed to control the animal and escaped. There was shooting from several directions. When it was over, Shadley lay dead. It was believed for years that Bill Dalton killed him. Dr. Pickering says no, and based on the evidence he discloses, the fatal shot could have been fired only by Arkansas Tom.

The Ingalls fight has to be considered a victory for the Doolin Gang. Doolin, Bitter Creek and Bill Dalton were wounded, but the only man they lost was Arkansas Tom, who was captured and sentenced to serve a term of years in prison.

There is no better way in which to separate fact from fiction regarding the Battle of Ingalls than to present the following fragments from the Pickering diary, as they appeared in the Oklahoma Historical Society's *Chronicles of Oklahoma*, in 1958:

"On the morning of Sept. 1st. there was 27 [certainly a typographical error] deputy marshals piloted into town in covered wagons. They caused no suspicion as there was hundred of Boomers moving the same way. 2 wagons stopped at Light's Black Smith Shop & one drove up by my house and they all proceeded to unload in a quite manner and take positions. Doolan [Doolin], Bitter Creek, Danimite [Dynamite] Dick, Tulsa Jack & Dalton was in Ransom & Murrys [Murray's] Saloon. Arkansas Tom was in bed at the Hotel. Bitter Creek got his horse & was riding up to a small building where Said Conly staid & the marshalls thinking he was known to the move fired on him. Dick Speed marshal from Perkins fired the first shot. The magazine was knocked of [f] his, Bitter Creek's, gun & he was shot in the leg. He made his escape to the southwest. Speed was shot about this time & instantly killed, also young Simonds mortally wounded. The fires of the Marshalls was centered on the Saloon & old man Ransom was shot in the leg. Murry in arm and side. Walker shot through liver.

"By this time the outlaws had got to the stable & saddled their horses. Doolan and Danimite went out at the back door & down a draw southwest. Dalton and Tulsa made a dash from the front door. As they came out Dalton's horse was hit on the jaw and he had a hard time getting him started, but finly succeeded."

Much of the foregoing I have already given.

"He [Dalton] went probably 75 yards when his horse got his leg broke. He then got off of him & walked on the opposite side for a ways, then left him but came back to his saddlepockets & got his wire cutters & cut a fence, then got behind one of the other boys & rode off. A great many say he shot Shadly but I seen Shadly run from my place to Dr. Call's fence & in going through it he was first shot. He then got to Ransom's house & was debating with Mrs. Ransom, she ordering him to leave when he got his last shots. He fell there and crawled to Selph's cave.

"A great many believe that Dalton shot him; in fact he [Shadley] thot so for when I and Dr. Selph was working with him in the cave he said Dalton shot him 3 times quicker than he could turn around, but I think I know better, taking the lay of the ground in consideration & I saw Dalton most of the time & never saw him fire once & Shadly was hit in the right hip & all the balls tended downward. If Dalton had of shot him he would of been shot in front & balls ranged up.

"The outlaws crossed the draw south of town & stopped a few minutes shooting up the street my house is on. One of these shots hit Frank Briggs in the shoulder but a slight flesh wound. I took him to my cave and dressed his wound, then went to Walker & gave him Tempory [sic] aid, from there to Murry's & laid his wound open and removed the shattered bone. Some of the doctors wanted me to amputate but I fought for his arm.; 2 inches radius was shot away, eight flesh wounds in his side.

"About this time I was called aside & told to go to the Hotel, that Jones [Arkansas Tom's local alias] was up there either wounded or killed. I and Alva Peirce & boy by the name of Wendell, boy about 12 years old, went over. I went in and called but got no answer & was about to leave when he [Arkansas Tom] came to top of stairs & says 'is that you Dock?' and I told him it was. I asked him if he was hurt & he said no. He said for me to come up & I told him if he wasn't hurt I would not but he insisted. So I went up. He had his coat and vest of [f] also his boots. Had his Winchester in his hands & revolvers lying on the bed. I said Tom come down and surrender. He says 'I can't do it for I won't get justice.' He says: 'Where is the boys?' [the gang]. I told him they had gone. He said he did not think they would leave him. It hurt him bad. I never saw a man wilt so in my life. He staid in Hotel till after 2 o'clock & then surrendered to a Mr. Mason, a preacher. They took him off right away.

"Of the wounded, Simonds died at 6 P.M. Shadly and Huston was taken to Stillwater, both died in three or four days. Walker shot through the liver died the 16th. All the rest recovered. The outlaws staid close to town as Bitter Creek could not travel. Dr. Bland of Cushion [Cushing] tended him. I loaned him instruments to work on wound with although I did not know just where he [Bitter Creek] was at. A piece of magazine [from his rifle] was blown in his leg. It eventually worked out and he got able to ride again. Tom was indicted for the killing of Huston, Speed & Shadly, was tried on the Huston case and was convicted of manslaughter in the 1st degree with no leniency of the court. Judge dale sentenced him to 50 years at hard labor in the Lansing [Michigan] Peniteniary."

Arkansas Tom served less than seventeen years of his long sentence. His brother, a minister, devoted himself to securing his release. Marshal Bill Tilghman was one of Tom's stanchest supporters. After he was pardoned, Tom returned to Oklahoma and operated a restaurant at Drumright for a time, but he slipped back into outlawry, robbed a bank at Ashbury, Missouri, and was killed while resisting arrest in Joplin.

25

Rose of the Cimarron—
Fact and Fiction

❧

Today Old Ingalls is a ghost town, save for the northwest corner that has been annexed by the new town of Signet, with its oil derricks. On State Highway 51, several miles away, a historical marker records the outlaw battle of September 1, 1893. In the old town itself, at the main street intersection, stands a monument erected by "Citizens of Ingalls in 1938" dedicated to the memory of the three marshals who gave their lives in the famous battle. Grass and weeds cover the streets and what is left of the residue of the old buildings. Though the passing years bring fewer and fewer visitors, it is unlikely that old Ingalls will ever be forgotten —not because brave men once died there. The romantic legend surrounding the beautiful Rose of the Cimarron will keep its memory green.

"Many of the most exaggerated stories have been invented by out-of-town writers or some romantically inclined individuals," Leslie McRill wrote in 1958. "Poets and writers have seized the opportunity to make interesting reading, regardless of facts. One writer [Richard S. Graves] has woven a tale of one Cimarron Rose, giving lurid and daring actions on her part during the fight. How she saw Bitter Creek, wounded and snapping his empty pistol at the marshals—at which pastime he would have lasted five seconds at the most—and how she lowered his ammunition from the upper story of the Pierce Hotel, then lowered herself by means of a sheet, and went to his rescue. This one makes all the old-timers smile, as none of them believes she was in Ingalls that day, and it was known at that time that Bitter Creek was interested in another girl who stayed at the hotel.

"As the Guthrie paper *(The Daily Oklahoma State Capital)* suggested in a review of the Ingalls fight, 'There were romantic tales of what happened or might have happened. The one regarding the Cimarron Rose has persisted until it has gained credence and insinuated itself into both romantic fiction and poetry of the state. Old-timers say the girl was not in Ingalls the day of the fight. She was about fourteen or fifteen years of age. Her home was in Ingalls, but as she did not always agree with her step-father (Dr. Call), she stayed at the Bee Dunn ranch part of the time. That ranch was a mile east and a mile south of town. About fifteen years after the fight, the tale began to spread that she was Bitter Creek's girl. The outlaws did stay at the Dunn ranch occasionally, so there was some semblance of the connection suggested."

Let us go back to the beginning (in print) of the "Cimarron Rose" myth. Though it already had a good start by word-of-mouth telling, it was not until about 1915 that "Cimarron Rose" became "Rose of the Cimarron" in a little paperback, entitled *Oklahoma Outlaws—A Graphic History,* published locally in Oklahoma City, that related how she had slid down some bedsheets to succor her wounded outlaw sweetheart and drag him to safety. Cattle Annie and Little Breeches, the two girl bandits, who were real enough, also attained the dignity of the printed page.

Shortly thereafter, a motion picture of the independent, home-made variety was produced in Oklahoma, under the title of *The Passing of the Oklahoma Outlaws.* The intention had been to produce a "thriller," but even by the standards of that day, when not too much was to be expected in the way of entertainment, the picture was so loosely put together and the acting so crude, that it suffered from its own mediocrity. Its principal characters bore the names of well-known outlaws, many long since dead. There was one notable exception: Henry Starr, who had not yet reached the end of his criminal career, played himself, as did Marshals Bill Tilghman, Chris Madsen and Bud Ledbetter. Who wrote the "story," I do not know. It could have been Graves, for his paperback *Oklahoma Outlaws—A Graphic History* was huckstered in connection with the showing of the film and used to promote it.

Writing in *Life* several years ago, Zoe Tilghman, the marshal's widow, said: "Bill turned to making a movie, based largely on facts of his career. He exhibited this film *The Passing of the Oklahoma Outlaws,* in cities all over the country." Financially involved with him in the venture were others, among them Fred Sutton, the Oklahoma City banker and co-author of *Hands Up!* and former U.S. Marshal E. D. Nix. It was Tilghman who traveled with the picture, appearing on the stage and giving a brief talk at all showings, which has given rise to the mistaken idea that he was only hired to exploit it.

One of the recurring facets of the Rose of the Cimarron legend is that those who knew her true identity refused to reveal it because she later married and became a good wife and mother. Wellman refers to it as "mumbo jumbo," and I agree with him. They had nothing to conceal or reveal. Rose of the Cimarron was not created until twenty years and more later. There was Rose Dunn, Dr. Call's stepdaughter, of course. There was no secrecy about the fact that she was one of a score of Ingalls' citizens who were brought into Guthrie and held for questioning about their connection with the Doolin Gang. Because two of her brothers and her cousin Will Dunn bore unsavory reputations, she must have been a prime suspect. But, according to the *Oklahoma Capital,* all were released two days later, no evidence being found against them. But her name was Rose, she was young and pretty. Out of such material are legends born, waiting only for the alchemy of passing time to lend them credibility.

In an article in a recent issue of *The Brand Book,* the quarterly of the New York Westerners, Horan says: "Almost a decade ago, in my *Desperate Women* I was first to reveal that the Rose of the

Cimarron was in reality Rose Dunn. As a result I was promptly sued by Rose, but truth is the best defense weapon in a libel suit and after her lawyers saw my proof the suit was withdrawn." He is mistaken about being the first to make that statement; old Chris Madsen, still hale and hearty, had been saying it for years. However, Rose could have threatened him with a lawsuit. She was still alive and living quietly with her second husband, in Centralia, Washington. She was seventy-six years old when *Desperate Women* was published. But if she had reason to believe she was being libeled, it casts the gravest sort of doubt on the widely copied story in *Oklahombres* that she was arrested by Marshal Tilghman a few days after Bill Doolin escaped from the Guthrie prison in January, 1896, charged with carrying information to the Doolin Gang. Mrs. Tilghman has always insisted that the girl was never taken into custody by Bill. I do not accept it either. In fact, I question the entire incident of her being found guilty on that flimsy charge and being sentenced by Judge Andrew G. C. Bierer, at Perry, to two years in the Women's Reformatory, at Framingham (not Farmington, as some have it), Massachusetts—now called the Massachusetts Correctional Institution. (In an effort to learn if Rose Dunn was ever an inmate there, I appealed to a law enforcement acquaintance to get the information for me. The correspondence that followed failed to elicit the yes or no that I wanted, possibly because old prison records are no longer available or are incomplete.)

While I have an abiding respect for Evett Nix, *Oklahombres,* on which he permitted his name to be used as co-author, is so filled with errors that would have been apparent to him that I often wonder if he even bothered to read it. At the time of its publication, he was a successful banker in St. Louis, Missouri, and far removed by years from his early days in Oklahoma Territory. If Gordon Hines, who wrote the book, had supplied corroborative evidence regarding Rose Dunn being sentenced to two years in a Massachusetts reformatory, I would be much less skeptical. But that he fails to do. There is a presumption among investigators that, because in the years following the Ingalls fight the Doolins were often at the dugout of Will Dunn or Bee Dunn's ranch, some miles distant, where Rose sometimes stayed, she was impressed as a messenger to bring them medicines and possibly food. Very likely that is true. It could have been done at her brother's urging and not, as has often been said, to succor her alleged outlaw sweetheart, Bitter Creek.

When Rose Dunn was brought before Judge Bierer, in the spring of 1896, as has been stated, Perry was the rawest, toughest town of any size in the Territory, born on the first day of the great "run." On the townsite, where there had been nothing at dawn, eight thousand frenzied men and women were crowded together by nightfall. A mile away to the north at Wharton station, where the Dalton Gang had staged their first holdup, the late trains were disgorging additional thousands. To establish some semblance of law and order in that seething madhouse where food and water were not procurable and fifty tent saloons were doing a roaring business, Marshals Tilghman, Thomas and Madsen were rushed up from Guthrie. Since it was soon apparent that Perry was to become the most important town in the Strip, a federal court was established there and Andrew Bierer took the bench.

I know nothing about Bierer's qualifications, but if he followed the rules of legal jurisprudence, he had to hear evidence against a prisoner at the bar before he could find him guilty. Who was it that testified against Rose Dunn? They have never been identified. I would like to know who they were. And what was it they could have said against her? It must have been very damaging to have drawn from Judge Bierer that same sentence he had previously handed out to those two little she-wildcats, Cattle Annie (Annie McDougall) and Little Breeches (Jennie Metcalf) who were guilty of selling whisky to the Osages, stealing cattle and unmistakably acting as spies and lookouts for the Doolin Gang. They were no older than Rose, but they were range waifs, hard, vicious, ignorant, and always went armed with rifle and six-gun. When marshals Tilghman and Steve Burke finally cornered them at a ranch near Pawnee, they did their best to kill the two men. Even after they were disarmed, they fought with tooth and nail until they were subdued. Rose Dunn was none of those things. The worst that can be said against her is that she was the sister of Dal, George and Bee Dunn, and the cousin of Will Dunn—all hard cases and suspected horse thieves.

The real Rose Elizabeth Dunn was never a person of any importance; in legend she is tremendous—the subject of at least half a dozen books, countless magazine pieces and two major motion pictures. Mrs. Tilghman, a young girl herself at the time, was well acquainted with her. In an interview, she recalled their first meeting:

"The first time I met her was at a schoolhouse supper. The supper was followed by what was called an 'entertainment.' This kind of entertainment would be looked down on now, but in those simple days we enjoyed it very much. She was there with her sister-in-law, Mrs. Bee Dunn. Rose had dark hair and dark, luminous eyes, a good complexion, a fine figure and was, by far, the best-looking girl present. Boxes containing supper were raffled off; the owners of the boxes were not supposed to be known—you must take your chance. But the wink went round that a certain food-laden box was Rose's. It brought the highest price of the evening, and it was really hers."

She was born near Winfield, in Cowley County, Kansas, on September 5, 1878. It was not a large family for those days, five boys and one girl. Rose was the youngest. They were well-to-do, and though the Dunns were not Catholic, Rose was sent to a convent in Wichita for schooling for two years. When her father died, her mother married Dr. Call. Shortly after that she moved to Ingalls with her mother and stepfather. Her brother Bee was already there, and George, Dal and her cousin Will were living in Pawnee County, not far away. Bee was the most prosperous of the lot, and it was his prosperity that cast suspicion on the means by which it was achieved.

They were hard, rough men. Evidently Dr. Call was well enough acquainted with their secret activities to warn Rose that they were headed for trouble and to order her to keep away from them. The result was what might have been expected. Being an independent, high-spirited girl, she resented his efforts to turn her against her brothers, especially against Bee, always her favorite, and she willfully spent more time than ever at the ranch. It was the beginning of continuing dissention between her and her stepfather.

That was the situation when Bitter Creek Newcomb and the Doolins first appeared in Ingalls. Rose Dunn was fifteen. No one has ventured to say how old Bitter Creek was. The perpetrators of the Rose of the Cimarron–Bitter Creek legend refer to him as being a "boy," and help their case with the reminder that under another alias he was known as the "Slaughter Kid." The way I figure it, he was twenty-eight, or very likely twenty-nine—a ripe old age for a man of his experience to be romancing a girl of fifteen and making her his mistress.

Newcomb was born on a farm near Fort Scott, Kansas. After Wichita faded as a market for Texas longhorns, Caldwell got the business. For a Kansas boy with Texas on his mind, the best way of getting there was to ride into Caldwell and catch on with one of the big outfits that had finished shipping, and be sent down the Chisholm Trail with the trail crew that was returning to Texas. George Newcomb was sixteen or seventeen at the time. It is not likely that he made the long trip on his own. Colonel C. C. Slaughter shipped from Caldwell as late as 1881, which just about marked the finish of the Chisholm Trail, the big herds shifting to Doan's Store crossing on Red River and going up the new Western Trail to Dodge City. Newcomb may have gone down with some other outfit. Whether he did or not, he was soon working for Slaughter and stayed with him long enough to win the sobriquet of the "Slaughter Kid."

When he left Texas, he cowboyed on ranches in western Oklahoma Territory long before he went to work for Oscar Halsell on the H X Bar. He had left boyhood far behind him by that time. Further proof of it lies in the fact that Roy Daugherty (Arkansas Tom) the "baby" of the Doolin Gang was twenty-two at the time of the Ingalls fight.

Undoubtedly Rose met Newcomb at dances and such parties as Mrs. Tilghman described. But that does not warrant saying they were sweethearts; in a town as small as Ingalls, with its gossips and prying eyes, I doubt that girls of fifteen were having "affairs" with men almost twice their age.

Other cracks appear in the legend when carefully examined. In 1898, Rose married Charles Noble, of Lawson P. O., Payne County (not to be confused with the town of Lawton in Comanche County). He and his brother Thomas were blacksmiths and well-diggers. On information supplied by them, a posse of deputy marshals had cornered and killed Bill Doolin in September 1896. Bitter Creek was Doolin's loyal follower. Frontier ethics being what they were, I protest that had he and Rose Dunn been sweethearts, she never would have married a man who had had a hand in his chief's killing.

It was a long marriage and, there being no evidence to the contrary, presumably a happy one. Noble died in 1932. Rose continued to live on in Ingalls, and on June 18, 1946, she married Richard A. Fleming who, after an absence of many years, returned to Ingalls, where he had grown up with her. They left Oklahoma and after a brief stay at Mt. Ayr, New Mexico, moved to Washington, where she died and lies buried in the Salkum Cemetery at Chehalis—no one aware of what is idiotically described by some writers as her "lurid" past.

As befits a mythical figure, there are not and never were any photographs of the legendary Rose of the Cimarron. For thirty-five years an alleged photograph of her, showing a comely young girl in a homemade dress and wide-brimmed hat, fondling a six-shooter, has gone the rounds of books, newspaper and magazine pieces. Long ago, however, Mrs. Tilghman disclosed that it was a hoax, arranged by her husband to escape the clamorous demands of news photographers. The girl who did the posing, identity unknown, was a prisoner in the Guthrie jail at the time.

26

Empty Saddles

THE Cherokee Strip was thrown open to settlement at noon on September 16, 1893, barely more than two weeks after the Ingalls fight, and the chaos that Doolin had foreseen followed immediately. Marshal Nix and his deputies were so swamped with work that they were literally needed in a hundred places at once. With their hands full elsewhere, it was impossible to organize and prosecute a relentless search for the outlaw gang. Had the Doolins been in condition to ride, the situation would have been made to order for them. But they were not. The bullet that had cut through the back of Doolin's neck injured a nerve, and though the wound healed, it was to bother him for the rest of his life. Bitter Creek, weak from loss of blood and his leg swollen to twice its normal size, was much worse off. Bill Dalton was ailing, too. He had come out of the fight with a bullet in his shoulder.

Doolin ordered the gang to scatter until he called them together again. As previously stated, Dalton had bought or rented a small ranch some thirty miles west of Ardmore, far down in the Chickasaw country, where his wife was living. He joined her there. I can find no evidence that he ever rode with Doolin again. The latter, accompanied by Bitter Creek, went to Hot Springs, Arkansas, in the hope that the mineral baths would help them back to health.

By the end of the year, conditions in the new towns that had sprung up in the old Cherokee Strip, now part of Oklahoma Territory, were stable enough to permit Nix to resume his search for the Doolin Gang. They had killed three of his deputies, and he meant to have them for it. Some of the gang's old hide-outs were located, but it was evident that they had been deserted for months.

The game of hide-and-seek continued into spring without contact with the gang being made. By then, it was apparent that the Doolins had quit the Territory. They were in fact at that time—late May or early June—at rendezvous somewhere in northwest Arkansas, very likely along the Illinois River, east of Siloam Springs, in Benton County, which would have placed them in position for their next foray. In the meantime, Doolin had been slipping back into Payne County and courting Edith Ellsworth, daughter of a minister living near Lawson P. O. Whether they were married there or in Arkansas, or whether Edith Ellsworth knew she was marrying an outlaw, I have never learned. But they were married in the summer of 1894. That can be documented.

It was only a matter of weeks when Doolin turned from romance to business. In Wild West fashion, he led his men across the Arkansas line into Southwest City, Missouri, and robbed the Seaborn Bank, relieving it of approximately $15,000. J. C. Seaborn and his brother ran out into the street as the bandits were fleeing. One of them fired a shot that passed through the younger Seaborn's body doing little damage but boring into J. C. Seaborn, formerly state auditor, and killing him.

This bank had the distinction of having been touched up once before, by Texas Jack and his merry men.

Heading back to their old haunts, the Doolins turned aside momentarily and cleaned out the bank at Pawnee, getting $10,000.

As for money, they were in clover, but from the sources of information they had available—"tick birds who lived off outlaws," as Al Jennings once told me—they learned that the friendly brakes of the Cimarron no longer were a safe hiding place. Reluctantly they left the river and, with winter coming on, hid out briefly in different places, staying in each only long enough to confuse whoever might be trailing them, moving north one week and doubling back the next. Their wanderings ended at a lonely ranch in the wildest part of Pawnee County where, believing they had thrown off possible pursuit, they holed up in a dugout with the owner.

In presenting the saga of Bill Doolin, no writer has failed to underscore what happened at that dugout in the blackjack hills of Pawnee County. In the course of many retellings, some details have been added to heighten its dramatic impact. But it is basically true. I first heard it from Al Jennings more than forty years ago, and no one has ever told it better.

On a cold, blustery January day, a blizzard in the making, Bill Tilghman and Neal Brown drove up to the dugout in a wagon. If you have read that they did not know where they were, you have been misinformed. Tilghman had been there before; he knew the dugout belonged to Will Dunn. Some have it that he and Brown were accompanied by an Indian driver. This I doubt, for Neal Brown was a host in himself and a deputy marshal.

The two men were old acquaintances, dating back to their Dodge City days, where Brown, a half-blood Cherokee, had served as a policeman on several occasions and had the distinction of sitting as a member of the famous "Dodge City Peace Commission" —an honor not shared by Tilghman. The two of them had left Dodge together soon after the opening of Old Oklahoma.

Tilghman left Brown in the wagon, and, perhaps fortunately, also his rifle. While he knew where he was, he certainly was not prepared for what he was to find there. He and Brown had been on the move for days, trying without success to discover the whereabouts of the Doolin Gang. Knowing that the law could expect little help from Will Dunn and his cousins Bee, Dal and George, he nevertheless had stopped that stormy afternoon to put a few questions to him. He called out the usual halloo as he approached the door. Getting no answer, he pushed in. At the far end of the long room, with its dirt floor, a man sat crouched over at the fireplace, a rifle resting on his knees. The only light came from the flickering flames of the burning blackjack logs.

Tilghman called a greeting and got a surly response and walked up to the fire and turned his back to it to warm himself. As he stood there, his eyes adjusted themselves to the semidarkness of the dugout. Both sides of the room were lined with curtained double-decker bunks, in typical cow camp fashion—but there was a difference. Peering out from every bunk was the business end of a Winchester, and they were all trained on him. In a flash, he realized that he had blundered into the hide-out of the Doolin Gang. They were all here—all eight of them.

It was a moment calling for nerves of chilled steel. Tilghman proved that he had them. Unhurried, though his life hung in the balance, he said half-facetiously:

"Will, how does a man get out of here?"

"The same damn way he got in," was the growling answer.

Tilghman started walking. For the rest of his life, he said it was the longest walk he ever took.

As he neared the door, there was a scuffle behind him, but he did not glance back. Climbing into the wagon, he ordered Brown to "get away fast."

They drove into Pawnee that evening and found Deputy Marshal John Hale there. They organized a posse and, despite a howling blizzard, were back at the dugout at dawn. The gang had fled. To clear himself, Will Dunn claimed that the Doolins had moved in on him and taken possession of his place and that he was surly because he feared they would kill him if he seemed friendly to the law.

"They recognized you before you got out of the wagon," he told Tilghman. "When you was leaving, Red Buck leaped out of his bunk and was pulling down on you. Doolin stopped him. 'What the hell, Bill!' Red Buck snorted. 'We left him to you and now you're letting him get away.' 'That's all right,' Bill told him. 'Tilghman's too good a man to be shot in the back.' "

Tilghman never forgot it. He and Doolin were superior men. Though they were on opposite sides of the fence, they respected each other as a worthy foe.

Nothing more was heard of the Doolin Gang until noon on May 4, 1895, when they held up a Rock Island train at Dover, north of Kingfisher, where the Dalton family had lived for years. From the express safe and passengers, they collected several thousand dollars.

Marshal Chris Madsen, thirty-five miles away in El Reno, got news of the robbery off the wire a few minutes after it happened. The Rock Island put a locomotive and boxcar at his disposal. Into the car he loaded horses and men and steamed north at full speed. Two hours later, they were in Dover and on the trail of the bandits. The Doolins, not believing pursuit could be so quickly organized, pulled up in a wooded glen ten miles east of town, to blow their horses and divide their loot. They were caught by surprise when Madsen and his posse charged over a ridge several hundred yards away. Before the outlaws could get into the saddle, Red Buck Waightman's horse was struck and killed. Tulsa Jack's mount went down a moment later.

Doolin and the others dropped back into some timber. Red Buck and Tulsa Jack ran to join them. Red Buck made it; Tulsa Jack fell, dying. Bitter Creek swung in close to Red Buck, who got up behind. The posse followed the retreating outlaws into the timber, but many of its members lost some of their enthusiasm for chasing bandits as the slugs began to whine about their heads. A running fight was kept up until twilight descended. During the night the bandits made good their escape.

With daylight, Red Buck began looking for a horse. Passing a cabin, he saw an animal in a corral, and while the others waited, he went after it. In a small barn made of pickets, he found a saddle and bridle. As he was saddling up, an elderly man ran out of the cabin, protesting the stealing of his horse. Red Buck Waightman turned on the unarmed old-timer with a curse and, drawing his six-gun, put enough lead into him to have killed him three times over. It was wanton, cold-blooded murder.

When the band had ridden on for a mile, Doolin told his men to get down. He finished counting out the money from the Dover robbery and gave each man his share, then got to his feet and faced Red Buck. "Now you git!" he is reported to have said. "You had no reason to kill that old man. You're too damn low to associate with a high-class bunch of men. You git!"

This incident can not be documented. There was no one to report it; but it has appeared so often that I give it for what it is worth. This much is fact: Red Buck no longer rode with the Doolins.

Not long after Red Buck was driven out, the Doolin Gang crossed the Territory to Woodward, in the northwest corner of Oklahoma, intending to hold up a Sante Fe train. They camped several miles to the east of town, and Bitter Creek, Little Bill Raidler and Charlie Pierce were sent in to learn what they could about the express shipments that were going through. Their sleuthing disclosed that a shipment of money had reached Woodward on an evening train and was reposing over night in the express company's Woodward office. Seeing no need to make the long ride out to camp to inform the others, they kidnapped the agent and brought him down to the office, where he was forced to open the company safe. For this bit of brain work, they received something in the neighborhood of $6,000.

Shortly after the Woodward robbery, the gang scattered for a few months to give the hunt for them time to cool off. Doolin gave them a date and a place where they were to rendezvous with him. The place he named was Bee Dunn's ranch, near Ingalls. Whether this was by prearrangement, I do not know. Very likely it was, and it lends veracity to the tale that Bee owed Doolin nine hundred dollars which he could not repay. Using his ranch was, therefore, not simply a matter of hospitality.

The gang had disbanded temporarily on several previous occasions. As they parted, it hardly could have occurred to them that this parting was to be any different from the ones that had preceded it. But it was; as things fell out, they were never to "ride" together again.

Doolin had bought a small farm near Burden, Kansas. His wife and baby son were there. With great secrecy, he joined them. Adopting the alias of William J. Barry, he lived on the Burden farm for six months, unsuspected, law-abiding and church-going.

Some commentators say that he promised his wife that he was through with outlawry. Perhaps he did; but I have too much respect for the demonstrated intelligence of the man to believe that he ever seriously entertained the idea that he could divorce himself from the past simply by going straight. The law had so many grudges against him that sooner or later it would hunt him down and demand atonement.

Through the long, hot summer months of 1895 the hunt for the

Doolin Gang was pursued relentlessly but without success, even though Marshal Nix had assigned his top men to the job. By the end of August, it was obvious that the Doolins had scattered following the Woodward robbery, and to a certainty would be gathering again somewhere before September was very old. Shortly thereafter, another bank would be robbed or a train held up. Discovering where the gang was to rendezvous was now vitally important. One possible way of getting the desired information was through an unsavory character like Will Dunn. They were agreed that he was worthless and would do anything for money. He had harbored outlaws, and the offense could be used to whip him into line.

Tilghman was delegated to make the deal, whatever it was. It resulted in Will Dunn being secretly commissioned a deputy marshal. Resorting to black treachery, he rode to Bee's ranch, as he had done so many times before, and without disclosing his changed status, got his cousin to confide in him that Bitter Creek, Bill Raidler, Dynamite Dick and Charlie Pierce had been there earlier in the week, expecting to meet Doolin. Bill had not put in an appearance, and the others had left, informing Bee that they would be back in a few days.

Armed with this precious information, Will Dunn left the ranch ostensibly to ride into Ingalls. His real destination was Stillwater, twelve miles to the west, where Tilghman and Heck Thomas were headquartering. With time all-important, Tilghman swore in three possemen and, with them, Thomas and Will Dunn, left for Bee Dunn's place at once, arriving there at daylight.

At first, Bee denied knowing anything about the Doolins. Will Dunn confounded him by admitting that he had changed sides and was now riding with the law. Given the choice between arrest for consorting with known outlaws, based on the information he had given his cousin in confidence, and cooperating with the officers, Bee reluctantly chose the latter course. A trap was laid, and the marshals and possemen settled down to wait for the quarry to ride into their hands.

They had a long wait. Two days and nights passed without anyone coming. Inside the house, which was more commodious than most ranch houses of that time and country, Tilghman, Bee Dunn and two of the possemen kept watch at the front and west-side windows. A hailstorm had broken the window on the east side and it was boarded up. To overcome that handicap, a shallow pit was dug out in the yard and roofed over with poles and sod. In it Heck Thomas, Will Dunn and the third posseman lay concealed and watchful.

Late on the third night the waiting men caught the drumming of horses hoofs approaching from the east. The moonlight was bright, and presently two horsemen detached themselves from the shadows of the high brush and came pounding up to the house, in which no lights were burning. They slid down from their saddles and were tethering their horses, when Thomas called on them to surrender. For one paralyzed second the two men, Bitter Creek Newcomb and Charlie Pierce, stood rooted in their tracks. The next moment, without any thought of attempting to flee, they whipped up their six-guns. An orange streak from the makeshift rifle pit told them where the enemy lay hidden. They charged the pit, their pistols spitting lead.

It was revolvers against Winchesters and no contest. Bitter Creek was the first to go down. Charlie Pierce was within a foot or two of the riflemen when he pitched forward on his face. Tilghman and the others came running from the house and examined the two men as the thunder of gunfire died away on the far reaches of the prairie. Both were dead.

It was learned later that Dynamite Dick and Little Bill Raidler had intended to accompany Bitter Creek and Pierce. Only a drinking bout had kept them from it. When they learned what had happened, they separated at once, seeking places in which to hide. Unwittingly, Dynamite Dick rode right into the hands of Deputy Marshals Steve Burke, Bill Nix and Will Jones, at a country store on Black Bear Creek, west of Pawnee, where the marshals had stopped to eat lunch.

Burke recognized the bandit as the latter turned his horse into the hitch-rack in front of the store. And at the same moment, Dynamite Dick recognized him. Six-guns were chattering almost instantly. The split-second advantage of being the first to fire belonged to the marshals. When Dynamite Dick toppled out of the saddle, his right arm was shattered, another slug had broken his right hip and a third bullet had lodged in his lungs. He was taken by wagon to Perry and by train to Guthrie, and placed in jail, where pneumonia developed and he died.

Tilghman and Thomas were still on the hunt for Little Bill Raidler. In Pawhuska, a friendly Osage Indian informed them that the educated, poetry-quoting bandit was hiding out on the Sam Moore ranch, close to the Kansas line. The two marshals rode north to the Moore ranch and questioned Moore and his wife. They admitted that Little Bill was hid out somewhere in the hills, just where, they did not know, but that he was in the habit of showing up almost every evening and coming to the house for supper, after putting his horse in the corral.

As dusk settled into black night, Tilghman took a position at one of the rear corners of the cabin, Thomas at the other. Flattening themselves against the building, they peered out cautiously in the direction of the corral. After a short wait they heard a horse coming, just jogging along. It was Little Bill. He put his horse in the corral and started across the yard for the cabin. He was only a few yards away when Tilghman ordered him to throw up his hands. The unexpected summons had an electric effect on Raidler. He seemed to bound into the air, and when he came down he had a six-gun in each hand and they were firing.

Tilghman described that moment graphically, and thanks to Mrs. Tilghman it was recorded:

"Did you ever see a dog creep stealthily up on a cat sleeping in the sun, and suddenly bark, and the cat spring up in the air, with its back hunched, and spitting fire? That's the way Little Bill acted. When I shouted he went up in the air as if he'd been thrown from a springboard, and as he went he pulled a six-shooter in each hand, and he shot at me before he hit the ground. I never saw a man draw and shoot so quickly."

A bullet struck Tilghman in the shoulder, inflicting a slight wound—one of the very few times in all his years as an officer that he was wounded. He fired at Raidler, so did Thomas; the shots so nearly simultaneous that neither could be sure who dropped the bandit. The slug tore into Little Dick's body, just missing the lungs, it was discovered later. The marshals thought he was mortally wounded. He was placed in a wagon and driven to Elgin, Kansas, ten miles away, where the bullet was extracted. Two days later, still hovering between life and death, he was placed on a cot in a Missouri Pacific baggage car and, by way of Winfield and the Sante Fe Railroad, taken to Guthrie.

Little Bill proved that he was as tough as bullhide. He fought off pneumonia and recovered from his wound. He was tried and convicted of multiple robberies and sentenced to twenty-one years in the Ohio State Penitentiary, at Columbus, of which he served less than half when he was pardoned, largely through the intercession of Bill Tilghman, which subjected the latter to some criticism by the few who could not understand the magnanimity that impelled him to ask mercy for a confirmed outlaw.

In an almost unbroken skein of forty years, Bill Tilghman, in his various roles as deputy sheriff, town marshal of Dodge, chief of police of Oklahoma City and U.S. deputy marshal, was as responsible as any man for the taming of the wild and lawless West of his day. His career is too well-known to need recounting or embellishment. Of the man himself, less is known. It has always seemed to me that no better way to measure the caliber of Bill Tilghman can be found than in his feeling about the men whom he hunted so relentlessly. He had their respect, we know. In a way, they had his, for in his eyes the bad and the good in men were so badly scrambled that no man was all bad: there was something worth saving in even the worst of men; many, given a second chance, would come out of prison and make good citizens.

Arkansas Tom had failed him, and later, Henry Starr was to disappoint him. But not so Little Bill Raidler, who married soon after his release from prison and lived inside the law until his death, ten years later.

Presumably Doolin learned from the newspapers, if from no other source, how his gang was being cut down. He must have wondered who would be next to go. Possibly himself. The wound he had suffered in the Ingalls fight was bothering him more and more. A country doctor could not help him. He wanted to go to Wichita and consult a specialist, but he was afraid to risk it. Marshal Nix and his deputies had completely lost track of him.

Bill Dalton had disappeared just as mysteriously. He was neither seen nor heard of in months. And then one day, late in September, a case of whisky, carefully disguised, reached the express office at

Ardmore, prepaid and marked to be held until called for. It lay there for several days, and the agent became suspicious that it contained liquor. Under federal law it was a criminal offense to bring alcoholic beverages into the Chickasaw Nation. Deputy Loss Hart happened to be in Ardmore. The express agent consulted him.

On examining the case, Hart agreed that it very likely held whisky. He had no authority to open it, so he settled down to wait until someone called for it. Once the party had it in his possession, he would demand that it be opened for his inspection. If it held whisky, he would take the man into custody.

It was not a man who called for it, however. A woman drove up to the railroad station in a buggy and inquired for a box that her husband was expecting. The name she gave corresponded with the one on the shipment. As soon as she had receipted for it, Loss Hart identified himself and demanded that the box be opened. The flustered woman admitted the name on the case was an assumed one and that it contained whisky. When she refused to give her real name and state where she lived, Deputy Hart went to work on her. Trapped in her story, she was forced to acknowledge that she was Mrs. William Dalton and disclosed where she and Bill were living.

The marshal locked her up and swore in a posse. On the morning of September 25, he had the hide-out surrounded. When Dalton saw half a dozen armed men closing in on the house, he knew what it meant. Buckling on his gunbelt, he leaped through an open window in a desperate attempt to escape.

It has been said many times that only one shot was fired that morning and that it came from Loss Hart's Winchester. Loss caught Dalton on the wing, so to speak, and he was dead when he hit the ground. The last of the outlaw Daltons was now accounted for, and of the eleven members of the Doolin Gang, only three remained at large—castoff Red Buck Waightman, Little Dick West and Doolin himself.

When Dalton was killed, Chris Madsen was twenty miles west of Fort Sill. By chance, he encountered two Texas Rangers who had crossed Red River in pursuit of two men wanted for murder and highway robbery. They were beyond their jurisdiction, but that was not unusual, the ownership of part of Comanche, Kiowa and all of Greer County still being in dispute between Texas and Oklahoma Territory. The identity of one of the fugitives was known to the Rangers; the description they gave of his companion fitted Red Buck Waightman so closely that Madsen did not hesitate. Swearing in the Rangers as possemen to avoid any legal tangle, the three men headed north. Luck was with them, and in northern Comanche County they caught up with the pair they were trailing. One of them was Red Buck. There was a brief fight. Red Buck was wounded but escaped; the other man was killed. The Rangers turned back to Texas with the body and Madsen took up the trail of Red Buck.

Near Arapaho, in Custer County, he located the dugout in which Waightman was hiding. Putting together a posse, mostly Indian, he threw a ring of armed men around it. After some hours of watching, Red Buck came out with a bucket on his arm and started for the well. The bucket went flying when Madsen called out for him to throw up his hands, and in the same motion he drew his murderous pistols. Rifles cracked. Red Buck was dead before he could fire a shot.

27

The Law Catches Up

FOLLOWING THE KILLING of Red Buck, Marshal Nix called his top men together in Guthrie. It was premature, he contended, to regard the Doolin Gang as broken up as long as Bill Doolin, the leader, was still running free. The old gang had been cut to pieces, but unless he was captured or slain, he would very likely recruit a new gang, and it might be as formidable as the old. To find him, and quickly, was to be the first order of business.

Tilghman volunteered to run him down. He was the man Nix wanted for the job. He relieved him of other duties and left him free to proceed as he pleased.

The hocus-pocus offered by some writers as the means by which he picked up Doolin's trail is difficult to accept. They have Tilghman pressuring Mary Pierce (the Ingalls hotelkeeper) with arrest for harboring outlaws unless she told him what she knew about Doolin's whereabouts; they say that Mrs. Pierce turned informer and gave him the address and alias under which the outlaw leader was living in Kansas. This was in November 1895, two years after the Ingalls fight, when the alleged offense took place. It passes belief that if the law had any claim on Mrs. Pierce it would have waited that long before doing something about it. That Tilghman would have had any reason for suspecting she had information about Doolin is equally incredible. Of course, a reason is invented, and it is nothing short of absurd. The way the story goes, Mrs. Doolin visited Bill in Ingalls prior to the big fight and Mrs. Pierce became acquainted with her. (Which would have been impossible, for Bill and Edith Ellsworth were not married until a year later.) Mrs. Doolin had written Mrs. Pierce recently, asking her to forward a ring she had left at the hotel, instructing her to send it to "Mrs. Will Barry," Burden, Kansas.

I say "recently" because the Kansas address had been in effect for only three or four months. Does a woman seeking the recovery of a forgotten ring wait two years before asking a hotelkeeper to mail it to her? All this is lame invention. But Tilghman got the Burden address from someone, and I venture the surmise that he got it from Bee Dunn.

If anyone in or around Ingalls had any contact with Doolin, it was Bee Dunn. Remember that he owed Doolin nine hundred dollars, which the latter was undoubtedly demanding, coupling it with some understandable threats against Dunn for the traitorous part he played in the killing of Bitter Creek and Charlie Pierce. Fearful of the man's vengeance, no one had better reason for wanting to see the bandit leader put away. Remember, too, that he was born and raised near Winfield, half a dozen miles from Burden. He was in a position to give information that could be pinpointed.

Back in Guthrie, Nix tried to persuade Tilghman not to go to Kansas alone, but Tilghman insisted on it.

"If I take a posse with me, there'll be shooting and Doolin will be killed," he said. "I believe he saved my life once. I want to bring him in alive."

Armed with a federal warrant and garbed as a minister in a hard hat and a frock coat that concealed his pistol. he entrained for the north.

His first business in Burden was with the postmaster, who, when the marshal produced the credentials Nix had given him, informed him that Mrs. Barry was no longer receiving mail at Burden. She had left no forwarding address, but it was suggested to Tilghman that he try the Winfield post office. There he learned that she was receiving two or three letters a week postmarked Eureka Springs, a small health resort in the northwestern corner of Arkansas. Its baths were said to have a "magnetic" quality, beneficial in the treatment of nervous disorders.

Tilghman did not know that Doolin was ailing and had gone to the spa for his health; what he saw in sleepy Eureka Springs was an almost perfect hide-out for a notorious outlaw. He took the next train east and before noon of the following day, December 5, arrived at the health resort. After registering and being assigned a bathhouse, he walked through the lobby, intending to look the little town over, when he was amazed to see Doolin seated at one of the windows reading a newspaper. The bandit leader glanced the marshal's way but failed to recognize him in his ministerial garb.

Tilghman says he turned back to the men's room and examined his revolver. Coming out, he walked up to Doolin and said: "Bill, I'm arresting you."

Even then Doolin was slow to recognize him. When he did, he leaped to his feet and his right hand darted under his coat, reaching for the revolver he wore in a shoulder holster. The pressure of the business end of Tilghman's six-gun was hard against his stomach.

"Bill, don't make me kill you," said Tilghman, clutching the other's arm. "I haven't forgotten what you did for me in Will Dunn's dugout."

Doolin only struggled the harder. This was a battle of life and death, and both men realized it. Doolin's sleeve began to rip. Tilghman could feel it tearing beneath his fingers. A few inches more and the outlaw's hand would close on his gun. The marshal knew he could wait no longer; that he had to do what he did not want to do.

"Good-by, Bill," he panted, lungs heaving.

Their eyes held for an anguished split second, and Doolin realized that this was the end of the line; that death was only a moment away if he persisted.

"All right, you win," he jerked out.

Tilghman disarmed him and took him upstairs so he could

gather up his things. On the bureau, he saw a small pewter cup with the word "Baby" engraved on it. Doolin had bought it for his infant son.

"I wish you'd see that the little fellow gets it," said he.

"I will," Tilghman promised. "If you give me your word that you won't try to break away, I'll spare you the humiliation of being taken to Guthrie in handcuffs. Your word is all I want, Bill."

"You've got it, Marshal."

Word of Doolin's capture had been flashed to the capital, and when Tilghman arrived with his famous prisoner, several thousand people were at the station. Police had to clear a path for the two men. As they were passing, a young woman exclaimed, "You don't look so terrible, Mr. Doolin. I believe I could have captured you myself."

"I believe you could," Doolin assured her, a twinkle in his eyes.

Though he was in jail and certain to face multiple charges of armed robbery and murder, he seemed untroubled. He had many visitors and talked freely. Most of the Doolin lore that has come down to us was related by him at that time. He made friends with his jailers. If one of them wanted a laugh, he could always find it at the door of Doolin's cell. He told them fantastic stories of the loot he had buried in different places and almost, but not quite, told them where they could find it.

On a cold Sunday night, early in January 1896, a turnkey stopped at his cell. Doolin soon had him laughing convulsively, and as the man threw back his head in merriment, Doolin reached through the bars and relieved him of his revolver. Keeping the guard covered, he unlocked his cell door, traded places with him and proceeded to release every man in the jail. Most of those who escaped were quickly recaptured, but not Doolin. He walked out by himself and, a few blocks away, held up a young man and a girl in a rig, made them get out and drove to the outskirts of town, where he unhitched the horse and lit out for parts unknown. Seven months were to pass before the law caught up with him again.

As the months passed, Doolin was reported to be here and there. Bank robberies occurred and he was believed to have had a hand in them. When run down, these tales proved to have no substance, as did the rumors that he had made contact with Little Dick West, the only member of his original gang still alive and free, and that they were running together. As a matter of proven fact, nothing appears in the record between January and September to say where Doolin was and what he was doing. But in the absence of any evidence to the contrary, it is difficult to believe that he was inactive all that time. Even though he must have realized that conditions in the Territory were changing rapidly and that the era of the horseback outlaw was almost over, he hardly could have withstood the temptation to engage in the traditional "last job" that would provide him with a stake with which to get himself and his family out of the country. If he engaged in such a venture, he escaped being identified with it.

Mrs. Doolin had long since left the Burden farm and returned to her father's home near Lawson. Tilghman knew she was there. He must have visited her, for she had in her possession the pewter baby cup he had promised to deliver.

The house was watched for months in the belief that drawn by his love for his wife and two-year-old son, it was there, if anywhere, Doolin could be expected to appear. The presence of marshals in the neighborhood seemed always to be known to him. He visited his wife on several occasions and managed to slip away undetected. The surveillance having proved a failure, Marshal Heck Thomas was brought in and placed in charge. Resorting to cunning, he induced the Noble brothers, Thomas and Charles, the well-diggers and blacksmiths, to turn informers against Doolin. The marshal then withdrew with his posse and retired to Ingalls, twenty miles away.

Charles, the younger of the Noble brothers, was the man who married Rose Dunn. Whether it was money or a sense of duty that set them to watching the home of the Reverend Ellsworth has never been disclosed. However it was, their spying brought results, and late in August they got word to Heck Thomas that Doolin was visiting his wife and child and planning to leave the country with them. The marshal and a posse left for Lawson at once, and closed in on the house on the night of August 25.

The moon was bright, and standing at the front door, they saw a team hitched to a wagon that appeared to be loaded for a long trip, with a saddle horse tethered to the end-gate. They realized at once that they had arrived just in time; in another few minutes the quarry would have slipped through their fingers. As it was, they no more had the front and back of the house covered when Doolin stepped out, his rifle crooked in his arm. Though he had allowed his beard to grow, Thomas recognized him at once. The outlaw glanced around suspiciously as he waited for his wife to join him. She came out then, the sleeping baby in her arms. She too peered about nervously.

Doolin kissed both and helped them to get into the wagon. Mrs. Doolin placed the child in an improvised bed in back of the seat.

"Drive down to the creek," they heard him tell her. "I'll walk on ahead; there may be someone in the willows."

She picked up the reins and he started walking. Thomas, veteran man-hunter, knew it was now or never. He was carrying a heavy eight-bore shotgun loaded with buck. At thirty yards there was no more deadly weapon. With the gun half-raised, he stepped out of the shadows and commanded the bandit leader to throw up his hands. Doolin's rifle leaped to his shoulder as he whirled. His snap shot missed. Both barrels of the shotgun thundered then and Doolin went down, his chest and stomach literally riddled with buckshot. He was dead when the marshal and his possemen reached him. Mrs. Doolin leaped out of the wagon, screaming, and threw herself on her dead husband.

The marshals were sympathetic, but they had only done their duty. In the wagon Heck Thomas found the little pewter cup that Bill Tilghman had promised Doolin the baby should have.

The body was taken to Guthrie, where it was viewed by thousands, and not only by the morbidly curious. Oscar Halsell, Judge Dale, Marshal Nix, Bill Tilghman and the host of deputy marshals, who had warred against him for three years, attended his funeral and saw nothing incongruous in doing so.

I am not going to try to evaluate the character of Bill Doolin. Admittedly, he had many good qualities. But he robbed banks, held up trains and killed many men, though he killed only those who were trying to kill him. He was an outlaw, however, and richly deserved the end that overtook him. By every definition of the word, he was a criminal. If, as many claim, the criminal tendencies of the father are transmitted to his offspring, and we have criminals by heredity, then Bill Doolin's son should have grown up to become a supercriminal. But again the fallacious theory that men are born bad falls flat on its face.

John Doolin was two years old when his father was killed. His mother—a good woman who had the misfortune to fall in love with an outlaw—became the wife of a Methodist minister, the Reverend Jonathan Meeks, when the boy was four. Meeks adopted him, and as John Doolin Meeks he grew to manhood and at an early age entered the ministry himself, with a pastorate at Ponca City—an esteemed and respected member of the community.

In the wiping out of the Doolin Gang, the Territory passed a significant milestone in its turbulent history. It did not mean the end of outlawry, but lawlessness had received a setback from which it was never to recover. The population was increasing; new roads were being built and old ones improved; the railroads were branching out and reaching heretofore inaccessible places. The outlaw was on his way out, and so was his horse. But some mopping up remained to be done.

28

Rounding Up the Jennings Gang

Y OU'RE A LIAR!"

Those fighting words, uttered during the course of a civil suit being tried in the county courthouse at Woodward were the seed from which sprouted the Jennings Gang. The matter in dispute concerned the nonpayment of rental on county-owned rangeland, a suit brought by Sheriff Jack Love, who also was collecting fees as corporation commissioner as the result of a rather obvious bit of political skulduggery which was bitterly resented by the Jennings clan, headed by ex-Judge J. F. D. Jennings, who wanted the sinecure for one of their own.

Judge Jennings had four sons: Ed, John and Al were lawyers; Frank, at the time, was in Denver, Colorado, where he was a court clerk. Al, next to the youngest, and only five feet-two, had been for a time Canadian County prosecutor at El Reno. He had come up for the trial, in which he had a personal interest, his brother Ed having been retained as counsel for the defendant. But that was only part of it. Love, in his dual role of sheriff and corporation commissioner, had engaged Temple Houston, the long-time foe of the Jennings clan to prosecute his case.

Temple Houston was the youngest son (not the grandson, as Rascoe has it) of General Sam Houston, father of the Texas Republic, and he never let anyone forget it. In 1886, then only twenty-four, he had been appointed state's attorney for the unorganized counties of the Texas Panhandle, with his headquarters at Old Mobeetie. It was there that he developed a perpetual scowl and certain eccentricities, often appearing in fringed buckskins, snake-skin hatbands, and allowing his hair to grow long. Too inexperienced to be considered a good trial lawyer, he nevertheless quickly became an impressive courtroom orator. He had a big voice and he used it to infuriate opposing counsel. When he roared and shook his long mane, the effect, coupled with his self-avowed prowess with his pistols, was that few men could stand up against him. When he appeared in Oklahoma Territory ten years later, he was a swaggering, often offensive, extrovert.

Ed Jennings had a belligerent nature. He and Houston clashed repeatedly as the trial proceeded. In a heated argument over a legal technicality, the latter became so enraged that he pounded the table with his fist and shouted, "Your Honor, opposing counsel is grossly ignorant of the law!"

Al always said it was he who gave Houston the lie; he was never modest about such things. His brother Ed and Houston squared off at each other, but they were separated before any blows were struck or shots fired. Onlookers did not expect the matter to end there.

That evening, Ed and John Jennings were playing cards in a saloon when Houston walked in. Ed immediately drew a revolver. Houston shot and killed him before he could get out of his chair. John Jennings leaped up, a pistol in his hand, but Houston's second shot struck him in the shoulder and Jennings' six-guns clattered to the floor.

Temple Houston was tried for this shooting and, acting as his own lawyer, was acquitted on his plea of self-defense, witnesses swearing that Ed Jennings had been the first to draw.

Frank had come from Denver. He and Al attended the trial and were bitter over Houston's acquittal. Fortified with a few drinks,

Al made some threats against Houston. Frank got him away before anything came of it, and they went to Tecumseh, where their father was then sitting as judge of the Pottawatomie County court. He had previously been a judge at Woodward.

Al (Alfonso) Jennings, born in 1862, was a Virginian by birth, as were his brothers. The Judge had fought under Lee in the Army of Virginia. He was a man of excellent character, and though ruined financially by the War between the States, he had given his sons more advantages than most. Ed was the leader. Al's grandiose dreams of the future political and economic importance of the family were woven around him. If Ed had lived, they might have been realized. With his death, they vanished.

The full measure of Al Jennings' hatred of Temple Houston can be appreciated only when viewed from that angle. In the two books attributed to him, he says he "hunted" Houston, determined to kill him. This is to be doubted. Houston went where he pleased, and if Al was looking for him it was in places, such as the wilds of the Sac and Fox country, where the man was least likely to be.

It has become the fashion to downgrade Al Jennings as an outlaw and to portray him as a fumbling comic figure, confused, boastful, hungry for public acclaim, who was deluded into believing that the tales of derring-do he invented about himself were true. It is an opinion advanced by those writers who know him only through the several books which he co-authored. It is justified in part; as a bandit, he had little to recommend him, for as Marshal Nix had once told me, "Al was never half as bad as he thought he was." Perhaps it was just as well that he was not, since any man with a rifle in his hands is dangerous. But whatever Al Jennings' faults were, he paid for his mistakes.

After a few weeks in Tecumseh, he and Frank were broke. They fell in with two brothers, Morris and Pat O'Malley, who, if they could claim any occupation, were cowboys. They were between jobs and getting hungry enough to be reckless. Al has told two versions of who first broached the idea of filling their empty pockets by holding up a train. At one time, he said it was his suggestion; at another, that Morris O'Malley made it. Very likely it came from Al, for he had an ace up his sleeve in the person of Little

Dick West, the lone survivor of the Doolin Gang, whom he was confident he could get to throw in with them. They recruited another member of their so-called gang in Sam Baker, a worthless character. Baker was to prove to be one of Al's greatest mistakes.

The five of them left Tecumseh and, somewhere in the Sac and Fox country, met Little Dick. Jennings never disclosed where and how he first made contact with the wizened little runt for whom Nix and his deputies had been hunting for months. He is equally vague about where he, the O'Malley brothers and Baker met the hairy little man. "In the Sac and Fox country," which would be north of Tecumseh, is as close as he comes to saying.

Little Dick had come up from Texas with a herd of horses for the H X Bar. More out of pity for the friendless range stray than because he needed him, Oscar Halsell had kept him on. The little man proved his worth, for he had a way with horses. But he was ignorant, dirty, smelling more like a wild thing than a human being. He refused to sleep under a roof. Summer and winter, he unrolled his blankets on the ground.

Doolin and his clique tolerated him. He was ambidextrous and could draw a pair of six-guns with catlike swiftness and was deadly accurate with both hands. That was something they could admire. Later on, both Bill Tilghman and Heck Thomas were to have occasion to comment on the lightning speed with which Little Dick could draw and fire. Both said they had never seen his equal. He was hard and tough, and there was something deadly about him, all of which recommended him to Doolin; and when the latter left the H X Bar after the Coffeyville fiasco and began putting his own gang together, he took Little Dick with him.

One of the foremost commentators on the horseback outlaw wonders what persuaded Little Dick West, an accomplished, veteran bandit, to join a band of raw, inexperienced amateurs—and why he permitted Al Jennings, rather than himself, to become its leader. The circumstances would seem to be explanation enough. For months he had lived a friendless, lone-wolf existence, hunted from pillar to post. Undoubtedly he would have associated himself with anyone who offered to take him in. Leadership was beyond him; he was not geared for it. Had it been offered, it well might have aroused his wolfish wariness and warned him of what he was letting himself in for.

If Al can be believed, there was no talk of organizing an outlaw gang at that time; he and Frank were interested only in sticking up a train, making a stake and getting out of the country. As he tells it, they had no money and soon ran out of food. To remedy that extremity, they rode up to a crossroads store, determined to beg, borrow or steal enough grub to tide them over for a few days. While the others waited outside, he and Little Dick entered the store. The proprietor was waiting for them with a shotgun. As he shoved it across the counter, Little Dick killed him. They robbed the till, took what food they could carry, and rode off. It was a shabby beginning, but there was no turning back now; the Jennings Gang was born; they were outlaws. They began by holding up a Santa Fe train near Edmond, about halfway between Guthrie and Oklahoma City. Two of them climbed into the cab of the locomotive as it was taking on water, and forcced the engineer to pull out of town a mile. There the other members of the gang were waiting. The express car was entered and the strongbox broken open. It held only a few hundred dollars. Apparently unnerved by their own boldness, they neglected to relieve the passengers of their valuables. But it was a beginning.

Ten days later they attempted to hold up a Katy train at Bond Switch, between Muskogee and Braggs, by piling ties on the track. This was good outlaw practice, successfully used by the James-Youngers and the Daltons. There was nothing wrong with their technique, but the engineer saw the barricade in time, opened his throttle and the train plowed through, scattering ties right and left and leaving the discomfited bandits shaking their heads.

Shortly after this misadventure, Sam Baker left them and returned to Tecumseh. Though no longer a member of the gang, he kept in touch with them. He also kept in touch with the law, passing on information that enabled the marshals to keep one step ahead of the Jennings Gang who, in their inexperience, failed to suspect that Baker was betraying them.

Unaware that the finger was on them, they rode south, crossed the Canadian River and set up to stop another Santa Fe train at Purcell, in the Chickasaw country. The night was black, and as they waited on the siding in the gloom of a boxcar for the south-bound train to pull up at the water tank, they mistook a group of mounted men riding up the right-of-way for a posse. They did not linger to make certain, and it was just as well they did not, for Sam Baker had informed on them. Tilghman was riding in the cab with the engineer and fireman. In the express car another deputy marshal and several possemen were ready for the summons to "open up."

Not having had any luck stopping trains, Al led his men across country to Minco, a little town on the Rock Island, twenty-odd miles south of El Reno, to rob the bank. This was country he knew from his days as prosecuting attorney of Canadian County. They pulled up outside the town. Fearing he might be recognized in Minco, he sent Pat O'Malley in to reconnoiter the bank.

Pat was unknown there, which was fortunate for him. Minco was a one-street town, and as he rode past the bank, he noticed three or four armed men lounging in the doorways of buildings opposite. They seemed so alert that he was convinced they were watching the bank. He kept right on riding, circled the town and rejoined the others. They were no longer interested in Minco, when they heard what he had to say. Cursing their luck, they struck off back east the way they had come. Nothing was going right for them and they could not understand it. They were play-ing with a loaded deck, of course. Sam Baker had heard them talking about Minco on one of his visits to their camp with food and had promptly notified the officers, who had been guarding the bank for several days.

Instead of returning to their old haunts, the gang headed south. Far down in the Chickasaw Nation, at a place named Berwyn, ten miles north of Ardmore, they had a try at another Santa Fe train; and this time, not having Sam Baker around to divulge their plans, they hit the jackpot. Jennings always claimed that they got $35,000. Discounting his usual propensity for exaggeration, one may estimate that it likely amounted to no more than $20,000. But it was a stake. They cut up the loot and scattered for a few months. Al and his brother Frank got passage on a tramp steamer at Galveston and landed in Honduras, from which there was no extradition.

In the cantinas of Puerto Barrios they fell in with a shabby, overweight and congenial refugee from Texas who had fled his native country to escape an indictment for embezzling funds from an Austin bank. With pseudo-histrionic dignity, he informed them that he was William Sydney Porter. They had money and he a nagging thirst. The three of them embarked on a drunken carouse, lasting for weeks, and ending only when they ran out of funds.

Penniless when they sobered up, Al says he suggested robbing the Puerto Barrios bank. Porter refused to have a hand in it. He was going back to Texas, he said, and face the embezzlement charge that he claimed had been brought against him to cover the peculations of the bank's officers. (A point which his numerous biographers have always made.) He was found guilty, however, and sentenced to five years in the Ohio State Penitentiary, where, under the pen name of O. Henry he began writing the short stories that were to make him world-famous.

In the fall of 1897, the Jennings brothers were back in the Territory. The gang soon gathered again. They greeted treacherous Sam Baker as an old friend. If he learned where their next strike was to occur, he was too late in getting the information to the officers for them to have time to frustrate it. But the gang supplied their own frustration. It was to be a daylight robbery this time, and they bungled it with disgraceful amateurishness.

At noon on October 1, a section gang working on the Rock Island track near Pocasset, eleven miles north of Chickasha, saw five masked men gallop down on them, brandishing their rifles. The foreman was ordered to flag the train that was soon due, and the gang hid out in the brush. The foreman's red flag stopped the train. Frank Jennings and Pat O'Malley covered the engine crew; Morris O'Malley stood guard beside the express car. Al and Little Dick climbed inside. They found two safes, a small one resting on top of a large one. They attacked them with an ax but without results. They were plentifully supplied with dynamite, however. They pried up the smaller safe, Little Dick inserted a stick of dynamite under it, lit the fuse and jumped out of the car with Al and the express messenger to await the explosion.

Little Dick West, for all of his proficiency with his six-guns, was a rank novice when it came to using dynamite. In his haste to leap out of the car, he had left three or four sticks of it lying on the floor close to the safes. When one stick exploded, the detonation set off the others. The roof of the car was blown off and the safes catapulted into a ditch. But neither of them was broached by the blast.

Determined to get at least something, the bandits went through the coaches and collected some watches, jewelry and a few hundred dollars.

It was a humiliating fiasco that set them to quarreling among themselves, each blaming the other. Little Dick must have borne the brunt of it, for without saying a word, he saddled his horse one evening and rode off. It was the last they were to see of him.

The worst was yet to come. A number of passengers identified Al and the O'Malleys as they went through the coaches at Pocasset. The marshals were soon on their trail, and they had to run for it. After a week of being continuously on the go, their horses gave out. In order to keep moving, they stole a wagon and a team of plodding farm animals. In a beeline they were nearly a hundred miles northeast of Pocasset when they drove through Cushing, below the Cimarron.

They were without food and in tatters. The town was asleep. Throwing caution aside, they robbed a store, took clothing, food and a few dollars from the till. They could no longer regard themselves as bandits; they were just thieves. But they were too desperate to care.

In some manner Sam Baker learned that the fugitives were hiding at the ranch of a man named Harkless, in the Creek Nation, northeast of Okmulgee. He passed the information on to Deputy Marshal Bud Ledbetter, who was leading one of the posses pursuing the Jennings Gang. A day later, Ledbetter had the Harkless place surrounded. He permitted Mrs. Harkless and her Indian hired girl to leave the house. When the gang refused to come out with their hands raised, what Al describes as the "battle" began. The posse did most of the shooting, but as evening came on, the four fugitives helped themselves to Harkless' horses and managed to escape—which fringes on the incredible. Neither in his books nor by word of mouth to me was Al able to explain it to my satisfaction.

And now it was to Sam Baker, of all men, that they turned for succor. Al had a slug in his right leg below the knee. Frank had been slightly scratched. Baker took them in and rode the five miles to Checotah for a doctor and to get word to Ledbetter, telling him how and where he planned to turn the four men over to him.

As soon as Al was able to travel, Baker put him, his brother Frank and Pat O'Malley in a covered wagon. Morris O'Malley and he, both mounted, followed behind. As the wagon neared Carr Creek, Baker moved up alongside and spoke to Al, who was doing the driving, and told him not to turn off to the north until he was a mile beyond the crossing. Al nodded that he understood. Baker then turned back, and Morris O'Malley turned back with him.

The trap was set and Ledbetter was waiting. A log had been placed across the narrow dirt road. The team stopped on reaching it. Ledbetter stepped out from the brush and called on the occupants of the wagon to surrender. There was no resistance. The Jennings brothers and Pat O'Malley climbed out, leaving their rifles behind them.

Bud Ledbetter had boasted that he could take them single-handed. He had made good, but he was not taking any chances. He had a posse with him. Their presence was not disclosed, however, until after the shamefaced bandits had been taken into custody.

Morris O'Malley was picked up a few days later. All four served five-year sentences at Columbus, Ohio. Al had been sentenced to life imprisonment, but he came out with the others, freed on a presidential pardon. At Columbus, he was assigned to the dispensary, and there he met his friend from Honduras, William Sydney Porter, from which came many years later *Through the Shadows with O. Henry*, a shoddy attempt to capitalize on another man's misfortune and fame. Also into that little circle at Columbus came Bill Raidler.

They were a chastened crew when they came out. Al tried the lecture platform for a time, his theme "Crime Does Not Pay," and was moderately successful. He tried the law again, and in

1914 had the audacity to campaign for the Democratic nomination for governor of Oklahoma. He was soundly defeated.

Whatever else he was, he was an excellent storyteller, and his tales were seldom about himself. It has been said that O. Henry got some of his short stories from him. I know that I did—many of them. One of his most amusing anecdotes concerned his campaign for governor. I'll try to tell it in his words:

"I was going up to Guthrie to speak at a political rally. An elderly man in a faded green Prince Albert and a black hat got on the train at Seward. I knew right off that he was a minister. He looked around and then sat down beside me. To make conversation, I said: 'I suppose you're going up to Guthrie to hear the outlaw candidate speak.' 'I am not!' he snorted. 'Only the horse thieves will vote for that man.' 'I hope you're right,' I told him. 'If all the horse thieves in Oklahoma vote for him he'll be elected by an overwhelming majority.' "

Al was in his middle fifties when I became acquainted with him—a lean, wiry little man, with twinkling blue eyes in a grizzled face, and dyed red hair. He passed away in 1962, aged ninety-eight by his reckoning, projecting to the end the illusory image of himself that he had used for half a century and more to cancel out his frustrations.

Soon after he and the rest of his gang were captured, Sam Baker, who betrayed them, became involved in a violent argument with a neighbor named Torrence over the ownership of a wagon. It is a pleasure to report that Torrence killed him and was acquitted, a witness testifying that he had shot in self-defense.

For months after the breaking up of the Jennings Gang the marshals were at a loss to say what had become of Little Dick West. Tilghman, Heck Thomas and others, who had done their best to flush him out of hiding, expressed the opinion that he had left the Territory for Texas or Mexico. They were shocked when they discovered that for most of that time he had been no farther away from Guthrie than a dozen to fifteen miles. A woman's babbling led to his undoing.

If Little Dick had no friends, he at least had some acquaintances left from his cowboys days on the H X Bar. They knew that he was wanted and that they were going against the law in setting out food for him and his horse. But they did. Ironically enough, they were the ambitious, thrifty men whom Oscar Halsell had helped to set up as the owners of their own small spreads. Among them was Herman Arnett. He had bought a piece of range from Colonel Zack Mulhall, down Beaver Creek from the vast Mulhall holdings. Halsell had given him the nucleus of a herd on credit. Arnett did so well that in 1897 he took unto himself a wife, and it changed his life considerably, for he found he now had someone looking over his shoulder, telling him what not to do.

One of the things she objected to was her husband's insistence on taking in for a meal or two any range stray who appeared out of nowhere. She particularly objected to a hairy little man with an oversized mustache, who smelled to high heaven and had a pair of eyes that frightened her. He came at unpredictable intervals, but too often to be the cowboy down on his luck riding the grub line that Arnett said he was. When he came, he stabled his horse in the barn, and whatever the two men had to say to each other was said there. Mrs. Arnett expressed her fear of the little man to a neighbor woman, who passed it on to her friends. Eventually it reached the wife of the clerk of the U.S. District Court in Guthrie. He communicated at once with Marshal Nix.

Nix called in Bill Tilghman and Heck Thomas. Yes, they agreed, the description of Herman Arnett's visitor fitted Little Dick. But was it he? Marshal Nix ordered them to investigate and assigned deputies Frank Rinehart and William Fossett to accompany them.

It was incredible to Tilghman and Thomas that, after months of scouring the Territory for the little outlaw, they were to find him almost in their own backyard, so to speak. But until they knew to a certainty that Arnett's visitor was not Little Dick, they had to proceed in the firm conviction that he was. Being realists, they knew that death could be waiting for them at the end of this short ride. The chances that West, if it were he, lightning fast with his guns, could be taken alive were almost negligible. He would go down fighting, and it would be nothing short of a miracle if he did not take one or more of them along with him.

Dawn was breaking when the marshals came up Beaver Creek

on April 7, 1898. They left their horses in the willows that fringed the creek bottoms and proceeded cautiously on foot, coming up through the orchard in back of Arnett's barn.

There was a horse in the corral. A man came out of the barn and began grooming the animal with currycomb and brush. As the light strengthened, Tilghman and Thomas recognized him. It was Little Dick. They could have killed him without warning. But that was not their way.

"Hands up!" Tilghman called out.

The little outlaw shook his hands free of brush and comb and as they went flying, drew his pistols. The marshals did not give him a second chance. Their guns cracked and Little Dick went down, his .45's clutched in his stiffening fingers.

Tilghman retrieved the currycomb and brush.

"They were the difference," he said later. "If Little Dick hadn't lost a fraction of a second getting rid of them, he'd have downed one or two of us."

With the killing of Little Dick West, horseback outlawry in Oklahoma Territory had almost run its course—but not quite. Henry Starr was still in the penitentiary; but he was not to remain their long. To him was to go the distinction of being the last of the noted horseback outlaws.

29

Henry Starr—
Last of the Horsebackers

❧

Though perhaps not justified, I have always entertained a sentimental regard for Henry Starr. To me, he is the classic example of the man lost to outlawry who should have been saved for something better. He had the intelligence and personal charm to have taken him a long way.

I do not agree with those who say he was pushed into outlawry. True enough, he was unjustly accused of stealing a horse when he was barely eighteen, arrested by the Cherokee Indian police and taken to Nowata, where he suffered the humiliation of being led into the hotel dining room with his hands in irons and being chained to his bed that night. The charge was dropped before he came to trial, but eight months later he was arrested a second time on a similar charge. There appeared to be no evidence against him. He was held for trial, however, his cousin Kale Starr and J. C. Harris, a tribal chief, going bond for him.

The old Starr-Ross feud was still very much alive. Sam Starr, the patriarch of the Starr clan, had returned to his old bailiwick after serving a long sentence at the Southern Illinois Penitentiary, at Menard, for introducing and selling whisky in the Territory. The difficulties young Starr was having may well have been the work of the Ross faction. Apparently convinced that, innocent or not, he was about to be railroaded into prison, he jumped bail. When he failed to appear for his trial, the bond was forfeited and Harris and Kale Starr offered a reward for his capture. But he was already on the scout. He eluded the Indian police without difficulty and in the wilds of the Verdigris Valley met up with Bill Cook, Cherokee Bill and the Verdigris Kid, the charter members of the Bill Cook Gang, which was then being formed. Later, he was to join them and continue his self-propelled progress into outlawry.

Henry Starr is described by some as being all-Indian and by others as more white than red. The truth is that the only white blood he inherited from his father, Hop Starr, was the Scotch-Irish strain that had been in all the Starrs since their early contact with white men in their original homeland in the Carolinas and Georgia. His mother was a quarter-blood Cherokee. In appearance he was typically Indian, with his straight black hair, black eyes, aquiline nose and swarthy skin. Though he was a slight man, under six feet tall, he had the physique of an athlete, and, says Mac-Donald in *Hands Up!*, "moved with an aboriginal grace, could dog-trot for half a day, had the Indian instinct for finding his way, and could live on roots, berries and nuts and sleep on the ground for months at a time, if need be."

He was born at Fort Gibson on December 2, 1873, and attended the Indian school at Tahlequah. He was remarkably abstemious, never using liquor, tobacco, tea or coffee. He made friends easily, many of whom remained loyal to him after he was steeped in banditry. Everybody seems to have liked handsome, soft-spoken Henry Starr. The U.S. marshals, whose business it was to run him down, respected him, even befriended him at times. They knew he was "absolutely without fear, that he would fight like a wildcat if cornered."

Nothing infuriated him so much as to read in the trash that was written about him that he was the son of Belle Starr. She was his cousin, and only by marriage, his father and Sam Starr, Belle's husband, being brothers. He claimed he had never been acquainted with her, which may be true, for he was not yet sixteen when Belle was killed.

Though Henry Starr robbed a score of banks and faced the gunfire of marshals and irate citizens many times, it is a tribute to his coolness when the chips were down that only one killing appears on his record, and that occurred a few weeks after he jumped bail on the horse-stealing charge and was hiding out in the Verdigris Valley. Whether you believe Starr's version of what happened, or accept the testimony of two eyewitnesses, it was one of the strangest pistol duels ever recorded.

It took place on the Albert Dodge ranch, near Nowata. Starr was then nineteen. He had worked as a cowboy for Dodge the previous year, and it was at the Dodge ranch that he was arrested on the first horse-stealing charge and again on the second. When a store at Lenapah and the express office at Nowata were robbed, suspicion grew that it was the work of the fugitive Henry Starr. Floyd Wilson, a Parker deputy marshal, and H. E. Dickey, an express-company detective, rode to the Dodge ranch, hoping they might find young Starr there. Dodge informed them that he had not seen their man in weeks and did not expect to see him.

And now the incredible occurred, for as they were in the house drinking coffee, a rider came up, glanced in through the window, saw there were strangers present, and rode on. Later, under oath, Dodge said:

"I told them [Wilson and Dickey], 'There's the man you're looking for.'"

Wilson ran out of the house, leaped on a saddled horse and pursued Starr. A hundred yards away, the latter suddenly pulled up and dismounted. Wilson did the same when he came up to him, and Dodge and Dickey, back at the house, saw them confronting each other, not thirty feet apart, with pistols drawn. Wilson then fired a shot—"a warning shot, over Starr's head," said Dodge and Dickey. "Starr shot then; Wilson went down. Starr walked up to him and fired again, killing Wilson."

That was not the way Henry Starr told it. "When Wilson called on me to surrender I called back, 'You can't take me, Wilson; go away.'

" 'Throw away that gun and put up your hands or I'll kill you,' he replied. He probably thought I was only a kid and was afraid of him. I didn't want to kill him.

" 'All right,' I told him. 'I'll lower my gun and give you a chance to shoot first and you better make a clean job of it. If I kill you it will be in self-defense. Shoot!'

"Wilson took cool aim at me, fired, and the ball sang past my ear. Then I put a bullet through his heart, mounted my horse and rode away."

That was the story he eventually told a jury. They refused to believe him.

Slaying an officer was serious business, no matter what the circumstances. He would have an army of deputy marshals on his trail now. If captured, it would very likely mean that he would end up on the gallows at Fort Smith. No further persuasion was needed to send him scurrying off to join the Cook Gang.

He took part in at least three robberies with them. When winter put a temporary stop to their activities, he pulled away and began organizing his own gang. The men with whom he surrounded himself were older than he, two of them not inexperienced in the bandit business. They were Link Cumplin, Frank Cheney, Bud Tyler, Hank Watt, Kid Wilson and a character known only as Happy Jack. They were not "all cowboys," as one writer labels them; outside of Link Cumplin and Frank Cheney, the rest were cowboys only by adoption, range renegades who lived without visible means of support, not to be compared with the men Bill Doolin had recruited on the H X Bar.

At half-past two on the afternoon of June 5, 1893, Starr led them into Bentonville, Arkansas (about twenty-five miles beyond the Indian Territory line and about the same distance due west of Eureka Springs, where Tilghman had captured Bill Doolin), to rob the People's Bank. With the attention to detail that became his trademark, he had cased the town and the bank for several days. Each man knew what his position was to be when he reached his destination, and the route he was to take in making his getaway after the robbery.

Starr and Frank Cheney drove into town in a buggy, in which the gang's rifles were hidden. Tethered at the tailgate of the rig were two riding horses. Strung out some distance behind them so as not to attract attention, rode the others.

Bentonville went about its business, unsuspicious of what was about to happen. The bank stood on a corner. The bandits came up at the rear of the building. On Happy Jack fell the assignment of holding the seven mounts. The rifles were snatched out of the buggy. Bud Tyler and Hank Watt took their posts halfway between the horses and the bank corner. Link Cumplin, the trustiest man of the lot, stopped at the bank door, the position of greatest danger. Starr, Cheney and Kid Wilson, a young Indian, pushed on inside.

Cheney and Kid Wilson leaped over the counter as Starr lined up the six men who were in the bank and made them stand against the wall, intending to use them as a screen when Cheney, Wilson and he marched out. Cheney went into the vault. Wilson scooped up the money on the counter.

Years later, while he was a prisoner in the penitentiary at McAlester, Starr described those few minutes.

"Scores of people saw us enter and knew us for bandits. Shooting began the moment we entered the bank. I heard the shots, slap, bang, at Link, who was walking up and down in front, shooting at every head that showed. Every second of time now might mean the difference between life or death for each man of us. . . . It seemed to me we were an hour in that bank, but it couldn't have been more than a minute or two before Cheney and Wilson sprang over the counter with the money in a sack.

"I told the six men I had lined up to do exactly as I said and they wouldn't get hurt. We started out behind them, but when we reached the street, fifteen or twenty men were shooting at us; it was as dangerous to stay with us as it was to run, and those six men just melted like snowflakes in a puddle.

"Link was shot almost to rags—one eye shot out—an arm shot through in two places, but he had his six-shooter in his good hand and was still blazing away. I helped him to his horse, and we tore out of town, all seven of us, not a man lost. A big posse chased us, but I never did think that posse tried very hard to get within gunshot distance of us."

There was only $11,000 in the grain sack; divided seven ways, it meant little more than $1,500 apiece. "Trifling pay," as Starr said, "for such a desperate venture."

Of the six men who accompanied Starr on the Bentonville raid, none was to "ride" with him again. Link Cumplin went to Alaska and was killed in holding up an express messenger; Happy Jack was killed several months later by marshals in Indian Territory; Frank Cheney fell before their guns within the year; Hank Watt was shot down by a posse who caught him with stolen horses in his possession. Kid Wilson wound up in the penitentiary and, after being pardoned, went back to banditry and was killed. Of the six, only Bud Tyler died in bed.

With his share of the Bentonville loot, Starr married a girl named Mary Jones, a Cherokee mixblood, and took her to Colorado Springs. Kid Wilson accompanied them. There on July 3, less than a month after the Bentonville robbery, William Feurstine, a Fort Smith businessman, saw Starr on the street and notified the police, who discovered that Starr and his wife, registered under the name of Frank and Mary Jackson, and Kid Wilson, alias Frank Wilson, were staying at the Spaulding House. When Starr and his wife were taken into custody, between $1,800 and $2,000 was found hidden under Mrs. Starr's pillow. Kid Wilson was traced to a bawdyhouse and captured in the room of one of the inmates.

He and Starr were hustled back to Fort Smith. Wilson was sent up for fifteen years for armed robbery. Henry Starr faced a number of indictments, one of them for the slaying of Deputy Marshal Floyd Wilson. It was on the murder charge that prosecutor Clayton brought him to trial.

It was the only time he faced the famous Hanging Judge. He was convicted and sentenced to die on the gallows. It will be recalled how he dumbfounded Parker by breaking in on the longwinded harangue the latter was pronouncing before passing sentence.

The date set for Starr's execution was February 20, 1895. He was still very much alive when the day passed. His lawyer had appealed to the Supreme Court, which then was possible, to set aside the verdict on the ground that the trial had been conducted in a manner prejudicial to the defendant. As usual on such appeals, months dragged by before that august body rendered its decision. In the meantime, Henry Starr remained caged in the overcrowded, vermin-infested hell-hole that was the Fort Smith court's prison. He was still there on the evening of July 26, when Cherokee Bill killed Turnkey Eoff and set off the riot. For his bravery in going into Cherokee Bill's cell and disarming him, the charge against him was reduced to manslaughter, and he was sentenced to fifteen years in the Ohio State Penitentiary.

At Columbus, with fifteen years of confinement ahead of him, he began the self-education that he was to pursue for the rest of his life. In his thirst for learning, his reading took him into widely unrelated fields—political science, ancient history, criminology and the science of firearms, phases of the last, such as the velocity of discharged missiles, windage and trajectory, requiring some knowledge of mathematics to be understandable. If he was an outlaw at heart, and the record says he was, he also had the instincts of a gentleman.

He must have been a model prisoner. When he had served five years, the warden was convinced that Starr could safely be returned to society. He instituted proceedings for his pardon. President Theodore Roosevelt granted it.

On his return to the Territory, Starr found his wife and embarked in the real estate and insurance business in Tulsa. He was moderately successful. His son was born, and he named him Roosevelt for the man who had pardoned him. For five years he led a law-abiding existence, and then, when it appeared that he was a brand that had been saved from the burning, Oklahoma achieved statehood on November 16, 1907. It changed the course of his life and sent him careening back into outlawry.

Following the Bentonville robbery, Arkansas authorities had indicted him for armed robbery. All the time he was in prison, and afterward, fourteen years, they had kept it alive. But Tulsa was in Indian Territory, and they could not touch him. With statehood, he could be extradited, and they asked for it at once. Before going into hiding in the Osage Hills, he sent a friend to Guthrie (it remained the capital until 1910) to plead his case with Governor Haskell. "He was to tell him how I had been going straight for five years, and beg him not to let the Arkansas wolves get me. I did not know what the governor might do, but I was determined not to go to Arkansas, for there I would have been sent up for life.

"I stayed in hiding. Within a month several banks were robbed in Oklahoma. [This is a quote from *Hands Up!*]I had nothing to do with them, but the newspapers printed scare-head stories that I had got off the reservation again, with forty kinds of war paint on. One day the telephone rang and the message I got from Guthrie was 'He's granted it.' Well, what could I do? I had the name of robbing banks. I might as well have the game. So I decided to touch up a bank or two to get enough money to leave the country. I did that . . . and started for California on horseback."

On the way, he passed through the little town of Amity, Colorado, on the Arkansas River. Its one bank, patronized almost exclusively by farmers, looked so easy to rob that, in his words, it seemed a shame to pass it up.

He collected several thousand dollars and continued on his way, but was captured by a sheriff's posse east of Lamar and sent to the Cañon City penitentiary for twenty-five years. It was only then that he learned that Governor Haskell had not granted extradition on him; that he had misunderstood his friend, who had said, "He hasn't granted it," not "He has granted it." Of course, the truth came too late to save him.

This tale has withstood the test of time. When I first heard it many years ago, I was skeptical of it. In a way, I still am. I know there was a misunderstanding over the telephone message Starr received, but I doubt that it hinged on mistaking "has" for "hasn't." A conversation, however brief, would have corrected that error. I believe that Starr heard the man correctly and that the latter, in his haste to get word to him, had jumped the gun and was relaying information he did not actually have.

At Cañon City, Henry Starr was once more an exemplary prisoner. He was made a trusty and put in charge of a road gang of a hundred convicts. At the end of the prescribed five years, the warden signed his application for parole. It was granted, with the proviso that he was to report to the parole board once a month and was not to leave the state of Colorado. He was no sooner at liberty than he hurried back to Tulsa to find his wife. He discovered that she had divorced him.

It was at this time that a wealthy stockman, who still had faith in him and believed he could get straightened out if he got away from his Oklahoma environment, took him up to St. Louis, bought him expensive raiment and got him a job. All went well for a time, until Starr was invited to a party in Webster Groves, a suburb. By chance, he got off the trolley car in front of the bank. Once again it was a case of a bank looking easy to rob. A week or so later it was held up by a lone bandit in typical border fashion. Starr disappeared from St. Louis.

He was next heard from in Oklahoma. In the course of the two years that followed, a score of small banks were robbed, all daylight jobs, and always by a lone bandit. The cry went up that Henry Starr was responsible, and it became so insistent that the legislature posted a reward of a thousand dollars for his capture, dead or alive.

At Stroud, Oklahoma, a little town on the Frisco Railroad, a few miles east of Chandler, the county seat of Lincoln County, on March 27, 1915, its two banks were robbed in spectacular fashion, the twin robberies being accomplished in less than a quarter of an hour. In some ways it was a repetition of the feat that had ended so disastrously for the Daltons at Coffeyville. The Stroud extravaganza was, eventually, to prove almost as costly to its participants.

At noon of that cold, blustery March day, Henry Starr jogged into Stroud with five armed companions whom he had recruited in the Verdigris Valley and the Osage Hills, the breeding ground of outlaws and horse thieves for half a century. They were "unknowns" in the world of banditry at the time: Lewis Estes, Bud Maxfield, Claude Sawyer and Al Spencer, an undersized young punk who survived to become one of the F.B.I.'s most wanted Public Enemies in the era of "automobiles and automatics" that was soon to follow. Very likely the fifth man who rode into Stroud that day was Spencer's brother-in-law, Grover Durrell, a future Spencer mobster.

Starr had cased the town carefully and knew that the local

marshal went home to dinner promptly at noon, as did some of the employees of the banks. He had rehearsed the twin robberies with his men, and when they turned into the hitch-rack in front of a store less than half a block from the two banks, it was according to the prearranged plan. The reins of the six horses were turned over to Bud Maxfield. As he stood there alert, watchful, the others started up the plank sidewalk.

When they reached the first bank, Starr, Estes and Sawyer entered. The other two stopped at the door and fired a salvo of shots to clear the street and intimidate the townspeople. Across the way from where he was holding the horses, Maxfield saw a boy run into the butcher shop. He should have stopped him.

The robbing of the first bank was accomplished without difficulty. Starr and his two companions came out, and all five then crossed the street to the other bank. When their business there was finished, they began retreating down the middle of the street to their horses, Starr bringing up the rear, walking backwards and holding the town at bay.

Stroud was stunned. Several hundred people saw them, knew they were bandits and that they had just looted both banks; but no one did anything about stopping them from getting away. Paul Curry, the boy of sixteen who had darted into the butcher shop when the shooting began, picked up an old, sawed-off single-shot rifle, used for killing hogs, that stood in a corner behind the counter, and as the bandits passed the shop he ran to the door and fired at them. The heavy slug shattered Starr's hip. He collapsed, temporarily paralyzed from the waist down. The others turned back to help him. "I'm done for boys," he is reported to have told them. "Save yourselves." They left him lying there on the frozen street, and with them went the moneybag.

Thousands of bullets had been fired at Henry Starr. His clothing often had been punctured, but no bullet had ever struck him until now. He had no sooner been picked up and carried to the town jail than the cry of "Lynch him!" was raised by men who had been docile enough a few minutes earlier. The town marshal telephoned Oklahoma City for help. Tilghman responded. He was in Stroud three hours later, and his presence put an end to the lynch talk. Nevertheless, he removed Starr to the county jail at Chandler.

They were friendly enemies of long-standing.

"Henry, I'm becoming convinced that you are going to live and die a criminal," Tilghman recalled having told him. "You've broken every promise you ever made me. You told me you were through robbing banks, and here I find you pulling a double-header."

"Mr. Tilghman," he said, "when I came to Stroud to look things over, I saw it was just as easy to rob two banks as one, so I decided to kill two birds with one stone."

A posse led by Tilghman surprised Starr's accomplices a few days later, and in the fight that followed, Lewis Estes was killed and Bud Maxfield and Claude Sawyer were captured. Spencer and his brother-in-law (presuming it was he) escaped and made off with the loot.

When Starr was able to stand trial, he was found guilty and was sentenced to twenty-five years at McAlester. Maxfield and Sawyer went along with him.

McAlester was reputed to be a tough prison, but Starr had no trouble there. He behaved himself and soon was given many privileges. Friends on the outside worked for his release. He appeared to be contrite. He was forty-seven, his health broken. In December 1920, he was released on parole, having served only five years and six months.

In all, he had been sentenced to sixty-five years in prison, but he served only slightly more than fifteen.

He returned to Tulsa but had no luck finding a job. He went on to Oklahoma City and sought employment in some minor capacity with the state. His reputation was against him. Oklahoma was booming, and he was a relic of the past who had outlived his time. Automobiles were everywhere, and hard-surfaced roads were shooting out across the prairies in every direction. Oil was making millionaires of dirt farmers almost overnight.

Henry Starr was no longer the handsome figure he once had been. He walked with a limp, stoop-shouldered and old beyond his years. Suddenly he disappeared and dropped from sight for weeks. And then on February 18, 1921, he was back in the headlines. Accompanied by two armed men, he walked into the bank at Harrison, Arkansas, a hundred miles east of Bentonville, where he had cracked his first bank, and informed William J. Myers, the cashier, and a bookkeeper that it was a holdup.

Myers was prepared for just an emergency. When Starr ordered him and his bookkeeper to back into the vault, he consented readily enough, for just inside the vault door he had a double-barreled shotgun loaded with buckshot. It was the bandit's intention to loot the vault and lock the two men inside while he and his confederates made their getaway. But as he followed Myers into the vault, the shotgun roared and Starr crumpled to the floor. The two men he had with him, identity unknown, turned and fled.

Henry Starr, who had been among the first, and certainly was the last, of the noted horseback outlaws was dead. Waiting in the wings, ready to take over, was a new crop of bandits of a deadlier breed, mad dogs who killed without compunction. Armed with automatics, submachine guns and bombs, using speeding automobiles to make their get aways, they were to terrorize the country as the James-Youngers, the Daltons, the Doolins and the Henry Starrs never had.

Starr died without a dollar, but he was not buried in a pauper's grave. In his flush days in Tulsa he had arranged with a local undertaker for his burial. "Someday," he told him, "you'll read in the paper that Henry Starr has been killed. When you do, give me a decent burial." The compact was fulfilled. Starr's body was brought to Tulsa and given a Christian funeral and burial.

It was the end of the era of the outlaw on horseback.

Notes

CHAPTER 1.

¹ Whether Kansas Territory was to enter the Union as free or slave was solely responsible for the struggle, lasting for a decade and more, which resulted in the so-called Border Wars and brought the expression "bleeding Kansas" into our language. Missouri was proslavery, and across the line in Kansas there was a strong proslavery element, which was soon outnumbered seven to three by organized Free State emigration from eastern states. Both sides held conventions, elected officers and sent Andrew H. Reeder, the territorial governor, and James H. Lane, the organizer of the Free State party, to the United States Senate. They were not seated, the federal government refusing to recognize the election. With the help of bands of armed men from Missouri, the proslavery element organized a government and became, temporarily, the predominant party. Lawlessness became the order of the day, with both sides equally guilty of the excesses that followed.

² As news of his failure to win recognition from the War Department of the Confederacy spread throughout the South, it led to his repudiation by the great majority of Southerners and their sympathizers.

³ Lawrence was the headquarters of the New England Emigrant Aid Company, which was bringing in antislavery men by the hundred, as well as being the home of the two leading Abolitionist newspapers, the *Tribune Herald of Freedom* and the *Kansas Free Press*.

⁴ On January 29, 1861, Kansas was admitted to the Union as the thirty-

fourth state. The proslavery element was now in retreat. The Free Soilers adopted a new constitution and called for an election. Dr. Charles Robinson, the leader of the New England Emigrant Aid Company, was elected governor, and Samuel C. Pomeroy and Jim Lane, United States senators: This time they were seated.

CHAPTER 2.

1 Even those commentators most heavily biased in his favor have not been able to clear him of this charge. There is abundant evidence that he was a pronounced psychopath, the slave of a tortured ego that alternately filled him with a madman's exhilaration or plunged him into the blackest depths of depression. Eventually, he took his own life. In the days of his greatest prominence, he not only accepted responsibility for all the deeds attributed to him but appropriated many in which he had not taken part, wanting, it seems, to stand alone as the Great Avenger of all the wrongs, real and fancied, that Kansas was suffering.

2 Wendell H. Stephenson, in his biography of Lane, published by the Kansas State Historical Society in 1930, says of Lane's unheroic departure from Lawrence: "Lane escaped half clad through a cornfield, assembled a dozen men, and started in pursuit of the guerrillas." William Elsey Connelly, in his *Quantrill and the Border Wars,* does much better: "It was the intention of the guerrillas to capture Lane and take him to Missouri and publicly hang him in Jackson County. . . . At the first appearance of the bushwhackers Lane sprang from bed and wrenched off the [name] plate on his front door. Then, in his nightshirt only, he ran through the house and into a nearby field of growing corn. From this field he crossed a low hill to a deep ravine west of the present residence of Governor Stubbs. At a farm-house he procured a pair of trousers, the property of a very short fat man (Lane was a very lean, spare man, more than six feet high), a battered straw hat, and a pair of old shoes. Of another farmer he got a plow-horse with a 'blind' bridle, but no saddle. Thus garbed and mounted he rode southwest and alarmed the people, having eleven men assembled by the time the guerrillas marched out of town."

3 This was the third raid on Lawrence, if the threatened invasion, known locally as the "Wakarusa War" is to be counted as the first. In 1855, "border ruffians from Missouri" gathered on Wakarusa Creek for the purpose of sacking the town and "were deterred only by the intervention of Governor Wilson Shannon and United States troops from Fort Leavenworth." The second raid really got there. On May 21, 1856, an army of Missourians led by U.S. Marshal Donaldson met in Lecomptom, Kansas, to "help in the enforcement of law at Lawrence." Ostensibly a posse to help U.S. officers, it was a proslavery army commanded by General William P. Richardson, of the territorial militia. David R. Atchison, later senator, was in command of one battalion

—the Platte County Rifles; Colonel H. T. Titus commanded the rest, largely composed of Buford's Alabama troops. (A contingent of three hundred men had been sent north from that state to aid and abet the proslavery men.) They met little opposition in Lawrence. The plants of two newspapers were wrecked. Atchison trained the cannon they had brought with them on the Free State Hotel, but his aim was so bad that he was supplanted by another artillery "expert." The hotel was destroyed. Other fires were lighted and the plundering began. One, or possibly two, men were killed.

4 The infamous Order No. 11 was issued two days after the Lawrence massacre and understood by all to be in retaliation for what happened there. Though it bore General Ewing's signature (for the rest of his life he was unable to escape from the stigma it attached to his name) Jim Lane was its author. He may, as some have said, have actually written it. For at least a year, Ewing had been under pressure to pursue a scorched-earth policy against certain Missouri counties. He had refused to adopt it as being unnecessarily cruel and unwarranted. There is documentary evidence that, in obedience to Lane's demand, he conferred with him in a cabin on the Kaw River the afternoon before Order No. 11 was promulgated, and according to the statement of Ewing's military aide given at a later date, Lane threatened to have the general removed from his command unless he issued the drastic order the following day. This was no idle threat, for it was well known (though it has never been satisfactorily explained) that Lane exerted a strange influence on President Lincoln and Secretary of War Stanton. To save his own head, Ewing capitulated.

5 This is acknowledged by Dr. Charles Robinson, a sworn Abolitionist and the first governor of Kansas, which would seem to be sufficient documentation.

CHAPTER 3.

1 In his *The Daltons,* Harold Preece quotes Chris Madsen, the old and famous deputy U.S. marshal, as saying that he had evidence that Bill Doolin had quarreled with Bob Dalton and did not accompany the Dalton Gang on the Coffeyville raid. I do not take this seriously. On the morning of the raid, two different parties saw six men jogging toward Coffeyville. Half a dozen people saw the outlaws ride into town and swore they numbered only five. If the sixth, or missing, man was not Bill Doolin, who was he? In his old age Madsen made a number of statements that run contrary to the evidence—most notably that Rose of the Cimarron, who was Rose Dunn, according to him, was Doolin's sweetheart before she became Bitter Creek Newcomb's sweetheart, and that she came from Texas. He is mistaken on every count.

2 You will not find any private papers or letters left by the horseback outlaws, for by the very nature of their trade they left none. Aside from those

of Judge Parker's Fort Smith court and Judge William H. Wallace's journal, court records provide little information about the Long Riders of Oklahoma and Missouri, who seldom, and sometimes never, faced a judge and jury.

CHAPTER 8.

[1] Testimony developed at the trial of the Younger brothers definitely pinned the killing of young Gustavson on Cole Younger.

[2] It was from Frank Wilcox that the prosecution drew the story of what happened inside the bank. Wilcox had viewed the body of Charlie Pitts and identified him as one of the trio that had entered the First National Bank. It was the shorter of the other two, he said, who shot and killed cashier Heywood. It had to be Jesse.

[3] Young Wheeler, kneeling at the window in the Dampier House from which he had wounded Bob Younger, must have been in position to see what happened, but I find no mention of a statement made by him.

[4] As for Jesse having argued that they should kill Jim Younger to facilitate their escape, Frank never denied it. But more to the point, Cole Younger, in the paperback published by the Hennebery Company, in Chicago, in 1903, entitled *The Story of Cole Younger By Himself,* tells how Jesse proposed to shoot Jim. Also, G. W. Walrath, who was a member of the posse that captured Bob Younger, testified that Bob had told him personally that Jesse had wanted to kill Jim Younger. Walrath was foreman of the jury that indicted the Youngers.

[5] Frank James, in later life, confirmed this.

CHAPTER 9.

[1] Missouri historians are chary of saying that Governor Crittenden's alleged dealings with Bob Ford and the subsequent part he played in breaking up the James Gang blighted his political career. But it hardly can be denied that the James boys became a bitter political issue in Missouri. Writing in the *Missouri Historical Review,* in July 1942, William A. Settle, Jr., in an article entitled "The James Boys and Missouri Politics," says: "The Republicans in Missouri used the Jesse James affair to political advantage and pictured the Crittenden administration as the protector of Frank James when he was later pardoned . . . the James issue was apparently playing a direct part in State politics. The work of [prosecutor and judge] William H. Wallace in breaking up the band helped to prevent his nomination by the Democrats for representative in Congress from the fifth Missouri District. Although he (Crittenden) made an effort to obtain the honor, Governor Crittenden was not chosen by the Democratic State convention." Crittenden hung on for years as a party faithful, but only in appointive posts.

CHAPTER 20.

¹ This was the struggle that was to last for a decade and a half, snuff out the lives of a score of men, cover the Southern Pacific with such obloquy that the passing years have never completely erased it, and make the names of John Sontag and Chris Evans household words in Califorina to this day.

² If I seem to dwell overlong on Eye-Witness's story of the Alila robbery it is because, though probably false on a dozen counts, it has been so widely accepted, either wholly or in part, by almost every writer who has had anything to say about the Daltons.

First, there is the erroneous statement that Bill Dalton "was elected to the state (California) assembly." A careful checking of the *California Blue Book* (Sacramento, State Printing Office, 1958) fails to find an entry for William Dalton as ever being a member of either the Senate or Assembly. The *Sacramento Union,* in its March 19, 1891, issue, in a story on the Alila robbery says: "William Dalton resided near Livingston (Merced) for about five years, and was well-known. . . . No one ever suspected him of being in the train-robbing business. He was active in politics when here." No mention is made of his being or having been in the State Assembly.

Following the Alila holdup, sheriffs and deputies, who owed their official positions to the railroad company, rounded up a score of suspects. Any man who was a prominent enemy of the Southern Pacific was judged to be suspect. Bill Dalton was brought in for questioning and freed on the alibi he produced. The story in the *Sacramento Union* says "when he was here," which indicates that he was no longer in Merced County. This was on March 19, approximately six weeks after the Alila robbery. Why he sold his ranch and left California so suddenly with his wife has never been explained. Perhaps he realized that he was now a marked man as far as the all-powerful Southern Pacific was concerned. Whatever the reason, he disappears from history until October 7, 1892, two days after the disastrous Coffeyville raid by his brothers. It may have been during this long interval that he bought or rented the ranch near Ardmore, down in the Chickasaw country, where he was killed four years later, on September 25, 1895.

Before leaving California and the Daltons, let me include a bizarre incident in the aftermath of the Alila robbery, for which I am grateful to the ever-reliable Stewart Holbrook:

"There was no profit (in the Alila robbery) for Messenger C. C. Haswell defied the robbers and replied with profane and obscene words to their demands to open the express car. Haswell also started shooting, blindly yet wickedly, through the grating of the express car's side doors. The robbers fled. Fireman Radcliffe died of wounds from bullets fired either by the messenger or by the robbers, nobody ever knew which. But somebody had to be arrested and the cops, lacking a better victim arrested the heroic Haswell and charged him with murdering the fireman. Haswell had to stand trial, too, even though speedily acquitted."

[3] It is not of record that any of the Daltons played more than a very minor role in the conflict in the San Joaquin, and it was not until after the debacle at Coffeyville had given them nation-wide notoriety that local historians in the valley counties began fashioning conflicting and undocumented hearsay accounts of the doings of the Daltons in California, allegedly garnered from men who had been acquainted with them. When placed side by side, the writers were confounded by the fact that they had six to eight "Daltons" running wild in Fresno and Tulare counties. The only way they could explain it was to acknowledge that some men were using the name as an alias, which is absurd, for at the time there was no magic attached to it.

CHAPTER 21.

[1] In the best *Police Gazette* tradition, tales as lurid as anything ever written about Belle Starr, whom she is made to resemble, even to a fondness for wearing male attire, have appeared in print, always allegedly being "the true story of Daisy Bryant." They agree on some points, having her born in Cass County, Missouri, the daughter of poor but respectable parents. Running away from home, she is depicted as becoming a harlot and the mistress, not the sister, of Black-Faced Charley Bryant, until she took the eye of Bob Dalton, when Bryant stepped aside in his favor. After Dalton was killed, they have her reverting to her former trade of prostitute in Guthrie, using the alias "Eugenia Moore." A few months later they have her riding as "Tom King," the pseudo male leader of her own gang of desperadoes and horse thieves, until "this boldest of the West's lady outlaws" dies by gunfire, the year given as 1893, which unwittingly reveals the whole account as fiction. In 1893, Bob Dalton had been in his grave only a few months.

Bibliography

An abridged bibliography of books concerned with the outlawry of the prairies that the reader may find helpful:

Appler, Augustus C., *The Younger Brothers*
Barnard, Evan G., *A Rider of the Cherokee Strip*
Buel, J. W., *The Border Outlaws*
Connelley, William Elsey, *Quantrill and the Border Wars*
Croy, Homer, *Jesse James Was My Neighbor*
———, *Last of the Great Outlaws*
———, *He Hanged Them High*
Dalton, Emmett, and Jack Jungmeyer, *When the Daltons Rode*
Drago, Harry Sinclair, *Wild, Woolly and Wicked*
———, *Red River Valley*
Edwards, John N., *Noted Guerrillas*
"Eye-Witness," *The Dalton Brothers*
Harman, S. W., *Hell on the Border*
Harrington, Fred Harvey, *The Hanging Judge*
Hines, Gordon, and E. D. Nix, *Oklahombres*
Horan, James D., *Desperate Men*
———, *Desperate Women*
James, Marquis, *The Cherokee Strip*

Jennings, Al, *Through the Shadows with O. Henry*
——, *Beating Back,* with Will Irwin
Jones, W. F., *The Experiences of a Deputy U.S. Marshal of the Indian Territory*
Kansas Historical Society, *The Kansas Historical Quarterly*
Love, Robertus, *The Rise and Fall of Jesse James*
MacDonald, A. B., and Fred Sutton, *Hands Up!*
Oklahoma Historical Society Quarterly, *Chronicles of Oklahoma*
Preece, Harold, *The Daltons*
Rascoe, Burton, *Belle Starr*
Raine, William McLeod, *Famous Sheriffs and Western Outlaws*
Robinson, Charles, *The Kansas Conflict*
Shirley, Glenn, *Law West of Fort Smith*
Tilghman, Zoe A., *Outlaw Days*
Wallace, William H., *Speeches and Writings*
Wellman, Paul I., *A Dynasty of Western Outlaws*
Younger, Cole, *The Story of Cole Younger, by Himself*
And that rare treasure, if you can find access to one, a file of the old *National Police Gazette.*

Note: Roman numerals refer to Drago's "Introduction: Behind the Myths and Legends," which in the original edition began on page ix.

Index